# Art Therapy Theori

CW00765456

## A critical introduction

Susan Hogan

 Routledge
Taylor & Francis Group

LONDON AND NEW YORK

First published 2016
by Routledge
2 Park Square, Milton Park, Abingdon, Oxon, OX14 4RN

and by Routledge
711 Third Avenue, New York, NY 10017

*Routledge is an imprint of the Taylor & Francis Group, an informa business*

© 2016 Susan Hogan

The right of Susan Hogan to be identified as author of this work has
been asserted by her in accordance with sections 77 and 78 of the
Copyright, Designs and Patents Act 1988.

All rights reserved. No part of this book may be reprinted or
reproduced or utilised in any form or by any electronic, mechanical,
or other means, now known or hereafter invented, including
photocopying and recording, or in any information storage or
retrieval system, without permission in writing from the publishers.

*Trademark notice*: Product or corporate names may be trademarks
or registered trademarks, and are used only for identification and
explanation without intent to infringe.

*British Library Cataloguing in Publication Data*
A catalogue record for this book is available from the British Library

*Library of Congress Cataloging in Publication Data*
Hogan, Susan, 1961-
Art therapy theories : a critical introduction / Susan Hogan.
pages cm
1. Art therapy. I. Title.
RC489.A7H65 2016
616.89'1656—dc23
2015010681


ISBN: 978-0-415-83633-3 (hbk)
ISBN: 978-0-415-83634-0 (pbk)
ISBN: 978-1-315-73805-5 (ebk)


Typeset in Times New Roman
by Swales & Willis Ltd, Exeter, Devon, UK

This book is dedicated to my father Peter Hogan, who encouraged my curiosity.

# Contents

*Foreword by Professor Diane Waller OBE, President of*
*the British Association of Art Therapists*                      ix
*Acknowledgements*                                               xii
*Biographical note*                                             xiii

1 Introduction                                                     1

2 Cognitive behavioural art therapy                              10

3 Psychoanalytic art therapy                                     26

4 Analytical (Jungian) art therapy                               38

5 Gestalt art therapy                                            52

6 Person-centred art therapy                                     66

7 Mindfulness art therapy                                        80

8 Integrative art therapy: the group-interactive art
  therapy model                                                  93

9 Feminist approaches to art therapy                            108

10 Social art therapy: art therapy as social action and
   art therapy as research tool                                 126

11 A critical glossary of terms                                 142

*Bibliography*                                                  153
*Index*                                                         166

# Foreword

It has never been easy to respond to the question, 'What is art therapy?', still frequently asked by the public and fellow health and care professionals, even after the profession of art therapy has formally existed for over 50 years. Put on the spot, art therapists will usually come up with a comparison that might be more readily understood, such as 'It is rather like counselling only we encourage the client to use art materials to make images which we can use as a shared communication. The client might be able to express feelings more easily with images than through words.' Obviously a polite query just to get an idea of what goes on does not require a thorough analysis of the intervention, nor a lecture. However, now that art therapists are increasingly, and necessarily, subjecting their practice to scrutiny and evaluation and are conducting research, it is very important to make an analysis of where we are now concerning theory, practice and philosophical underpinnings. A similar movement can be observed in the professions of psychotherapy and counselling, where the demands of the evidence-based practice agenda, within the health and social care sector in particular, have led to more practitioners being prepared to (or required to) design and carry out research projects – to continue to fulfil the agenda put forward by Roth and Fonagy (2005) in their seminal *What Works for Whom? A Critical Review of Psychotherapy*. In designing research projects for art therapy, as with our colleagues in psychotherapy and counselling, we have to identify what approach to art therapy we are bringing to the research table in order to see whether or not it is having any impact on our clients. If it is helpful, we must ask why and how. If not, why, and would another approach to art therapy, another arts therapy or another intervention altogether be more effective? At this stage in the professional development of art therapy in the UK, being a regulated profession with considerable stability, we can tolerate outcomes that might show that the approach we used was not useful for that particular client or client group, whereas the same approach in another setting, with different people, might well be. The tendency towards 'propagandism' as one vice-chancellor of the 1990s unkindly put it, when referring to the lack of research in our profession, should be behind us.

As art therapists, we have the additional complication of the image to take into consideration and need to be careful that this essential ingredient of art therapy does not get sidelined or even ignored. In this respect, discussion of theory and sharing of methodology with our colleagues from the other arts therapies and from art and design will be helpful. Now that more attention is being given to practice-led research and research-led practice in the arts, led, for example, by McNiff (1998) and currently Smith and Dean (2014), art therapists may be able to find a way to prioritise the image within a favoured qualitative methodology, within the context of a soundly presented epistemology.

As Susan Hogan points out, in her timely book:

> Whilst art processes are at the core of art therapy, there are different concep-tualisations of the process, based on varied theories. These theories are not inconsequential since they posit different views as to what a human being is. Consequently, there are different opinions about the role of the art therapist. How the use of art materials is advocated can vary, as well as the way the materials may be used and the language chosen to explain the engagement.

This seems to me a vitally important yet surprisingly little studied or understood aspect of art therapy. Perhaps because of the long struggle to establish art therapy as a discipline and profession in the UK – and in many countries it is still hardly known about let alone practised – there has been a tendency to think about art therapy in a rather static way, as opposed to a set of processes that are in constant flux. I have been asked 'Are you a Jungian?', as this is a label that many people seem familiar with, or 'Do you do Gestalt?' to which, in my case, the answer would either be 'Not exactly, but I might use some techniques sometimes' as opposed to 'No' or 'Yes'. If I said I favoured 'process sociology' and don't like to be categorised, I might get some odd looks (unless in the unlikely event I was in a sociology department!) The same kind of reification has persisted within psychotherapy for very many decades. Until very recently, being attached to one modality has been a requirement for reg-istration with the main professional associations. This has not been the case in art therapy, where clearly many different modalities, approaches and philosophies have jogged along together with prioritisation of the art object linking us all together.

Susan Hogan points out that the idea of isolating theoretical perspectives seems an obvious one but has not existed previously in the form in which she has chosen to present her text. Questions arise for postgraduate students and researchers about their epistemological and ontological positions: something I confess until a few years ago I hadn't given much thought to. Yet when we consider the theoretical approaches dis-cussed in Susan Hogan's book, it is clear that the world view of the therapist is essen-tial to consider. Is the positivist attitude required to conduct a randomised controlled trial compatible with that of a researcher whose orientation is towards existentialism and phenomenology? Can a mixed methodology satisfy a pragmatist?

Can a social constructivist live happily in a research project based on surveys and statistical analysis? Can there be integration of theories, or could there be a pluralistic approach as outlined by Cooper and McCleod (2011) concerning psychotherapy research? By understanding the origins of the various theoretical approaches and how these manifest in practice, we will surely be able to explain more succinctly how our personal orientations as art therapists impact on our research choices.

Underpinning all this is, of course, the desire to offer our clients a rationale for coming to art therapy in the first place. We might strongly believe that 'being engaged in making art is therapeutic' (and indeed as a profession we have stated this more than once in our long history), but as to why it is, or might not be in some cases, this is more difficult. Curiously, we are now, as art therapists, having to counter the argument that 'art is good for you', which comes from those areas where the arts are seen as having an undeniable positive presence. Only recently I advised caution to a care home that was intending to introduce an art group run by volunteers, pointing out that image making can be very disturbing as well as beneficial, and it might be a good idea to have a qualified art therapist available to support the volunteers! The staff had not thought that images could be upsetting, possibly not suitable for the proposed public display, and were keen to take this advice. As to the theory behind the now popular view that engaging people with dementia in creative arts is a 'good thing', it would be unfriendly to discourage something that could well provide much needed meaningful activity and pleasure. But what is the theory underpinning this? As art therapists what could we say?

This book is important in many ways. It is based on years of practice, teaching and research in the UK and in Australia. The author has a track record of radical engagement with the challenging issues of difference – gender, race, culture, disabilities. She has researched, and continues to do so, on the theoretical origins of art therapy and is actively involved with teaching postgraduate art therapy trainees and in her own art therapy practice. Susan Hogan has managed to undertake a big task and present her thoughts in an accessible way, valuable to art therapy trainees, to fellow professionals, to potential clients and to researchers, providing much needed focus for debate and further development. I found the book really enlightening and strongly recommend it.

Professor Diane Waller OBE
Emeritus Professor of Art Psychotherapy, Goldsmiths, University of London
Hon. President, British Association of Art Therapists

## References

Cooper, M. and McLeod, J. (2011) *Pluralistic Counselling and Psychotherapy*, London: Sage.

McNiff, S. (1998) *Art-based Research*, London: Jessica Kingsley.

Roth, A. and Fonagy, P. (2005) *What Works for Whom? A Critical Review of Psychotherapy*, London and New York: Guilford Press.

Smith, H. and Dean, R. (2014) *Practice-led Research, Research-led Practice in the Creative Arts*, Edinburgh: Edinburgh University Press.

# Acknowledgements

A number of people have helped me by reading and commenting on specific chapters in which they have a particular interest, so thanks to John Birtchnell, Shelagh Cornish, Deborah Gibson, Rita Roberts and Diane Waller for these readings. Getting constructive criticism is essential and much appreciated for a sophisticated elaboration of each theory. Heartfelt gratitude must also go to my friend and ex-husband Phil Douglas for being prepared to read various chapters as a non-expert and for his subsequent, and often salutary, remarks on the comprehensibility of my prose. He must take a lot of the credit for the fluency of the text. I'd also like to remember friends and family who have helped me with my writing, especially Lizzie Burns, Andrew Campbell, Mary Douglas and Alan Rice. It is their critiques I have internalised. Indeed, I try to write as elegantly as Mary, though usually I fail.

Deep appreciation is also deserved for Professor Diane Waller's foreword. She is right to assert that we need to be able to distinguish between different art therapy practices, as these represent different attitudes towards the function of the art in the therapy process, the role of the therapist, as well as what constitutes a thriving self. Indeed, these different stances represent different ways of conceptualising what human beings are and what we should strive for. It is imperative for the development of our practice and for research that these distinctions are understood and clearly articulated and delineated.

I don't think I ever thank my students well enough; it is years of facilitating experiential training which have taught me so much and which I have attempted to share in this and my previous book, *The Introductory Guide to Art Therapy* (2014). Conducting such groups is a truly enriching experience. The glossary of terms is an extended version of that which appears in *The Introductory Guide*.

Art therapy is still widely misunderstood and it is my hope that these two volumes together will help in making the scope of the discipline more widely understood.

# Biographical note

**Susan Hogan** has a BA Degree in fine art, a postgraduate diploma in art therapy, a Master's Degree in Arts Administration (Arts Policy and Management) and a further Master's Degree in Social Science Research Methods (Social Policy and Sociology, specialising in visual methods). Her PhD was in Cultural History from Aberdeen University, and looked at the history of ideas around madness and the use of the arts. Susan has also studied art history at Sydney University. Additionally, Susan undertook further training in group-psychoanalytic psychotherapy. She served for six years as a Health Professions Council (UK) 'visitor' (now HCPC). She is a former Vice-President of ANATA (Australian National Art Therapy Association, now ANZATA), and has twice served as a regional coordinator for the British Association of Art Therapists (BAAT). She has been instrumental in setting up several art therapy training courses, and also courses in dance-movement and drama therapy.

Professor Hogan qualified as an art therapist in 1985. She has a particular interest in group work and experiential learning, following early employment with Peter Edwards MD, an exceptional psychiatrist who had worked with Maxwell Jones, a psychiatrist who is associated with the 'therapeutic community movement' in Britain. She is currently Professor in Cultural Studies and Art Therapy at the University of Derby, in which role, for many years, she facilitated experiential workshops and the closed-group component of the art therapy training. This closed-group training has been based on the group-interactive approach described by Professor Diane Waller (summarised in this book). Now most of her time is spent supervising research at MA and PhD levels, and conducting research.

Susan has also undertaken work with pregnant women and women who have recently given birth, offering art therapy groups to give support to women, and an opportunity for them to explore their changed sense of self-identity and sexuality as a result of pregnancy and motherhood. She has published extensively on this subject.

Susan Hogan has worked mainly in academia since 1983 for a number of institutions, including the University of New South Wales, College of Fine Art; the University of Technology, Sydney; Macquarie University and the National Art School, Sydney.

Professor Hogan is currently conducting research with several partner institutions, including co-researching women's experience of ageing with sociologists from the University of Sheffield using visual research methods. She is a Professorial Fellow of the Institute of Mental Health of the University of Nottingham. In addition to all the above, she has also published a number of both scholarly and polemical papers on women and theories of insanity.

Particularly influenced by the anthropological work of her late mother-in-law, Professor Dame Mary Douglas, Hogan's work has been innovative in its application of social anthropological and sociological ideas to art therapy; also distinctive is her unwavering challenge to reductive psychological theorising.

Her books are:

- *Feminist Approaches to Art Therapy* (as editor, 1997);
- *Healing Arts: The History of Art Therapy* (2001);
- *Gender Issues in Art Therapy* (as editor, 2003);
- *Conception Diary: Thinking About Pregnancy and Motherhood* (2006);
- *Revisiting Feminist Approaches to Art Therapy* (as editor, 2012);
- *The Introductory Guide to Art Therapy* (with Coulter, 2014).

# Chapter 1

# Introduction

Art therapists have a considerable understanding of art techniques and are proficient in using materials to facilitate non-verbal communication. Metaphors, symbols and the expressive use of art materials combine to create a rich language for self-expression and the opportunity for the translation of strong emotions into a pictorial expression which can be visceral in its intensity. Differences in scale or perspective, tone and colour, along with the use of metaphors, allow for a potentially sophisticated articulation of thoughts and feelings.

Symbolism is multi-faceted and able to contain manifold and contradictory meanings. Indeed, a veritable constellation of meanings can be generated at the meeting point of several symbols. The use of symbols enables the expression of moods and immaterial ideas or qualities, which would otherwise be hard to articulate.

Tacit embodied feelings can be sensed and explored through the manipulation of materials. The process of making art works is in itself potentially revelatory, triggering strong feelings and revealing previously unexpressed issues. The materials themselves, their very substance, can be evocative. It is a sensory process in which the movements of the body and the tactile sensation of the materials are evocative. Another embodied dimension of the art therapy process could include aspects of *prosopopeia* in which a part of oneself, or an imaginary or absent person, is represented as speaking or acting. There could be an inner dialogue stimulated by engagement with the art work, or it might be spoken. Moving around an object can uncover different dimensions, different potential dialogues.

The images produced can be enlightening and provoking in unpremeditated, startling ways. The revealing image unburdens complex representations. Furthermore, many works placed together can collectively create unforeseen narratives. The space in which they are experienced can also have an influence, as well as the relationship of the works to the maker and to the viewer in how they are seen, displayed or hidden from easy view. How the works are subsequently engaged with can generate significance. The art works, the space and the viewer can interact to create new meanings. The art work can become a powerful container; showing the piece to others is potentially transformational. The pictorial content may be immutable – it assails. Finally, the disposal of works can have strongly revitalising consequences.

Whilst art processes are at the core of art therapy, there are different conceptualisations of the process, based on varied theories. These theories are not inconsequential since they posit different views as to what a human being is. Consequently, there are different opinions about the role of the art therapist. How the use of art materials is advocated can vary, as well as the way the materials may be used and the language chosen to explain the engagement.

The aim of this book is to provide an introduction and give an overview of the main theoretical models of art therapy. Without 'dumbing down' the different approaches, the book will attempt to explain them in clear and concise English, avoiding jargon, and elucidating difficult terms and concepts as they arise.

Each chapter provides an analytical synopsis of one different approach. This book will be particularly aimed at trainee art therapists in the English-speaking world, who need when training to be able to demonstrate that they have a grasp of theory.

The idea of isolating theoretical perspectives seems an obvious one, but, surprisingly, an overview of theoretical approaches did not exist previously. It is therefore hoped that this small volume will be extremely popular, especially with trainees and with an international audience. The non-judgemental tone adopted is intended to ensure widespread adoption.

## Terminology

This book uses art therapy as the generic term. It does not make the distinction, made by some North American colleagues, between art therapy and art psychotherapy, as there is no consistent dichotomy in the use of such terms in Europe and Australia, or in most historic writing on the subject. There is a glossary of terms included.

## Contents: further details

In each of the following chapters the particular features of one method will be elucidated and the underlying theory explained.

### Chapter 2. Cognitive behavioural art therapy

In cognitive behavioural therapy (CBT) there is a focus on distorted thought processes, which give rise to emotions and behaviours. The task of cognitive therapy is to identify patterns of understandings that are unfounded and regarded as inaccurate; these are challenged and more adaptive ways of thinking and behaving are formulated. Malchiodi describes CBT thus:

> The basic goal of CBT is to help the client identify the false and negative rules and assumptions governing his or her actions and then find ways to replace or restructure assumptions with more realistic and positive rules and expectations. A collaborative relationship between the client and the therapist

is at the foundation of this approach and treatment is generally time limited and psycho-educational in nature.

(2012, pp. 89–90)

In CBT there is a tradition of using mental images to envisage new emotional responses and ways of being. Art therapy can be instrumental in aiding these processes.

Negative thinking is identified, as well as triggers for such negative thinking. 'Automatic negative thoughts' or 'negative self-talk' are identified with contexts and situations and are challenged (Corey 2009). Art is used in conjunction with this framework: for example, in exploring and reframing traumatic events. In CBT, clients are asked to imagine themselves thinking, behaving and feeling differently using mental images. Clients can make actual images of these imagined scenes (Malchiodi 2012, pp. 90–1).

This model will be elaborated in further detail, from initial goal setting through to termination of treatment. The views of some of the principal exponents of these ideas, such as Roth (2001) and Rosal (2001), will be presented. This model is more developed in North America and Canada than in the UK, and with pressure for evidence-based practice and shorter-term interventions, this model is likely to be further developed and adopted in Britain. Included in this chapter will be a section on solution-focused brief art therapy (SFBT).

The solution-focused technique will be elaborated on. Although philosophically located within a constructivist framework, this is essentially a behavioural technique in which the individual identifies aspects of her or his life she or he wishes to change. The therapist assists by asking questions that help the beneficiary to clarify possible solutions and the means of achieving them. The technique focuses on what the individual desires to achieve; it is a method that attempts to utilise the strengths and capacities of the individual. Identifying such strengths might entail some analysis of previous situations or events in which the recipient successfully generated a solution. However, generally, it is future-focused and 'goal-orientated'.

'Scaling questions' are frequently employed, allowing individuals to analyse aspects of their lives on a scale of 0 to 10, where 10 equals the achievement of all targets and zero is the worst possible scenario. The person undergoing SFBT is asked to identify his or her current position and the point at which there might be adequate fulfilment. Within this structure it is possible to define ultimate objectives (Iveson 2002). This approach is also particularly associated with the 'miracle question', which is explained below.

Mindfulness as a technique is being used by CBT arts-based practitioners in conjunction with other CBT methods, but these will be discussed in a separate chapter.

### Chapter 3. Psychoanalytic art therapy

In this chapter, the distinctive features of psychoanalytic art therapy will be explored and applied to practical work. Psychoanalytic theory will be explained in further detail in a comprehensible manner. This is one of the areas in which students often struggle, as the theory is particularly complex, but it can be articulated clearly without reductionism.

Psychodynamic therapy has arisen out of psychoanalysis, and sees inter-psychic conflicts as a form of stress which can result in psychological disturbance. It is an approach which is interested in the fundamental psychological forces governing human behaviour. These forces are seen as resulting in human action in a way that is not always obvious to the individual. The underlying forces are seen as being in a state of fluctuation (hence 'dynamic').

The personality (or psyche) of the individual is seen as being comprised of three main elements which are in a state of constant tension. The super-ego is the moral part of the self which responds to the demands of civilisation and includes such ideas as conscience, discipline, self-restraint and self-sacrifice.

The ego is viewed as the conscious, rational part of the mind that negotiates with the other parts of the psyche and is seen as attempting to create a compromise between conflicting impulses. If the ego has good strength then it will succeed in maintaining balance; if the ego is weak, the personality may become unbalanced and consequently too ruled by either the super-ego or the id. The ego is seen as having various 'mechanisms' at its disposal to maintain this balance, which will be elaborated on. For example, 'repression' is explained as the ego's attempts to thrust painful memories deep down into the unconscious mind so that they are effectively forgotten (though they may be rekindled later and cause problems). Another important mechanism is that of 'projection', in which thoughts are attributed to someone or something else. Freud saw a number of mechanisms at play to do with flows of psychic instinctual energy and conflicting internal forces.

The third part of the mind is called the id. The id is the primitive part of the self. Instinctual behaviours and basic needs are viewed as arising from the id. The id is seen as demanding immediate satisfaction and pleasure; it is interested in the gratification of needs, and is not interested in morality, and is therefore in conflict with the super-ego.

Developmentally, the id is seen as infantile and as developing in early childhood; the ego then develops, and then lastly the super-ego. These theoretical constructs allow for a mobile or 'dynamic' view of the mind and have been immensely influential. These ideas permeate twentieth-century thought and culture, though the technicalities of psychoanalytic theory are not always well understood.

Other psychodynamic approaches have evolved from psychoanalysis. In psychodynamic art psychotherapy, clients become increasingly aware of the dynamic conflicts and tensions that are being revealed as symptoms or stress in their lives; whilst this approach has evolved from psychoanalysis, psychodynamic therapy is not necessarily *explicitly* Freudian and may not use all the conceptual apparatus Freud postulated to explain how the ego functions. The term 'psychodynamic' is used for explanatory schemas and methods interested in interrogating dynamic emotional processes.

Psychodynamic principles are evident in several models of modern art therapy, as will be elucidated: as Malchiodi explains, 'most contemporary practitioners do not take a strictly psychoanalytic, analytic or object-relations approach to art therapy, elements of these philosophies are present in many contemporary art therapy approaches to treatment' (2012, pp. 72–3).

That 'psychoanalytic' and 'psychodynamic' are used synonymously by some writers adds to the general confusion. Nevertheless, there are art therapists whose practice is clearly located within the psychoanalytical tradition and who subscribe to the psychoanalytical view of symbolism, so this will be articulated. As this is also the theoretical basis for subsequent theoretical developments and challenges, these ideas are significant and need to be properly understood.

'Object-relations' theory is a development of psychoanalytic ideas and is explored. In this model of thought, the internal representations acquired in child-hood are seen as playing out later in life through relationships. There is usually a particular emphasis on exploring how such representations are projected outwards, particularly to the art therapist; hence, the main focus of therapy becomes the exploration of this transference relationship.

## Chapter 4. Analytical (Jungian) art therapy

This chapter will explore art therapy derived from analytical psychology. The term 'analytic' will refer to analytical psychology. Important art therapy techniques that stem from analytic psychology, such as 'amplification', will be explained.

There has been a tendency among some British art therapists to refer to psychoanalytic art therapy as 'analytical'. Analytical psychology is properly 'Jungian', deriving from the work of Carl Gustav Jung, and is a distinctive departure from psychoanalysis, especially in respect to its attitude towards images.

In analytic art therapy, pictorial symbolism, emerging from the unconscious, acts as a 'compensation' or complement to the conscious psyche, potentially bringing into focus aspects of the person not to the fore. Jung felt that good health was best achieved by giving voice to the unconscious aspects of the self and that the less conscious aspects of a person's total nature could appear in dreams or art work. Symbolism is seen as a bridge between the conscious and unconscious realms. The production of images is seen as assisting in creating equilibrium and as playing a regulatory role upon consciousness.

As well as the theoretical underpinnings of the analytic approach, studio-focused analytic art therapy techniques will also be explored. This way of providing art therapy is focused on the aesthetic dimensions of the production of art works and the relationship of the subject to her or his work. Thus, analytical studio work has an emphasis on non-verbal aspects of art making. Believing the psyche to be a self-regulating system that is capable of balancing and adjusting itself as necessary, art therapy is thought to be efficacious without verbal analysis. Indeed, art is regarded as therapy.

### Chapter 5. Gestalt art therapy

Gestalt theory is a branch of humanistic psychology which has a particular emphasis on working in the present. Gestalt art therapy has also integrated some psychodynamic aspects into its practice.

Using images as an adjunct to verbal psychotherapy is a technique employed by some art therapists. Gestalt art therapy is essentially a verbal psychotherapy that employs drama therapy methods into which image making is then incorporated. It employs a focused use of imagery that is often rather directive.

The art work in the Gestalt approach is usually a brief sketch rather than an involved piece. The art work is usually made at the same time as speaking, or is used to stimulate discourse. Part of the process is an opportunity to look at how the present is affected by the past. As John Birtchnell puts it: 'Talking to the picture, particularly in the here and now, is the most powerful device I know' (1998, p. 149).

This chapter will explore ideas from psychodrama and verbal psychotherapy that have been incorporated into this distinctive mode of art therapy. It's theory and practice will be illuminated. The views of its principal exponents will be explicated.

### Chapter 6. Person-centred art therapy

The person-centred art therapy model will be explained, and delineated in terms of its similarities and differences. This model of working and its underlying theory will be elucidated, with reference to the work of Carl Rogers (1902–87) in particular. The humanistic roots of the model will be described, along with the key features of Rogerian art therapy.

Humanism is interested in an individual's subjective conscious perception and understanding of the world. It does not look for 'unconscious' motivations. It has been described as a 'third way': an alternative to both behaviourism and psychoanalytic (and psychodynamic) orientations.

The 'non-directive', or 'person-centred', approach assumes that the client has the resources to deal with her or his problem, if given the opportunity, in the context of an authentic, empathetic relationship, and to be aware of his or her own feelings and desires. This authentic relationship is described as being 'congruent'. Being non-directive is thought to give power to the client to deal with what she or he considers important, and to set the pace, and is a distinctive feature of this approach. Clients are seen as having 'deep strengths' which can be released and freed in a permissive, supportive environment (Rogers, 1946).

The work of art therapist Liesl Silverstone (1997, 2009), who has sought to promote a person-centred approach, will receive mention.

### Chapter 7. Mindfulness art therapy

Mindfulness art therapy will also be mentioned here. Art therapists have sought to incorporate ideas from Buddhism into their practice (Monti *et al.* 2006). There are several variations of Buddhism; a common practice is to still the mind, then to note the kind of thoughts that arise: to take note of them, but not to follow or elaborate them. This takes a bit of practice, but using this basic meditation technique can enable the practitioner to begin to notice what the mind is doing, and to identify patterns of mind, including the sort of negative inner speech that CBT also identifies (see Chapter 2).

Buddhism also urges compassion towards all beings as a core value. Whilst CBT doesn't go this far, there are parallels in developing compassion towards the self, in rejecting damaging self-appraisal. Self-analysis through mindfulness has core aspects in common with a behavioural approach, but also with other psychotherapeutic approaches. Mindfulness as a technique is being used by CBT practitioners in conjunction with other CBT methods, but now mindfulness-based methods are being used with a range of theoretical orientations and are beginning to emerge as a distinct approach.

### Chapter 8. Integrative art therapy: the group-interactive art therapy model

The group-interactive art therapy model is a distinctive style of art therapy that is widely used in Britain. Theoretically, this is an eclectic approach which draws from a wide range of theory to develop a unique model of working. The most important strands of this approach are social psychology, existential philosophy combined with group theory (from systems theory) and psychodynamic theory, all of which will be explained for readers coming fresh to these subjects.

The basic idea behind the group-interactive approach is that during interactions with others individuals reveal their 'characteristic patterns of interaction': these are seen as constraining people in their everyday lives (Waller 1993, p. 23). These 'patterns of interaction' are acknowledged and reflected upon, and provide a focus for group analysis. Therefore, the method employed involves an analysis of clients' here-and-now behaviour in the group. This is not a simple discussion of clients' issues, so much as a *revelation* of their present constraints. Such constraints, or habitual ways of being and thinking, can be *revealed* through interactions with other members of the group or depicted in art works. 'Feedback' from participants is an important part of this method: 'Feedback from members of the group illuminates aspects of self which have become obvious to others but which are not recognised by oneself' (Waller 1991, p. 23). This is a complex model, so this account should not claim to be the definitive interpretation. It is a model which is likely to be practised with modifications according to the orientation of the art therapist. However, this summary should give a good sense of it as a working model.

### Chapter 9. Feminist approaches to art therapy

Feminism is the principle of advocating social, political and other rights of women as being equal to those of men. Feminist art therapy is necessarily interested in the question of equality (Hogan 2012a, 2013a). In academic writing, feminism refers to a mode of analysis that seeks to examine the function of gender in societal relations, and to explore the particular experience of women. This mode of analysis sees the construction of gender (or writers may use the term 'sex' to indicate that they reject the theoretical division of cultural 'gender' from biological 'sex') as historically and geographically situated and subject to change, and as being generated by culture, rather than biologically determined.

In terms of feminist art therapy, the construction of sex can become a focus; this is manifested primarily in an enhanced awareness of women's issues and an acute awareness of misogynist discourses (particularly those negative psychiatric discourses about women's 'instability', which are pervasive). Developing a critical awareness of these discourses is potentially empowering.

Sometimes, when using task-led 'directive' art therapy, it is possible to introduce exercises that can help participants reflect on their sex and sexual orientation. For example, I offer a workshop in which I ask men and women to bring in two images from any sources of a person, one image they like and another that makes them feel uncomfortable. These images form the basis of the session, and are analysed in place of made images. This exercise presents an opportunity to look at how people are represented, and to explore how participants feel about these images which surround us in our daily lives (Hogan 2014).

Some art therapists work with women-only groups to allow them to explore unique aspects of their experience, such as pregnancy and childbirth (Hogan 1997, 2003, 2012a, 2012b), collective trauma such as breast cancer (Malchiodi 1997), rape, childhood sexual abuse (McGee 2012) or the experience of ageing (Hogan and Warren 2012). However, 'maintaining a feminist awareness is, arguably, an important aspect of good practice in general and should form an integral part of training' (Hogan 2011b, p. 87).

Feminist art therapy is a form of 'social art therapy', but it is also an approach which can be seen as distinctive, though a feminist awareness can be incorporated into any of the above models of art therapy more or less comfortably.

### Chapter 10. Social art therapy: art therapy as social action and art therapy as research tool

Increasingly, art therapy is being used as part of social action (Hogan 1997, 2003, 2012a; Kaplan 2007) and social change (Levine and Levine 2011). Individuals may wish to speak out. Art may be made for both personal and political purposes; the highlighting of the AIDS pandemic was an example of this, with art being displayed to raise awareness. Similarly, work with traumatised domestically abused women has been exhibited to de-stigmatise being the recipient of violence.

Some social art therapy blurs the line between art therapy and participatory arts, employing art therapy techniques to facilitate art elicitation groups (Hogan and Warren 2012).

Art therapy is also being used as a social science research method (Hogan 2012c; Hogan and Pink 2010; McNiff 1998; Pink et al. 2011). This chapter will outline current work in this area.

*Chapter 11. A critical glossary of terms*

Key concepts have been defined and discussed separately.

## The intention of the book

Many art therapists are eclectic in their practice, taking a technique from Gestalt art therapy here and working with a concept derived from psychoanalysis there. The chapters in this book could be thought of as colours on an artist's palette for those who wish to pursue such an eclectic approach. However, this book is an attempt to disentangle the different theoretical approaches and to present them in a coherent manner so that they are easier to understand and so that there is more clarity in general. Hopefully, art therapists can use this book to think more carefully about the nuances of their practice, and to understand better the origins of the ideas in use.

Art therapy students can use this book to help them articulate their position in a more intelligible manner, to gain insight into the development of these ideas, and to make the conceptual leap from these different stances to how they represent different ways of conceptualising what human beings are.

In relation to theory, art therapists vary. Some will work very comfortably with not knowing, and be very circumspect and sensitive to not foreclosing potential meanings; they will be like the best kind of anthropologists visiting an unfamiliar people and trying to fathom unfamiliar complexity, not wishing to impose their own schemas. Theory is almost put to the side (or is so assimilated into practice that it is performed unobtrusively). Other art therapists might feel much more comfortable working in a relatively tight disciplinary conceptual framework such as person-centred or CBT. That might be right for them and the people who select for that.

I wrote each chapter with enthusiasm, and in so doing convinced myself that each of these approaches, if sensitively executed, could be efficacious. I hope this book will help art therapists enrich their practice.

For introductory reading on art therapy, see Hogan, S. and Coulter, A. (2014) *The Introductory Guide to Art Therapy*, London: Routledge.

# Chapter 2

# Cognitive behavioural art therapy

This chapter will outline the theory and practice of cognitive behavioural art therapy; it will then include a mini-chapter on solution-focused brief art therapy (SFBT).

The idea of behavioural therapy is often attributed to the work of Russian psychologist Ivan Pavlov (1849–1936), who began work in the 1890s with dogs; he was interested in how the dogs could become 'conditioned' to respond in certain ways to particular stimuli (most famously to the sound of a bell). He fed the dogs whilst subjecting them to a particular stimulus (such as a flashing light, or a particular sound) and then noted that the stimulus on its own produced increased salivation, because the stimulus had become associated with eating.

Behavioural therapy emerged in the 1950s and worked with the ideas of conditioning and deconditioning. It seemed to work well with phobias where the feared object or situation could be gradually introduced, often following a period of relaxation. Cognitive behavioural therapy (CBT) was developed in the 1970s and emerged as a prominent treatment method later in the 1980s (Hall and Iqbal 2010, p. 7). In England, the Layard report described CBT as the most developed of the short-term, evidence-based therapies on offer; these new therapies, Layard wrote, 'are short, forward-looking treatments that enable people to challenge their negative thinking and build on the positive side of their personalities and situations. The most developed of these therapies is cognitive behavioural therapy (CBT)' (2006, p. 4). This report gave a boost to CBT provision following its publication.

The basis of cognitive therapy is a focus on distorted thought processes, which give rise to emotions and behaviours. There is more than one specific approach, but what they have in common is a belief 'that it is not events per se but rather the person's assumptions, expectations, and interpretations of events that are responsible for the production of negative emotions' (Malchiodi and Rozum 2012, p. 89).

Assumptions, expectations and interpretations are analysed. The task of cognitive therapy is to identify patterns of understanding that are unfounded and possibly inaccurate; these are challenged and more adaptive ways to think and behave are formulated. In this definition the positive aspects are highlighted.

We can immediately see that such an approach is philosophically, and potentially ethically, problematic. A religious believer may interpret events as signs from God, but in a social context where such interpretations are tolerated, or even encouraged (the 'Bible Belt' of North America, for example), is this an 'unfounded' or 'inaccurate' way of perceiving the world? Surely it is the interpretation which will be valorised and endorsed by others, affording social support and social integration?

Actually, potentially 'unfounded' beliefs may be perfectly acceptable and even adaptive in certain social contexts. For example, I may get out of bed in the morning and say a positive affirmation to myself. I've been told by behavioural psychologists that using positive affirmations will boost my confidence, so I stand in front of my bathroom mirror and say, 'Susan you are a very beautiful and lovely human being.' I hope this will perk me up for my forthcoming morning. Nine out of ten people given a continuum of boxes to tick would probably not tick the 'very beautiful' box, opting instead for the 'attractive' or 'somewhat attractive' options (depending on their ideals of beauty). So is this fundamentally 'unfounded' self-affirmation a problem? Can some 'faulty' thinking be adaptive and useful? Beck, without irony, gives the example of a patient who was diagnosed with 'dependent-personality disorder and obsessive-compulsive disorder', who told him 'The best time of my life was in the army. I didn't have to worry about what to wear, what to do, where to go, or what to eat' (Beck *et al.* 2004, p. 6). Clearly, his 'disorders' had been adaptive during his successful military career.

Perhaps it is not 'inaccurate' thinking per se that is the problem here, as so many CBT writers might have us believe, not to mention the awkward task of deciding what might be 'faulty' cognitive processes. However, it is entirely plausible that our assumptions and expectations will influence our interpretations of events. We view the world through a personal lens. Furthermore, we are continually engaged in a process of what psychologists call 'self-reinforcement', so an attempt towards the production of 'rational, adaptive thought patterns' is surely warranted and potentially useful (Rubin 2001, p. 212). Again, as I have highlighted above, there may be disunity between what is adaptive and what may be deemed rational. We need to work with the knowledge that understandings of rationality are 'situated'. I am not suggesting absolute relativism, as reason may have persuasive or apodictic force; however, our 'thought styles' are always, necessarily, culturally situated (Douglas 1996).

Art therapist Malchiodi describes CBT thus:

> The basic goal of CBT is to help the client identify the false and negative rules and assumptions governing his or her actions and then find ways to replace or restructure assumptions with more realistic and positive rules and expectations. A collaborative relationship between the client and the therapist is at the foundation of this approach and treatment is generally time limited and psycho-educational in nature.
>
> (2012, pp. 89–90)

Malchiodi and Rozum (2012, p. 90) identify the key components of CBT as:

1   identification of problematic thinking;
2   restructuring of negative thoughts;
3   or elimination of such thoughts;
4   clarification of when feelings of anxiety or panic elicit automatic responses, and learning to control these;
5   mastering basic skills to remain symptom free.

Advocates of CBT point out that it is pragmatic in focus and avoids excessive jargon. CBT is interested in how thoughts stimulate feelings, which in-turn generate physiological responses, which then lead to behaviours and further thinking. 'It is a psychological treatment that addresses the interactions between how we think, feel and behave' (Somers and Querée 2007, p. 3).

Rubin posits the overriding goal of CBT as the gaining of self-control:

> For adults, cognitive-behavioural art therapy helps to decrease behavioural problems, increase awareness of triggers leading to socially inappropriate behaviours, and improve locus of control . . . Children in cognitive-behavioural art therapy can learn to manage aspects of their own behaviour. For people of all ages, increased self-control can lead to more personal choice and freedom; and personal power, in turn, can lead to a richer and more meaningful life.
>
> (2001, p. 218)

This definition of CBT focuses on reinforcing positive behaviour and learning; 'CBT is a process of teaching, coaching, and reinforcing positive behaviours. CBT helps people to identify cognitive patterns or thoughts and emotions that are linked with behaviours' (Somers and Querée 2007, p. 7). The authors then move on to talk about 'dysfunctional thoughts':

> Different people can think differently about the same event. The way in which we think about an event influences how we feel and how we act . . . People do not have to continue to think about their experiences in the same way for their entire lives. By identifying dysfunctional thoughts and by learning to think differently about their experiences, people can feel differently about these experiences, and in turn, behave differently.
>
> (2007, p. 8)

With regard to triggers, these may be context driven and activated by specific tasks (public speaking, in disagreement or refusal, or decision making, for example). Beck points out that levels of awareness at referral vary enormously; some people present with disorders such as depression, but underlying this are what have become dubbed 'personality disorders'. Others 'are very much aware of the self-defeating elements of their problems (e.g. overdependence, inhibition, and excessive avoidance) but remain unaware of the personality aspects or the role of personal volition in change' (Beck *et al.* 2004, p. 5). Beck *et al.* give examples of the 'schemas' that people develop:

> A person entering a group including unfamiliar people may think, 'I'll look stupid', and hang back. Another person may respond with the thought, 'I can entertain them'. A third may think, 'They're unfriendly and may try to manipulate me', and will be on guard. When differing responses are characteristics of individuals, they reflect important structural differences represented in their basic beliefs (or schemas). The basic beliefs, respectively, would be: 'I am vulnerable because I am inept in new situations', 'I am entertaining to all people', and 'I am vulnerable because people are unfriendly'.
>
> (2004, p. 14)

Somers and Querée elaborate on the idea of 'faulty cognitions' which create schemas:

> Most of the time people believe things about themselves and the people around them because they have good evidence for their beliefs. However, people are often very selective in the evidence that they focus on (or what they believe to be 'fact'). A depressed individual may remember the person who ignored her in a conversation but not remember the person who found her interesting. Therefore, she may conclude, 'I am a boring person'. Cognitive-behavioural practitioners help people understand how, by selecting particular evidence to focus on, they can end up forming beliefs that are 'cognitive distortions'. The individual may not even be aware that they have formed these beliefs. Such cognitive distortions are problematic, not only because they can be inaccurate, but also because they contribute (more than necessary) to debilitating negative emotions or avoidance of troubling situations. People can learn to recognize their automatic thoughts, monitor and scrutinize these thoughts, and pay attention to evidence that supports alternative beliefs (for example, 'Some people find me pleasant and interesting to talk to').
>
> (2007, p. 8)

Table 2.1 gives another example of how structural differences can result in different feelings. The table shows possible reactions to the same event, that of a friend not arriving when expected for dinner. Such schemas are widespread, but in those with personality disorders certain beliefs can be more pronounced, repetitive, compulsive, insistent, entrenched and resistant to change. Underlying beliefs which maintain schemas are identified (Beck *et al.* 2004, p. 30). Often these are negative self-appraisals which occur as 'automatic thoughts' called NATs (Beck *et al.* 2004, p. 31). Information may be processed selectively to maintain these outlooks; there is therefore a loss of 'rational modes' of cognitive function (Beck *et al.* 2004, p. 32).

*Table 2.1*

| Thoughts | 'How dare she do this to me! She is so inconsiderate and rude!' | 'She probably didn't want to come because she doesn't really like me. I'm such a loser.' | 'What if she's had an accident? She could be seriously hurt.' | 'I expect she's stuck in traffic. At least I have extra time to prepare dinner.' |
|---|---|---|---|---|
| Feelings | Angry | Depressed | Anxious | Relieved |
| Possible behaviours | Tell her off or act chilly when she arrives. | Withdraw from people and stop asking them over. | Phone local hospitals. | Continue preparing dinner. |

Source: 10MinuteCBT (www.10minutecbt.co.uk/?More_about_CBT:Basic_Principles_of_CBT).

Beck *et al.* suggest that reinvigorating the 'reality-testing' function is of prime importance in CBT and that the therapist takes on this function as 'auxiliary reality tester' for the person (2004, p. 32). They suggest that those subject to depression, for example, are good at incorporating negative information about themselves, but block positive information, hence their cognitive function is 'dysfunctional' (Beck *et al.* 2004, p. 32). How data are processed depends on our 'personality organisation'; however, states are seen as potentially mobile and a personality disorder is seen as able to shift into an anxiety state, which in-turn could lead to depression. Repetitive cycles may become established. Certain patterns of behaviour tend to be overdeveloped at the expense of others, thus an obsessive-disordered individual would be characterised by 'an excessive emphasis on control, responsibility, and systematization and a relative deficiency in spontaneity and playfulness' (Beck *et al.* 2004, p. 35).

## CBT in practice

Key aspects of the approach are a collaborative identification of issues, leading to agenda setting and goal setting. In CBT assessment questions are asked that aim to examine thoughts, feelings and behaviours. Simmons and Griffiths (2009) explain that a 'formulation' is different from a diagnosis because it seeks to proffer an explanation and is not a 'label' as such. Sheldon (2011) points out that a formulation is more than a summary as the 'working out' is shown; this includes 'best guesses on the likely origins, patterns of development and present-day manifestations' of presenting problems – 'A good formulation is both a summary of main aetiological elements . . . but it has dynamic features too' (p. 184).

The following illustration concerns children who were tearful and fractious at leaving school time, so were referred to Social Services via the school. Though not using quite the same structure as that recommended by Simmons and Griffiths (2009) below, Sheldon gives this as a good example of a case formulation because it shows the students' thinking:

Because of his lack of experience with children and his anxieties about discipline, Mr A. tended, on joining the family, to crack down severely on minor infringements of rules – what he calls 'starting as you mean to go on'. However, the children's relationship with him is not sufficiently well developed that they are willing to accept this as his legitimate role. They see it instead as a rejection of them; as a desire to dominate them, and to replace their natural father. Discussion of this problem with the family and the drafting out of a simple agreement describing the obligations and expectations of both adults and children may be a useful temporary measure to reduce the present high level of conflict (rows and slaps) between Mr A. and the children. A separate series of meetings with Mr A. and Mrs L. aiming at teaching Mr A. how to express his positive feelings towards the children in a way that they can accept (including how to deal with rebuffs) should enable him to cope better in joint activities. It would be a good sign if these increased beyond their present low level.

(Anonymous trainee in Sheldon 2011, p. 184)

The formulation should be open to revision in relation to new information or developments; it's a working document. Thus, a 'formulation' is a model of the individual's problems and what might be contributing to them. According to Simmons and Griffiths (2009, p. 47), key aspects of a formulation could include:

- *Predisposing factors*. Aspects which help to address the 'why me' question. Core beliefs are noted. This might entail looking at the past.
- *Precipitants*. Information is solicited about what was happening just before the individual developed symptoms.
- *Triggers*. As noted above, these are any factors which activate symptoms on a regular basis. For someone anxious about going out, the trigger might be opening the front door or stepping over the threshold.
- *Symptoms*. These are divided up into physical symptoms (hyperventilation, a racing heart etc.); thoughts ('no one likes me'); feelings (sadness, anxiety etc.) and behaviour (e.g. not going out).
- *Maintenance cycles*. These are how all of the above information fits together. Once the maintenance cycles have been ascertained, ways of breaking them can be considered.

A formulation is often developed through the use of a written record or log. Part of the formulation is identification of the 'maintenance cycle'. Here is an example from Simmons and Griffiths (2009, p. 78) of one for a man diagnosed with agoraphobia, showing a cyclical pattern:

- thoughts (I will collapse in front of everyone);
- feelings/emotions (anxiety; fear of embarrassment);
- feelings/physical sensations (heart beats fast; feels hot);

- behaviour(s) (avoids going out);
- he does NOT learn that he would not have collapsed, but thinks he had a lucky escape, thus leaving the original thought reinforced;
- thoughts (I will collapse in front of everyone).

A formulation will include sections on: predisposing factors – the why me?; precipitating factors – the why now?; and protective factors – what helps? It will identify core beliefs, core assumptions, trigger situations and resulting problems. It will also identify key thoughts, emotions, physical sensations and behaviours. Conducting a formulation is an essential competency for cognitive behavioural therapists. A maintenance cycle is also devised as part of the formulation, which is shared with the client (Simmons and Griffiths 2009, p. 75).

Logs and diaries analysing links between perceptions, emotions, sensations and behaviours are an important part of this process. 'The logs can chart thoughts, feelings, behaviours, bodily changes, events and other people's behaviour' (Somers and Querée 2007, p. 12). Coping strategies are identified as part of this process (though not immediately challenged):

> The formulation looks to the links among these elements to explain what keeps a problem going. For example, in an individual with paranoia, being looked at by a stranger ([an]other's behaviour) may trigger the thought, 'He is going to attack me', which leads the individual to run away immediately (behaviour). If the individual runs away every time he sees a stranger look at him, he will never find out that the stranger would actually pass him by, and so he remains afraid. Part of the therapy would involve helping the individual to look at strangers, despite his fear. After looking at several strangers who do not attack him, he will gradually realize that his thought or belief about strangers is unfounded. There can be several formulations if the individual has more than one problem (for example, depression and a fear of going out in public).
>
> (Somers and Querée 2007, p. 12)

Self-monitoring through the use of diary sheets is also often used to measure behaviour (for example the number of times someone suffering from obsessive anxiety might check that the oven is turned off), also noting the intensity of feeling associated with the action. According to Simmons and Griffiths (2009, p. 53), diary sheets tend to be used once an intervention is under way, but they can also be used to help generate new formulations.

Formulations can change as the individual presents new information and experiences through the course of treatment (Somers and Querée 2007, p. 12). The actual sessions are typically very structured:

> At the start of each session (or in preparation for the next session), the qualified CBT practitioner and individual seeking treatment draw up an agenda of what topics they plan to cover and then attempt to work through them systematically.

Between-session practice is also structured, as are future expectations, to achieve specific goals the person in treatment desires. The use of structure promotes accountability, organization, and ultimately, progress in treatment.

(Somers and Querée 2007, p. 11)

The logs mentioned above play an important part in this process:

The logs might ask the person to keep track of beliefs he has (for example, 'I am boring'), the feelings associated with the belief (for example, 'I feel unloved'), the evidence he has for the belief (for example, 'I don't have as many friends as my brother which means that people don't find me interesting') and alternate evidence (for example, 'I do have a few close friends who want to see me regularly so they must find me fun to be with').

(Somers and Querée 2007, p. 11)

Here is an example of the sort of material that can be contained on a thought-evaluation sheet:

1    Situation. Where were you? Who was there? What were you doing? When?
2    Emotion(s). What did you feel at the time? How strongly did you feel it? (0–10)
3    Thoughts and/or Images. How strongly do you believe the thought? (0–10)
4    Evidence for the thought. What direct evidence do you have to support it?
5    Evidence against the thought. What direct evidence do you have against it?
6    Alternative (balanced) thoughts. Rate how strongly you believe this alternative. (0–10)

(Simmons and Griffiths 2009, p. 137)

As we can see, this is a simple tool which functions to enable CBT clients to start to identify and challenge their own negative automatic thoughts (aptly abbreviated as NATs); these sheets are viewed in the CBT session and if, in the evidence box (number 4 above), another NAT has been entered, that might be challenged. In completing section 5, the clients are forced to challenge their own negative thinking, and in the final section to replace it with a more balanced thought. This is something a lot of people do quite reflexively (she walks into kitchen, looks at the mess and thinks: 'I am turning into a slob . . . Oh, I mustn't be so hard on myself; my kitchen is usually immaculate and people often comment on how nice it is, so it must look good. Yes, that's true'). In psychotherapy, a client will very often say something self-depreciating and then self-correct in precisely this way, and the psychotherapist can prompt towards finding the counter-evidence (or even provide the counter-evidence based on her or his knowledge of the client), as well as facilitating exploration of the negative inner dialogue. We can see how this tool can teach someone to start to do this and break a cycle of internal self-criticism, and aid in the practice of replacing such thoughts with a more balanced assessment.

Here are some questions recommended for the evaluation of NATs:

- Am I only noticing the 'down' side of things?
- Am I expecting myself to be perfect?
- What would I say to one of my friends if they were thinking like this?
- What would one of my closest friends say about this?
- Am I assuming that my way of looking at things is the only way?
- Am I assuming that my way of looking at things is the right way?
- Am I blaming myself for something that is not my fault?
- Am I judging myself more harshly than I would judge others?
- What are the pros and cons of thinking this thought?
- Am I feeling hopeless about the possibility of changing things?
- What is the evidence for the thought?
- Am I making any thinking errors?
- Do I often think like this when in a certain state of mind?
- When I am feeling different do I think differently about things?
- Are there certain situations or times when I see things differently?
- Are there any experiences I have had that contradict this thought?

(Simmons and Griffiths 2009, p. 138)

These tools are used to enable the client to achieve her or his own goals. Tasks should start simply and be achievable, and specific. 'I don't want to feel shy any more' doesn't provide a specific goal, for example, but 'I will talk to one colleague during the coffee break' is more definite. They should be positive in orientation, moving towards a desired outcome (rather than 'away' from a negative aspect) so that the goal is framed in a way that allows it to be worked towards tangibly. Goals need to be recorded to plot progress over time and therefore need to be measurable (the logs and diary sheets noted above are used). Time-limited goals are particularly recommended; 'I'll go to the super-market and walk up one aisle in the next month', is an example given. So, to summarise, goals should be:

- graded
- specific
- positive
- measurable
- realistic
- time-limited.

(Simmons and Griffiths 2009, p. 85)

Another important part of CBT is often described as psycho-education. This involves getting clients to think about different types of thinking biases in order to be better able to identify their own NATs. The most common sorts of thinking disorders are identified as follows:

**Catastrophising**
*When the worst possible outcome is predicted and magnified.*
If I make a mistake I will lose my job.
I can feel my heart beating fast; I am going to die.

**Mind-reading**
*Guessing another person's thoughts.*
They thought I looked stupid.
She didn't really want to meet up with me.

**Fortune-telling**
*Predicting a bleak future, without evidence for it.*
There is no point, I will just fail at it.
I am always going to be like this.
No one will ever love me.

**All-or-nothing (black and white) thinking**
*Only seeing the extremes, being unable to see the grey areas.*
If I don't get 100 per cent I am a failure.
If he doesn't phone me every day he doesn't love me.

**Discounting the positive**
*When positives are viewed as worthless or meaningless.*
He was just saying that to be nice.
Anyone could have done that.
N.B. Look out for 'yes buts' in response to positive information.

**Overgeneralisation**
*A single negative event is viewed as affecting everything, or as a signal that everything will go wrong.*
The bus didn't turn up. Everything is going wrong.
I burnt the cake. The whole party is a disaster.

**Personalisation**
*Feeling responsible when not at fault.*
It's my fault no one is enjoying themselves.
They cancelled the trip because they don't want to go with me.

(Simmons and Griffiths 2009, p. 128)

## Cognitive behavioural art therapy

Negative imagery can form part of many disorders, from distorted body images in eating disorders, to social phobia. To give some examples:

if a woman with an eating disorder sees herself in her mind's eye as disgustingly fat and ugly, and this image is associated with her core beliefs about herself as being unacceptable and worthless, the constant repetition of the image may be a powerful driver of the disorder. Likewise, the man with social phobia who pictures himself dripping with sweat and bright red while he tries to hold a conversation with a new acquaintance will fear social interaction because his image of himself represents a feared self that he does not want others to see, as well as a belief that he will be rejected or humiliated if other people do see this self.

As well as the very specific images of self, in many disorders there are images of fearful situations, which range from vivid memories of traumatic situations to images of a feared object such as a snake or spider. Although the self may not be directly represented in these images, the individual's beliefs about the meaning and consequences of these feared images often have negative consequences for the self. So for example, the person with PTSD [post-traumatic stress disorder] who has constant intrusive images of the trauma may fear that he or she is going mad, or losing control.

(Stopa 2009, pp. 65–6)

In art therapy there is the opportunity to explore images pictorially using art materials. Schaverien (1998), for example, discusses how art works can allow 'previously terrifying' images to become assimilated. She notes that the art work may 'come to be experienced by its maker as the embodiment of the image it carries . . . It may temporarily be experienced as 'live' (p. 167).

In CBT this may be called 'imaginal exposure'; exposure to feared stimuli or feared situations has been a critical component of behavioural therapy, in two forms: *in vivo* (exposure to the live stimulus) and imaginal exposure, which is exposure via the imagination, typically through visualisation (Stopa 2009, p. 72). Guided imagery could be used, in which a story is told and the client is asked to imagine the scenes.

Images can be multi-sensory, with remembered sounds and tastes and bodily responses; often with PTSD a particular smell can be the trigger. Frequently, CBT practitioners ask for a description of a feared situation – this could be drawn or painted. Stopa gives the example of Layden's open questioning: 'Do you see a picture? Are you seeing something? Is there something flashing through your mind? In the image, where are you? Is there anyone else there? What are you doing, saying, thinking, feeling?' (Stopa 2009, p. 69). Layden argues that, because early abuse or neglect is often implicated in personality disorders, 'critical meanings about the self are often encoded pre-verbally and therefore contain sensory and perceptual rather than verbal information. Imagery can provide a route to accessing and changing the meaning of these stored experiences' (cited in Stopa 2009, p. 69). It is noted that patients with personality disorders may experience high levels of distress and arousal when they are doing imagery exercises. Arguably, using art materials might give the client more control over the pace of such visual exploration, which is otherwise potentially re-traumatising. (Layden's open questioning also sounds a lot like Gestalt technique, which will be discussed in a later chapter.) CBT practitioners have ways to help with experienced distress; for example, having a 'safe space' to return to after the imagery exercise, or at any point if the client feels unable to continue. This is elaborated on in some depth, focusing on sensory details. Sopa puts it thus: 'starting off by creating a safe place in imagery can provide the patient with confidence in the method as well as the knowledge that he or she can create a powerful refuge in the imagination' (Stopa 2009, pp. 70–1).

In CBT there is a tradition of using mental images to envisage new emotional responses and ways of being. This is called 'imagery rescripting':

> Here, the core of the technique is its focus on changing a person's memory in his or her imagination through the use of imagery. This can be done in a number of ways, which can include imagining a different ending to the event or bringing an adult into a memory of childhood abuse . . . There can also be transformations of either the victim or the perpetrator, such as making a child grow bigger and turn into an adult, or shrinking a perpetrator such as a school bully . . . Imagery rescripting differs from prolonged exposure in that it is an explicit attempt to change the nature and thus the meaning of the memory within the imagery process itself. It also differs critically from guided exposure in that the patient generates the solution . . . the therapist's role is to help the client discover his or her own resolution rather than suggesting or prescribing an alternative scenario or attempting to rescue the client.
>
> (Stopa 2009, p. 85)

At the end of the imagery rescripting session, client and therapist can explore shifts in perception that may have arisen.

Art therapy can be used in a way that is instrumental in aiding these processes. Clients are often asked to envision themselves behaving differently in different situations, and this can be done imaginatively and through the use of art materials.

Negative thinking and its triggers are identified. Negative automatic thoughts (NATs) or 'negative self-talk' are identified with contexts and situations and are challenged (Corey 2009). Art is used within this framework: for example, in exploring and reframing traumatic events. As with CBT, in which clients are asked to imagine themselves behaving, thinking and feeling differently by using mental images, clients can make actual images which can then be manipulated (Malchiodi and Rozum 2012). Malchiodi and Rozum recommend that the art therapist starts off by asking the client to make an image rather than a list, and then asks questions to help the client define his or her problem, such as:

> 'What is the problem?'
>
> 'What does the image tell the viewer about the problem?'
>
> 'What thoughts came up during the making of the image?'
>
> 'What thoughts are you having now?'
>
> (2012, p. 92)

They make the following recommendations for the use of images in treatment, including any or all of the following:

- *Make an image of a 'stressor'.* Identifying stressors that trigger negative feelings is a key to understanding and developing strategies about how to cope. The therapist may direct the client to keep an imagery journal of events, situations, or people that initiate negative behaviours or self-talk.
- *Making an image of 'How I can prepare for a stressor'.* For example, if being in a social setting is stressful, a client may be asked to create an image of 'what I can do' or 'how would I look if I were successfully meeting this challenge'.
- *Make an image of 'step-by-step management' of a problem.* For some individuals it is helpful to break down the problem or stressor into steps to a solution. Making an image or series of images that illustrate how the problem can be divided into more manageable parts or components can visually assist some clients in learning how to master difficult situations and any problem behaviours that result from these experiences.
- *Making imagery for stress reduction.* The very act of making images – whether drawing or constructing a collage – can be used as 'time out' from negative experiences and may be useful in inducing a relaxation response . . . A therapist may also suggest to clients that they collect photo images that they find self-soothing from magazines or other sources and put these into a visual journal or keep them in a prominent place such as the office where they can regularly be seen.

(Malchiodi and Rozum 2012, pp. 92–3)

Art techniques can be usefully integrated into those forms of CBT that use a relaxation period as part of the process, in conjunction with soothing music, smoothing and manipulating soft clay or Plasticine, or combining large brush strokes with breathing exercises (Lusebrink 1990; Rosal 2001). Images can be used to examine 'inner speech'; the inner speech can be depicted and then manipulated: 'According to cognitive behavioural theory, an adaptation of the external message will ease the adoption of an internal adjustment' (Rosal 2001, p. 217).

Malchiodi and Rozum point out that 'homework' between sessions can be visual (2012, p. 93). Internalised self-messages can be recorded pictorially: 'As part of the assigned homework, the client may be asked to visually chart dysfunctional thoughts and feelings (a standard assignment) and also produce at least one image a day that represents the most pervasive thought the client experienced' (2012, p. 93). After recognition of negative thoughts, mental schemas can be identified, and then challenged.

Rosal argues that the art-making process can be used as a form of cognitive behavioural art therapy. She suggests that it is a misconception that CBT practitioners just focus on thoughts (as already noted mental images are important), but she thinks this is why more art therapists have not embraced the CBT model.

She argues that 'when cognitive processes are used in art therapy the emotional components of experiences are not only included, but are an integral part of understanding a person's cognitive process system' (Rosal 2001, p. 213). Furthermore, she suggests that:

> Art therapy is particularly suited to CBT, because making art is an inherently cognitive process. When creating a piece of art, the artist must be involved in uncovering mental images and messages, recalling memories, making decisions, and generating solutions. Whether drawing or sculpting, creating art involves instant feedback systems and the ongoing reinforcement of satisfying behaviours. Each brush stroke that appears on the paper can suggest or promote further action (feedback) as well as delight (reinforce) the artist. Creating art means that there is a concrete record of inner processes. This concrete record can be discussed, altered, and redrawn to satisfaction. It can also be used to recall past events and as a reminder of positive emotional experiences.
>
> (Rosal 2001, p. 217)

Malchiodi and Rozum concur, suggesting that: 'Once the therapist has led the client through the process of analysing thoughts and schemas, the client may develop more positive assumptions by experimenting with physically altering a negative image through art expression' (2012, p. 93). Although this model is more developed in North America and Canada than in the UK, with pressure for evidence-based practice and shorter-term interventions, this model is likely to be further developed and adopted in Britain.

Simmons and Griffiths (2009, p. 100) suggest that mindfulness can be used as a part of CBT and that exercises can be used such as handling a particular textured material, listening to sounds or observing colours in a room. This will be discussed further in the chapter on mindfulness approaches.

## Solution-focused brief art therapy

Solution-focused brief therapy (SFBT) will be briefly elaborated on. Although philosophically located within a constructivist framework, this is essentially a behavioural technique in which the individual identifies aspects of her or his life that she or he wishes to change. The therapist assists by asking questions that help the recipient to clarify possible solutions and the means of achieving them. The technique focuses on what the individual desires to achieve; it is a method that attempts to utilise the strengths and capacities of the individual. Identifying such strengths might entail some analysis of previous situations, or events, in which the recipient successfully generated a solution. However, generally, it is future-focused and 'goal-orientated'. Often, an incremental approach is used, with small manageable steps being taken. The assumption here is that small changes lead to further changes, and eventually to a key change, but without major disruption as the changes have been small; 'Thus, small steps toward making things better help the client move gradually and gracefully forward to accomplish desired changes in their life and to subsequently be able to describe things as "better enough" for therapy to end' (Shazer and Dolan 2007, p. 2). Another core idea is that the solution is not necessarily connected to the problem. Whilst many approaches have problem-leading-to-solution sequences, a solution-focused approach, as the name suggests, develops solutions by first eliciting an understanding of what will be different were the problem solved. Shazer and Dolan (2007) explain that this leads to a therapy which spends very little time looking at the origins of problems (dysfunctions or pathology). The language used is positive and avoids 'problem-talk'. This in turn indicates the often transient nature of problems and embraces the idea that people are not necessarily locked into particular patterns of interactions and ways of being. In this sense, it is almost antithetical in technique to core aspects of CBT and the formulation in particular. The future is seen as created and negotiable and one in which the individual has control over his or her destiny; it is hopeful. People are seen as resilient. The past is relevant only insofar as solutions previously used may be recounted and reflected upon.

Unlike other types of therapy, solution-focused therapists do not proffer interpretations, nor do they confront their clients, nor do they delve into areas which seem unproblematic to look at deeper meanings or structures. Questions are the primary tool used in this model. As noted above, questions are present- or future-focused. What is already working and how the client would like his or her life to be is the emphasis. Validation of what is going well and acknowledgement of how difficult problems are, give encouragement and also underline the fact that the therapist is listening and is receptive to his or her client's situation (Shazer and Dolan 2007, p. 5). Clear goals are paramount.

Scaling questions are frequently employed. To help analyse aspects of their lives, individuals are frequently asked to access them on a scale of 0 to 10, where 10 equals the achievement of all targets and zero is the worst possible scenario. The person undergoing SFBT is asked to identify his or her current position and the point at which there might be adequate fulfilment. Within this structure it is possible to define ultimate objectives (Iveson 2002). This approach is also particularly associated with the 'miracle question', which is explained below. There are variations on this but here is the version that is reproduced by Shazer and Dolan:

> I am going to ask you a rather strange question. After we talk, you will go back to your work (home, school) and you will do whatever you need to do the rest of today, such as taking care of the children, cooking dinner, watching TV, giving the children a bath, and so on. It will come time to go to bed. Everyone in your household is quiet, and you are sleeping in peace. In the middle of the night, a miracle happens and the problem that prompted you to talk to me today is solved! But because this happens when you are sleeping, you have no way of knowing that there was an overnight miracle that solved the problem.

So, when you wake up tomorrow morning, what might be the small change that will make you say to yourself 'Wow something must have happened – the problem is gone!'

(Berg and Dolan 2001, p. 7, cited in Shazer and Dolan 2007, p. 6)

Or, put another way:

A miracle happens while you're sleeping and the miracle makes the problems that brought you here disappear.

But this happens while you're sleeping so you can't know it happened.

How do you and people close to you discover this miracle happened?

(Shazer and Dolan 2007, p. 38)

Given enough time to reflect, most people can ascertain some things that would have to be different; identifying these changes allows goals to be ascertained. Some of these goals might be pictured. The miracle question is also called the 'reality question' because the client needs to think about tangible things which would indicate that something had changed; it is not about wishful thinking, and it assumes that the client has the capacity to think of his or her own solution, to set goals and to work towards them (Shazer and Dolan 2007, p. 38).

To summarise, this chapter has articulated the philosophical and theoretical underpinnings of cognitive behavioural therapy and outlined the idea of psychological schemas. The chapter then described CBT in practice, explaining the key concept of the formulation. Various ways in which CBT is used were articulated. Key ideas such as triggers, goals and maintenance cycles were explained. The role of logs and diary sheets for self-analysis was articulated. The chapter then moved on to look at how imagery is used in CBT and also gave some examples of what cognitive behavioural art therapy might look like. A further mini-chapter followed on the cognitive behaviourally orientated approach of solution-focused brief art therapy, which can form a part of CBT or be used as a distinctive modality. In a further chapter, some parallels between CBT and mindfulness techniques will be drawn.

# Chapter 3

# Psychoanalytic art therapy

## The basic principles of psychoanalysis

In the psychoanalytic schema the human mind is often compared to an iceberg floating in the sea. The bit above the waterline is consciousness. Just below is the pre-conscious, and deep below, in the murky depths, is the unconscious.

The personality (or psyche) of the individual is seen as comprising three main structural elements: the super-ego, the ego and the id, which are in a state of constant dynamic tension. The *super-ego* is the moral part of the self which responds to the demands of civilisation, and includes the ideas of a conscience, discipline, self-restraint and self-sacrifice. It is learnt, and appears later developmentally; it is where parental *introjects* are seen as located, as Freud saw self-observation as developing out of a process of *internalisation* of the parents, or split-off parts of the parents (*object-representations*), which become *internal objects* (Rycroft 1968, p. 160). Internal objects are a crucial part of the psyche; these are *object-representations* which have acquired the significance of external reality or, to put it another way, they are mental representations of an external object (or part object) which is experienced 'inside'. This is called variously an *introject, introjected object* or *internal object*, and can take symbolic forms (Rycroft 1968, p. 77).

The concept of the *super-ego* was developed as an embellishment of the ego. This is the part of the mind that indulges in self-criticism and self-scrutiny: 'conscience is one of its functions and . . . self-observation, which is an essential preliminary to the judging activity of conscience, is another of them' (Freud 1973, p. 91). Freud described it as 'a special critical and prohibiting agency' (1973, p. 57).

The *ego* is viewed as the conscious, rational part of the mind that negotiates with the other parts of the psyche and is seen as attempting to create a compromise between conflicting impulses. The ego represents reason and common sense. If there is good ego strength then the ego will succeed in maintaining balance; if the ego is weak, the personality may become unbalanced and consequently too ruled by either the super-ego or by the *id*.

Sigmund Freud (1856–1939) gives the example of an overactive super-ego, implicated, he believed, in episodes of melancholia; it becomes:

> over-severe, abuses the poor ego, humiliates it and ill-treats it, threatens it with the direst punishments, reproaches it for actions in the remotest past

which had been taken lightly at the time – as though it had spent the whole interval in collecting accusations and had only been waiting for its present access of strength in order to bring them up and make a condemnatory judgement on their basis. The super-ego applies the strictest moral standard to the helpless ego which is at its mercy.

(1973, p. 92)

Alternatively, Freud postulates a 'shattered' ego (1973, p. 90).

The ego is seen as having various 'mechanisms' at its disposal to maintain this balance, which will be elaborated on. For example, the idea of '*repression*' is the idea of the ego's attempts to thrust painful memories deep down into the unconscious mind so that they are effectively forgotten (though they may be rekindled later and cause problems). Another important defence mechanism is that of *projection*, in which thoughts are attributed to someone or something else. Freud saw a number of mechanisms at play to do with flows of psychic energy and conflicting internal forces.

The third part of the tripartite model of the mind is called the *id*. The id is the primitive part of the self. Instinctual behaviours and basic needs are viewed as being governed by the id. The id is seen as demanding immediate satisfaction and pleasure. It is interested in the gratification of needs, rather than morality (and is therefore in conflict with the super-ego). To talk of the id containing unconscious thought is a misnomer perhaps, as it is psychic energy which is not readily available as conscious material, so the term 'thought' is misleading. Freud describes it as dark and inaccessible, as unorganised, emotional, oblivious to space and time, ungoverned and ungovernable; in many respects it is the antithesis of the ego. It is governed by the *pleasure-principle.* A person too dominated by the id would tend towards being sociopathic and amoral.

Developmentally, the id is seen during infanthood (and it remains infantile in the adult); the ego then develops, and lastly the super-ego. These theoretical constructs allow for a mobile or 'dynamic' view of the mind and have been immensely influential. The parts of the mind are seen as dynamic, insofar as they are constantly active. Psychoanalysis (and *psychodynamic theory* arising from psychoanalysis) sees inter-psychic conflicts as a form of stress that can result in psychological disturbance.

Sigmund Freud revised his ideas many times, and they have subsequently been debated and fought over. It is not possible to present a definitive account of psychoanalytic theory in one chapter, but I shall attempt to give the reader an understanding of the sophistication of Freud's thinking, which has had profound reach and influence on twentieth-century thought.

## The importance of the unconscious in psychoanalytic thinking

This is an approach that theorises basic psychological forces governing human behaviour through the above outlined structures. These energies are seen as underlying human action in a way that is not always obvious to the individual: repressed thoughts, *beyond our conscious note or recall*, are believed to 'give rise to behaviours and experiences which seem to come from "somewhere else"' (Frosh 2002, p. 15).

Being unconscious is not realising the existence or occurrence of something, being 'temporarily insensible' (Oxford Dictionaries 1973, p. 2406). In psychoanalytical theory, however, unconscious processes refer to psychic material, which is only rarely accessible to awareness and which is repressed or pre-conscious (the latter may arise into consciousness more easily). It is believed that such psychic material can have a profound influence upon behaviour.

The unconscious is not, therefore, a psychic dustbin. Unconscious material is considered to govern our behaviour. Thus the unconscious mind is viewed as 'primary and causal; it makes us what we are', as Frosh (2002, p. 13) asserts. Furthermore, repressed material can fight its way out of the unconscious, often becoming distorted en route, through a mechanism that Freud calls '*displacement*'. Displacement is a 'process by which energy (*cathexis*) is transferred from one mental image to another' (Rycroft 1968, p. 35). This idea is important to the psychoanalytic theory of symbolism, which will be discussed. *Repression*, already mentioned in passing, is a *defence mechanism* by which an intolerable impulse or idea is rendered unconscious. It can involve the displacement of energy to a less threatening idea or object (*sublimation*). There is not a consensus among modern psychoanalysts about what material is repressed. Repression (primary repression) is an adaptive mechanism allowing adjustment to context and ego development. Rycroft puts it like this: 'repression resembles a dam holding back the flow of a river' (1968, p. 142). However, repression, if excessive, may lead to problems of ego development and symptoms rather than sublimations. Here is an explanation of this:

> Because repression is unconscious, it manifests itself through a symptom, or series of symptoms, sometimes called the 'return of the repressed'. A repressed sexual desire, for example, might re-surface in the form of a nervous cough or a slip of the tongue. In this way, although the subject is not conscious of the desire and so cannot speak it out loud, the subject's body can still articulate the forbidden desire through the symptom.
>
> (*New World Encyclopedia* 2013)

'When used loosely, the unconscious is a metaphorical, almost anthropomorphic concept, an entity influencing the SELF unbeknownst to itself' (Rycroft 1968, p. 173). In the 1920s Freud renamed the conscious mind as the 'ego' and the unconscious mind as the 'id' (a potentially useful distinction), the id, as noted above, being associated with 'instinctual' energy, and the gratification of basic needs, the 'ego' being the more cultivated civilised and socialised aspects of the psyche. Rycroft discusses why the use of the term 'unconscious' is potentially problematic:

First it can be and is used to obliterate a number of other distinctions, e.g. voluntary and involuntary, unwitting and deliberate, unself-conscious and self-aware. Secondly, it can be used to create states of sceptical confusion; if a person (patient) accepts the general proposition that he may have unconscious motives, he may then find himself unable to disagree with some particular statement made about himself, since the fact that it does not correspond to anything of which he is aware does not preclude the possibility that it correctly states something of which he is unaware. As a result he may formally agree to propositions (interpretations) without in fact assenting or subscribing to them.

(1968, p. 173)

It is potentially problematic for art therapists to offer interpretations for precisely these reasons, because the therapist's view may be hard to resist, especially if unconscious motivations are invoked. Rycroft also discusses the potential problem that a client may 'entertain an indefinite number of hypotheses about their unconscious motives without having any idea how to decide which of them are true' (p. 173). It makes much more sense, I'd maintain, for any interpretation of an art work to be undertaken by the art therapy participant, as thoughts and feelings reach his or her awareness. The other, very serious reason for avoiding focusing on 'unconscious' motivations for clients' behaviour is, as Rycroft suggests above, that it is simply too crude and can distract from the more helpful task of enabling clients to explore their own psychological motivations and complexities (Hogan 2012a). It is not my intention to try to re-convert the psychoanalytically inclined here, so much as to point out the conceptual pitfalls associated with the use of this term. Making assumptions about what might be unconscious in art or discourse is potentially problematic and art therapists need to be aware of this (Hogan 2012a, 2014).

## Symbolism

It is not possible to have a proper understanding of psychoanalytic art therapy without an understanding of symbolism, so this section will explain the difference between analogies, similes and symbols, though it is acknowledged that this is the language of artistic endeavour so tends to be familiar to art therapists.

Symbols, similes and analogies are sometimes confused. A simile is the explicit comparison of two *unlike* things: for example, 'she was like a rose'. An analogy gives a correspondence; it is the illustration of an idea by means of a more familiar, but *similar* or equal idea: the analogy between a heart and a piston pump, for example. Analogies may be presented in the form of an extended simile (Baldick 2001).

A symbol, in contrast, is 'a material object representing something immaterial; an emblem, token or sign . . . Something that expresses, through suggestion, an idea or mood which would otherwise remain inexpressible or incomprehensible; the meeting point of many analogies' (*Macquarie Dictionary* 1981, p. 1720).

'Something that stands for, represents, or denotes something else (not by exact resemblance, but by vague suggestion, or by some accidental or conventional relation); esp. a material object representing or taken to represent something immaterial or abstract' (Oxford Dictionaries 1973, p. 2220), for example a wedding ring is a symbol of marriage.

In psychoanalytic theory, symbolism is seen as arising out of an inter-psychic conflict between the repressing tendencies of the unconscious mind and the repressed – 'only what is repressed is symbolised; only what is repressed needs to be symbolised' (Jones 1916, cited in Rycroft 1968, p. 162). This is a key idea. Furthermore, the object or activity symbolised is theorised as being, 'always one of basic, instinctual, or biological interest' (p. 163). Symbolism is seen as generated from particular material. Therefore, the word 'symbolic' is used in a particular way by psychoanalytically orientated writers. There is also a term in psychoanalytic thinking – *condensation* – for when a single word or image represents several thoughts or images. It has multiple meanings. It has become particularly 'loaded'.

Symbolic representation is immensely important in all forms of art therapy (not just psychoanalytically orientated work), as feeling states and ideas which would be difficult or impossible to articulate verbally can be represented by symbols and metaphors. Symbols are often 'mysteriously indeterminate' with many possible meanings, or multiple meanings. Baldick speaks of literary symbols, but his point applies equally to images when he suggests that it is, 'usually too simple to say that a literary symbol "stands for" some idea as if it were just a convenient substitute for a fixed meaning; *it is usually a substantial image in its own right around which further significances may gather* according to differing interpretations' (Baldick 2001, p. 252; my italics). Thus symbols offer a rich and complex mode of communication.

## The psychoanalytic theory of symbolism

It has already been noted above, first, that symbolism is seen as arising out of conflict between the repressing tendencies of the unconscious mind and the repressed but still active material there; second, that only what is repressed is symbolised; and, third, that a symbol is the result of intrapsychic conflict. It is early infantile material which is posited as having been repressed, especially the manifestation of infantile sexual life; 'these infantile experiences have attached to them all the imperishable, unfulfilled instinctual wishes which throughout life provide the energy for the construction of dreams' (Freud 1973, p. 58). With these unfulfilled wishes may also arise other buried events, which are swept upwards, buoyed along in the psychic current, 'in their mighty uprush, of forcing to the surface, along with the rest, the material of distressing events' (Freud 1973, p. 58).

It has been noted that repressed material may reach consciousness through a process of *displacement* (the process by which a mental image with a 'weak charge' of psychic energy takes over the charge from a mental image with more energy, enabling it to force its way into consciousness). Displacement is the part of the conceptual apparatus (called a *primary process*) that allows one image to symbolise another; however, the resulting symbols are not conscious thoughts, the process of their production is believed to be quite unconscious. Whilst some theorists posit that symbols are not 'formed' during displacement, because they already exist in the unconscious, the act of displacement would seem to allow for transformations of form and content.

In this schema, symbols are an unconsciously produced 'substitute' for something else:

> This approach is often characterised as 'regressive' . . . What is important here is the unconscious nature of the symbolic process, and the 'primary' nature of what is symbolised . . . the classical psychoanalytical position, as expressed by Freud, and supported by Jones, restricts the term 'symbolism' to cases where the substitutive process operates largely unconsciously and in the service of defence . . . Symbolism and symbolic activity is the result of a compromise between repressed and repressing forces.
>
> (Petocz 1999, p. 10)

Freud discusses in his *New Introductory Lectures* (1932–3) how repressed instinctual impulses can become hallucinations; the impulse unable to be expressed by action while the subject is sleeping is transformed 'into a collection of sensory images and visual scenes' (1973, p. 48). Such sensory and visual scenes are called *phantasies*.

He also acknowledges how difficult it is to interpret such imagery as the forces of repression act against this with active *resistance*. In his own words, 'The copious employment of symbols, which have become alien to conscious thinking, for representing certain objects and processes is in harmony alike with the anarchic regression in the mental apparatus and with the demands of censorship' (Freud 1973, p. 49). The relationship of repression to symbolism was not entirely evident and, in the 1930s, Freud acknowledges being baffled by the ubiquity of symbolic material in dreams:

> One of the tasks of psychoanalysis, as you know, is to lift the veil of amnesia which hides the earliest years of childhood and to bring to conscious memory the manifestations of early infantile sexual life which are contained in them. Now these sexual experiences of a child are linked to painful impressions of anxiety, prohibition, disappointment and punishment. We can understand their having been repressed; but, that being so, we cannot understand how it is that they have such free access to dream-life.
>
> (Freud 1973, p. 58)

But he then counters his uncertainty and suggests that through a process of wish-fulfilment dreams may eradicate distress and transform disappointment into attainment.

## Summary and discussion

So to summarise, symbolism arises where there are opposing psychical forces. Thus, an unacceptable unconscious desire may be transformed into a symbol (via *displacement*), or indeed a physical symptom (via a process called *conversion*). Dream images and symptoms are examples of symbol formation, born out of a similar process. Furthermore, these psychic constructions are seen by some psychoanalysts as unique to the individual:

> 'True' or psychoanalytical symbolism, in fact, resembles dreaming and symptom-formation in that they are private constructions, the meaning of which is discoverable only in terms of the individual experience of the subject and not by reference to dictionaries or social conventions.
>
> (Rycroft 1968, pp. 162–3)

There is some tension between Rycroft's assertion and a suggestion explored by Freud (and embraced by Jung) that symbols are phylogenetically transmitted and are part of our archaic cultural heritage. This idea led Freud and others to look for constant and universal meanings in symbols. Freud gives numerous dogmatic examples in his *The Interpretation of Dreams* (1901). Both ideas are evident in his writings. In later work he notes that in his *associative* method, simple translations are seldom possible, and it is clear that he considers a more individualistic understanding of symbols, even if they are seen as rooted in the archaic remnants of collective symbolic language. Symbols are certainly seen as a residue of archaic thinking and 'an inherited, archaic, primitive, regressive mode of expression' (Petocz 1999, p. 29).

By the 1890s Freud had developed parallels in his work between primitive and neurotic behaviour (Wallace 1983, p. 22). He pathologised 'primitive' or 'atavistic' tendencies, writing in 1900, 'a good deal of symbolism is shared by dreams with psychoneurosis' (Freud 1900, p. 343, cited in Wallace 1983, p. 26). In *The Introductory Lectures in Psycho-Analysis* (1916–17), Freud conceptualised dream symbolism explicitly as a survival of prehistoric modes of expression (Wallace 1983, p. 12). He drew on the work of philologist, Hans Sperber (1912), who suggested that sexual needs played an important part in the development of human speech. The first speech summoned the speaker's sexual partner, and when speech was later used in other contexts it retained its sexual connotations. Thus 'sexual interest became attached to work' which was accompanied by rhythmically repeating utterances (Freud 1963, p. 167). Freud applied these ideas to dream symbolism:

> We should understand why dreams, which preserve something of the earliest conditions, have such an extraordinarily large number of sexual symbols, and why, in general, weapons and tools always stand for what is male, while materials and things that are worked upon stand for what is female. The symbolic

relation would be the residue of an ancient verbal identity; things which were once called by the same name as the genitals could now serve as symbols for them in dreams.

(Freud 1963, p. 167)

A sentiment that is perhaps absurd to the modern reader.

Freud's theory of symbol formation, as described in *The Interpretation of Dreams*, is complicated, but commonly symbols in dreams are seen as 'disguised representations' of 'latent thoughts' (Freud 1977, p. 280), especially 'wish fulfilments' (Freud 1977, p. 280). Involuntary ideas, with a repressed sexual aetiology, he argued, would often emerge in a visual form in dreams (Freud 1977, pp. 470–3). Such images arise from the primary processes that contain 'wishful impulses from infancy, which can neither be destroyed nor inhibited'; these 'irrational' primary processes force their way through the repressing tendencies of the secondary processes and are 'charged with uninhibited energy from the unconscious' (Freud 1977, pp. 763–8). Freud expressed his interest in the 'regressive archaic character of the expression of thoughts in dreams' (cited in Forrester 1980, pp. 469–70).

An analogy between madness and artistic symbolism became established. The implications of such theorising are essentially negative, as expressive art work may be seen as pathological (Hogan 2001). The corollary of such theoretical links was rather frighteningly played out in Freud's own lifetime via the Nazi destruction of 'degenerate art' from public and private collections (Hogan 2001). However, psychoanalysis did set a precedent for exploring mental illness through an elaboration and exploration of symbolism, so this can be seen as one tributary leading to the development of a modern art therapy.

The exploration of symbolism in psychoanalysis is done via a technique which has become known as *free association*, in which the patient is asked to articulate any ideas that come spontaneously to mind, without reservation and making no attempt to concentrate (the latter was supposed to minimise *resistance*). The technique is based on the premise that what is significant will emerge and that 'therapeutic need' will also influence the direction of the work. The technique is thought to relax the censoring mechanisms of the psyche. The therapist helps the patient to reflect on the material.

The Symbolism art movement (*c.*1885–1900) laid great emphasis on the importance of imagination and fantasy, with an focus in art on feelings and sensations, and with an aim to evoke subjective states of mind in visual forms (Chipp 1968, p. 49). In its broader sense, Expressionism became the predominant form of new artistic movements of the twentieth century; its emphasis on a highly subjective, spontaneous form of self-expression is typical of a range of modern art movements (Hogan and Coulter 2014). The Surrealist art movement was a response to free association, claiming to throw off the shackles of the intellect with a technique called 'pure psychic automatism', described by André Breton in 1924 in the *Premier Manifeste* as a process in which the artist should 'express, verbally, in writing, or by other means, the real process of thought, without any control exercised by reason, outside of all aesthetic or moral preoccupations' (Hogan 2001, p. 94). Notwithstanding the difficulty of the quest, here we have a translation of Freudian ideas into artistic endeavour, although the primary aim is not therapeutic.

## The object-relations turn

There has also been a turn towards *object-relations* among many post-Freudians; as noted earlier, Freud saw self-observation as developing out of a process of *internalisation* of the parents, or split-off parts of the parents (*object-representations*), which become *internal objects* (Rycroft 1968, p. 160) or, indeed, *part objects*. Part objects, born out of infantile instincts, were postulated as 'bits' of the care giver; if developed as part of the oral drive, for example, it could be the mother's breast. Or if part of exhibitionist impulses, it could be the mother-as-looker, rather than the 'whole' person (Greenburg and Mitchell 1983, p. 41). Another important idea is that of *splitting*, where two contradictory feelings are split off from each other and one becomes the focus. These ideas were further developed by other theorists, especially by Melanie Klein.

Certainly, the notion of *self-representation*, which is how an individual feels herself to be in relation to significant others in terms of her inner representation, is something that many art therapists would work with. Though some theorists modified Freud's work, others have sought to replace his theory of drives with one founded on *object-relations*; the latter is a 'fundamentally different conceptual framework in which relations with others constitute the fundamental building-blocks of mental life. The creation, or recreation, of specific modes of relatedness with others replaces drive discharge as the force motivating human behaviour' (Greenburg and Mitchell 1983, p. 3).

Object-relations theory has been criticised in general terms for putting too much emphasis on the very early stages of development and for framing this in a particular way which blames the mother. There is no doubt that traumatic disruptions early in childhood can have an impact on development (particularly extreme neglect); however, object-relations theory sees a sustained 'good-enough' connection with the mother, which is internalised, as essential, otherwise further stages of development can be impaired. This is rather deterministic and the language used is often misogynistic, as the mother (even a conscientious and responsive mother) is invariably conceived as problematic; she can be 'too engulfing', 'not allowing space for separation', 'distancing and not allowing connection' (Kavaler-Adler 2011), or she can be even 'too good' and denying her infant the vital experience of frustration (Hopkins 1996, p. 410)! That an infant might be 'too well understood' (Hopkins 1996, p. 412) points to a theoretical underpinning in which, '*there is no such thing as a good enough mother*' and I have pointed out that this has implications for the mental health of new mothers who are left feeling that they can't get it right (Hogan 2012b, p. 79). It is also a red herring.

Many art therapists today work with a mix of psychoanalytic and object-relational ideas in a psychodynamic framework. Others work with a more open integrative model which will be described later.

## Psychoanalytic art therapy

'At root, psychoanalysis is formulated as a discipline devoted to uncovering hidden meanings, reaching below the surface of action and consciousness to reveal the disturbing elements of unconscious life' (Frosh 2002, p. 74). The role of the analyst is towards *facilitating* the patient's self-expression; the belief in modern practice is a 'belief that the stream of associations would eventually lead to the recall, more or less spontaneously, of emotionally charged memories surrounding important and significant events of the patient's past' (Sandler *et al.* 1973, p. 105). Frosh suggests that this leads the patient 'to a form of linguistically mediated self knowledge which gives her or him more control over experience' (Frosh 2002, p. 81).

There is also some confusion over terminology, with 'psychoanalytic' and 'psychodynamic' being used interchangeably; as illustrated above, these terms are not synonymous. David Edwards suggests that modern psychoanalytically inclined art therapists tend to use the term 'unconscious' to refer to the contents of the mind that are not present in consciousness at any given moment. He asserts that:

> In practice, art therapy is often concerned with gaining access to and making sense of this unknown or unacknowledged 'inner world' and the ways in which it influences relationships in the external world. The ways of working developed by art therapists are based largely upon the belief that through making images and objects, and the relationship between the art therapist and the client, long-buried conflicts and feelings may find expression. By facilitating the emergence of inner experiences, within the secure environment provided by the art therapist, the client is offered an opportunity to further their self-understanding. Through externalising internal experience it becomes possible to stand apart from, think about and change it. Psychoanalysis has played such an important role in the development of art therapy largely because it offers both a method and body of ideas for accessing and understanding the unconscious mind.
>
> (Edwards 2004, p. 44)

Many art therapists are psychodynamic rather than classically psychoanalytic, as they reject the basic premise that symbols are the result of repressed, unconscious conflicts; rather, they articulate the view, following the view of Suzanne Langer, that symbols are a fundamental and intrinsic form of self-expression. Milner, for example, argued that symbols were able to integrate and transform experience and should be regarded positively. Anna Freud said of Milner's book:

> It is fascinating for the reader to follow the author's attempts to rid herself of the obstacles which prevent her painting, and to compare this fight for freedom of artistic expression with the battle for free association and the

uncovering of the unconscious mind which make up the core of the analyst's therapeutic work.

(Freud 1957, preface to Milner 1957, p. xiii)

Grace Pailthorpe used object-relations theory as the basis of her interpretations, drawing on the work of Melanie Klein. She asserted that 'every mark, shape and colour is *intended* by the unconscious and has its meaning' (Pailthorpe 1938–9, p. 16). The following is an example of an interpretation of a painting which depicts a house on a hill, foregrounded by a large leafless tree, which leans to the right. In a small dark doorway sits a symmetrical white ball. To the left of the doorway is a figure on a balcony walking or running towards the doorway. The interpretation produced bears little relation to the actual pictorial content:

> The house is a symbol of a mother. He has stolen the ball, a breast symbol, and the father tree is after him to punish him for the theft. The branch projecting from the tree in the direction of the ball is the father's hand stretching forward to feel the breast-ball to see if he, the child, has damaged it.
>
> (Pailthorpe 1938–9, p. 11)

Unfortunately, such interpretation illustrates how the reductive and dogmatic application of object-relations theory can overwhelm pictorial content. Art therapists will encourage the use of art materials, and then facilitate a dialogue in relation to the image. Few now offer interpretations of the art work, such as that above. However, here is an example of an art therapist's interpretation:

> At root it came from her perception of a split-off bad part of her 'internal object' . . . Paddy shot a fearful glance at me, as if she had just recognised me as the bad witch, and as if she was experiencing me in the same way that the infant part of herself has experienced the persecuting mother. When I put this to her she became quite frightened and moved away to a table at the far end of the room . . . the witch mother image had been made real. In order to escape these feelings of persecution Paddy's ego attempted to transfer her 'projected sadism' from something of her own creation.
>
> (Weir 1987, p. 112)

Here is an extract from my critique of that: 'It is just possible that Paddy's fear was due to the strange interpretation of the therapist who seemed not to be interested in what she was really trying to express' (Hogan 1997, p. 41).

I have suggested elsewhere that reductive dogmatic interpretations based on particular psychological schemas are counterproductive, and I have reproduced numerous undesirable examples (Hogan 1997, 2001, 2003, 2012a, 2012b, 2013a). I have conducted a detailed critique of Freudian (Hogan 1997, 2001, 2012a) and object-relational theory-based interpretations (2012b), suggesting how the interpretations given were problematic; for readers who would like to think about this in further fine detail, I refer you to these critiques.

Many art therapists have been critical of the interpretative method; among the most articulate is David Maclagan, who suggests that:

> By conjuring up the mirage of an alternative 'unconscious' intentionality which is in competition with consciousness, psychoanalysis (at least in the classical, Freudian forms) sets up modes of explaining a painting's hidden meaning that in effect act out a rivalry with the creative work they are purporting to analyse . . . the psychoanalytic privileging of depth over surface also had the effect of splitting the 'superficial' aesthetic level of a painting from its deep unconscious meaning.
>
> (2001, p. 13)

Frosh (2002) too acknowledges interpretation as problematic; 'how one works out whether an interpretation is a "good" or "bad" one, let alone "true" or "false", is deeply problematic' (p. 82). In the end he concurs with Karl Menninger, that psychoanalysts:

> are not oracles, not wizards, not linguists, not detectives, not great wise men . . . who 'interpret' dreams – but quiet observers, listeners, and occasionally commentators . . . their *occasional* active participation is better called intervention. It may or may not 'interpret' something. It may or may not be an interruption. But whenever the analyst speaks he contributes to a process.
>
> (Menninger 1958, cited in Frosh 2002, p. 82)

# Chapter 4

# Analytical (Jungian) art therapy

Analytical psychology is properly 'Jungian', deriving from the work of Carl Gustav Jung (1875–1961), and is a distinctive departure from the Freudian school of thought which coined the word psychoanalysis. Jung's break with Freud took place in 1913, by which time Jung had developed his distinctive style. This chapter will explore the theory and development of this approach and in particular how it was developed by Dr Irene Champernowne (1901–76), a Jungian analyst who developed an arts-based approach. Differences between Freud's psychoanalysis and Jung's analytic psychology are clearly seen with respect to their respective attitudes towards images, which are distinctive in the two approaches (Hogan 2001). In a nutshell, Jung's idea of *libido* was different from that of Freud and, as a consequence, there are important implications for how symbolism is perceived. Furth, attempting to elucidate Jung's 'libido', provided this useful analogy:

> By libido Jung meant psychic energy, 'the intensity of a psychic process, its psychological value' (Jung 1976, pp. 455–6) . . . Jung compares the progressive nature of psychic energy to a flow of water. Essentially, water that is flowing cannot be stopped. Water flows from a higher level to a lower level. In theory if sufficient water is collected and the water backed up, we would have regression. The water could be channelled elsewhere, or the water could be stored, eventually reaching a maximum level of its own accord flowing off into a new direction. This is seen psychologically as a progressive movement. There must be both a progression and a regression of libido. Opposites exist, producing a balancing effect. Without one the other does not exist . . . A therapist needs to be alert to the flow of energy from a patient's unconscious. This can be ascertained through pictures from the unconscious.
>
> (Furth 2002, p. 4)

Compensatory energy is seen as emerging in symbols; the compensatory symbol is seen as useful. Pictorial symbolism, emerging from the unconscious, acts as a compensation or complement to the conscious psyche in this model, potentially bringing into focus aspects of the person not to the fore. This attitude towards symbolism has important implications for how analytic art therapy is theorised and practised. Jung's theory of compensation will be explored in further detail and linked to art therapy practice. Like Freud, Jung wrote a large body of work over which there is still plenty of argument. This chapter will therefore focus in particular on the reception and use of Jung's ideas by analytic art therapists – those art therapists following his ideas and building on them to create an art therapy practice.

## The development of the analytic art therapy model

Withymead was Britain's first art therapy-based therapeutic community. As it would have been difficult to maintain a serious interest in art therapy in Britain in the late 1940s and 1950s without being aware of Withymead, this is a logical starting point for this exploration of the development of analytic art therapy, which was the dominant explanatory schema in the period in which art therapy emerged as a distinctive profession. It was established in 1942, rather spontaneously, following heavy bombardment of Exeter, which left some of those who had been undergoing therapy without homes, and destroyed. Withymead's founder, Irene Champernowne's private-practice rooms. It was a pragmatic development in the context of extreme wartime conditions (although therapeutic community experiments were taking place at the time). Champernowne was also involved in early developments towards the professionalisation of art therapy, attending some of the National Association of Mental Health (NAMH) working parties. The community was undoubtedly the single most important institution in the development of art as therapy in this period in Britain, and arguably towards art therapy as a profession.

All staff had to undergo in-depth 'Jungian' analysis as a condition of their employment. It was possible, and not at all unusual, for a person to arrive at Withymead seeking help and end up, having undergone sufficient analysis, a member of staff helping others (Hogan 2001, pp. 220–31). Professional people such as therapists and artists also came to Withymead seeking 'analytical help for a deeper and more creative insight into their work' and thus Withymead provided early informal art therapy training (Champernowne and Lewis 1966, p. 164). Indeed, Champernowne is quite clear on this point saying, 'no one who has not experienced something of the power of healing within these modes of expression is really fit to be a healing teacher or art therapist' (1963, p. 104). The lack of a tidy boundary between patients and therapists (all could be called 'residents' if residential) was a distinct feature; this was also evident in the analytical psychology establishment, in which 'analysands' could attend meetings of the Zurich Psychological Club (1913–48); a reflection of this could be seen in Withymead (Hogan 2001, p. 231). Withymead was also in close contact with the Analytical Psychology Club in London.

The work of the community centred around a weekly community staff committee meeting at which every patient was discussed, so that the 'depth of crisis or problem' was to be understood by all, in relation to the events and subtleties of community life. The underlying assumption was that different parts of the patient's personality could be manifested in his or her different relationships with various members of staff, such that 'transference' might be exhibited. To get a total picture of a person, it was necessary to think about the totality of her or his relations. Transactions between people were considered. Free discussion among the members was thought to resolve personal difficulties which, 'if unrecognised, might adversely affect patients' (Champernowne and Lewis 1966, p. 165).

If we think of the Latin *'trans'* for 'across' (in this case between people), and 'transact' as meaning to manage and settle affairs, then we can see the community staff meeting providing a place where the emotional affairs of the community were managed and settled. 'The development of "transference" was encouraged as a way of allowing patients to fully express their personality. It was regarded as positive so long as close communication between staff members allowed them to build up a total picture of the patient' (Hogan 2001, p. 249). Changing an emotional element in relation to a person could change that person. So this was the very particular 'frame' in which art therapy practice developed, one in which psychodynamic analysis was key.

## Underpinning theory: compensation

To understand fully how art therapy functioned in the studios, it is necessary to elaborate the idea of the 'compensatory function' of the unconscious mind. This has been defined as 'the self-regulatory (homeostatic) functions of the organism. Compensation means balancing, adjusting, supplementing' (Samuels *et al.* 1986, p. 32).

Furth elaborates the basic idea:

> An example is an individual who is easy-going, amiable, has no ego identification, is sometimes 'tred upon' [trod upon], and thus may become, at times, angry at an unconscious level. This person never displays his anger, but remains silent. He then reports dreams of fighting, bombing, and physical violation of other dream characters. These dreams would be seen as compensatory; they compensate for his overly-passive conscious attitude and keep his psyche in balance by allowing the energy of the anger to flow.
>
> (2002, p. 9)

Corrie, an important proponent of Jung's work, suggested that 'Every exaggerated quality in the conscious will be compensated for in the unconscious by its opposite' (1927, pp. 14–15).

Jung believed that repressed contents of the mind are 'excluded and inhibited by the conscious orientation of the individual lapse into unconsciousness and there form a counter-pole to consciousness . . . He regarded the compensatory activity of the unconscious as balancing any tendency towards one-sidedness on the part of consciousness' (Samuels *et al.* 1986, p. 32). So, as the conscious inhibition strengthens, so does its counter in the unconscious, eventually breaking through to consciousness:

This counter-position strengthens with any increase of emphasis upon the conscious attitude until it interferes with the activity of consciousness itself. Finally, repressed unconscious contents gather a sufficient energy charge to break through in the form of dreams, spontaneous images or symptoms. The objective of the compensatory process seems to be to link, as with a bridge, two psychological worlds. That bridge is a symbol; though symbols, if they are to be effective, must be acknowledged and understood by the conscious mind, i.e. assimilated and integrated.

(Samuels *et al.* 1986, p. 32)

This idea of symbols being a link between worlds is rather different from the psychoanalytic view of symbolism as we have seen. Furthermore, the idea that images might aid in creating equilibrium is a positive view of their role.

Constance Long, an important proponent of Jung's early work, explained this understanding of the unconscious, pointing out that the creative mind has a general balancing function, which is not driven by a limited range of primary instincts concerned with wish-fulfilment, as in the psychoanalytic model:

He regards it as being the creative mind, and as having a balancing tendency also . . . repression is not referred to sexuality and the primitive instincts alone, but to all the neglected and under-valued material belonging to the various psychological functions of thinking, sensation, and intuition.

(Long 1920, p. iv)

Shamdasani (1995) suggests that Long and Corrie's work together constituted the dominant English understanding of Jung's work and 'hence reflect[s] how Jung would have been understood in England at the time' (1995, p. 1).

Long explains the difference between 'Jungian' analytic psychology and 'Freudian' psychoanalytic perspectives. She argues that in Freud's view the unconscious knows no other aim than the fulfilment of wishes – it exhibits only 'primitive tendencies', whereas Jung's idea is that *all* psychic phenomena, including the dream and the neurosis, are manifestations of psychic energy or 'libido' (which can be loosely defined as 'life force' in his special usage of the term) (Corrie 1927, p. 19). The unconscious is seen as providing significant information which can compensate for the 'one sidedness of consciousness' (Jung 1953, p. 73).

Withymead also worked with the idea that people have a dominant personality type: intuitive, feeling, sensationalist or thinking, and that the less conscious aspects of their total nature could appear in dreams or art work. Jung felt that good health was best achieved by giving voice to the unconscious aspects of the self, as these could play a regulatory role upon consciousness if they are not repressed. Indeed, Corrie explained that if an aspect of the personality became too neglected it could 'sink to a low level of the unconscious to a primitive condition of culture' and thus become a 'destructive force' (1927, p. 56).

Modern writers on analytic art therapy also use this idea of compensation. Here is Furth's explanation of its implications for therapy:

> Jung's theory of compensation is based on his theory of opposites. A therapist should not try to impose any particular behaviour upon the patient, but rather must be willing to accompany the individual's unconscious on its journey. Believing the psyche to be a self-regulating system that is balancing and adjusting itself as necessary, the therapist follows the patient's unconscious as it deals with life. Jung's theory of compensation suggests that the unconscious either complements or compensates for the conscious, thus always striving for balance.
>
> (Furth 2002, p. 8)

Furth elaborates on the analytic attitude towards imagery:

> A symbol from the unconscious always acts in a compensatory or complementary relationship to the conscious status of the psyche at a given moment in life. If the conscious attitude is one-sided, so involved with one aspect of life as to exclude another, then this compensatory energy emerges as a symbol from the unconscious. A compensatory symbol expresses the neglected area, either in a dream or fantasy or in a drawing, in an attempt to bring it to the attention of consciousness and promote a change in conscious attitude. The neglected area always demands attention in some way. Thus the symbol has a healing influence, striving for balance and wholeness.
>
> (Furth 2002, p. 9)

This is an important difference in attitude between psychoanalysis and analytic psychology to the role of symbolism, and towards unconscious material more broadly; in the latter, the Jungian model, the emergence of unconscious material in art works is viewed positively as life enhancing, rather than negatively as evidence of psychopathology, wish fulfilment or unresolved sexual fantasies, as in the Freudian system of thought. 'The attitude of analytic psychology is therefore much more sympathetic to the production of art work than the Freudian theoretical framework' (Hogan 2001, p. 239).

This section has suggested that there are fundamental and irreconcilable differences of approach when it comes to the reception, theorisation and explication of patients' imagery between analytic psychology and psychoanalysis. Corrie suggests that the views of Freud and Jung are 'largely irreconcilable' (1927, p. ix).

## Underlying theory: collective meaning and symbolism

Early analytic art therapists rejected the notion of an a priori interpretation of symbolic meanings, though common symbols might be seen as archetypal (containing universal mythic figures). Nonetheless, both Freud and Jung thought about the collective meaning of symbols; Freud's early psychoanalytic work is full of dogmatic interpretations, based on the interpretation of symbols based on a priori assumptions. In *The Interpretation of Dreams*, Freud suggests that the erect male organ, for example, may be represented by a tree trunk, umbrella, knife, dagger or pike (1977, p. 470). Similarly, the uterus may be represented by boxes, cases, chests, cupboards and ovens (Freud 1977, p. 471). Generalisations include that, 'rooms in dreams are usually women'. It is on this absurd level of generalisation that Freud's work on symbol interpretation is most open to question. Here is an example from *The Interpretation of Dreams*, first published in 1900:

> a dream of going through a suite of rooms is a brothel or a harem dream . . . steps, ladders or staircases, or, as the case may be, walking up and down them, are representations of the sexual act. Smooth walls over which the dreamer climbs, the facades of houses, down which he lowers himself – often in great anxiety – correspond to erect human bodies, and are probably repeating in the dream recollection of a baby's climbing up his parents or nurse. The 'smooth' walls are men . . . tables, tables laid for a meal, and boards also stand for women . . . a woman's hat can often be interpreted with certainty as a genital organ. In men's dreams a neck tie often appears as a symbol for the penis.
>
> (Freud 1977, pp. 471–3)

Similarly, Freud asserts that castration is depicted symbolically in a variety of ways which include hair cutting, decapitation and the falling out of teeth! Clearly, there is a huge difference in approach to unconscious imagery between Long's assertion that there are no fixed meanings to symbols and Freud's dogmatic early interpretations, and although Freud may have modified his views in later work (see chapter above), some of his followers did not (Hogan 1997).

There was some reductive interpretation evident in the Jungian camp too. However, Long asserted: 'For the Swiss School, the meaning of dream symbols is individual and manifold. There are no symbols with absolutely fixed meanings, though there are many typical ones, which appear everywhere. These "typical" symbols are "archetypes"'(Long 1920, p. 120).

There has been considerable debate on this topic, which it is not possible to encapsulate here. Without wishing to get too bogged down in a mass of definition and theory, it is easy to see a possible tension between analytical ideas that all dream symbolism is 'individual' but may also be 'archetypal' and 'collective' (Hogan 2001, p. 241). Archetypes are viewed as a sort of 'racial history' linked to our 'primitive history' and to the 'primordial images and instincts comprised in the collective unconscious' (Long 1920, p. 200). Corrie's understanding of the 'collective unconscious' has it as containing 'traces of experience lived through ancestrally, and repeated millions of times' which are 'imprinted in the structure of the brain, and, handed down through the centuries, [can] reappear in dreams'

(Corrie 1927, p. 16). Thus, the brain of an infant is not seen as a tabula rasa, but as imprinted with 'primordial images' or 'archetypes' which evolve into myths.

To acknowledge that symbols have culturally derived meanings is, on the face of it, a reasonable thing to do. However, some theorists pushed this idea of the 'collective unconscious' rather too far. H.G. Baynes, one of the early leading exponents of Jung's work, explores the ways images can represent psychic states in archetypal categories such as the 'maternal aspect' or 'heroic combat'. These sorts of generalisations provoked Ernst Kris to accuse Jung of working within a 'vulgarised conceptual framework' (Kris 1953, p. 15).

Nor did Campernowne regard symbolic material as just evincing archetypal significance; she also 'continually sought to find literal, personal meanings in her images' (Henderson 1980, p. 2). 'It is therefore not insignificant that she finally succeeded in convincing both Jung and her own analyst, Toni Wolff, that her painting had particular significance in pointing to unconscious aspects of her relationship with Wolff' (Henderson 1980, p. 2). If this is true, then it indicates that both Jung and Wolff were willing to concede that art therapy could provide information which is both factual and personal (Henderson 1980, p. 1). In other words, Jung was willing to rethink his ideas about the archetypal nature of symbols in relation to art works and to reconsider his theory of amplification, which sought to link personal contexts with mythic themes to clarify and make obvious (or 'make ample' – hence amplify) the metaphorical content of symbolism.

Although Jung continued to think that images could contain an archaic character, especially when dealing with mythological motifs, which he thought derived from the collective unconscious, he also acknowledged the possibility of personal images: 'A personal image has neither an archaic character nor a collective significance, but expresses contents of the personal unconscious and a personally conditioned conscious situation' (Jung 1976, p. 443).

However, this view that symbolic material could be personal seems not to have been accepted by the Jungian institutes established by that time, with which Jung had little contact in the final decade of his life (Hogan 2001, p. 242). How Withymead used the concept of amplification will be elaborated on in the next section. It is Long's (1920) view, that *there are no symbols with absolutely fixed meanings*, that prevailed with the first generation of analytic art therapists. Furthermore, their use of the term 'amplification' also reflects this difference in view.

Furth talks of *feeling the meaning* behind the symbol:

A symbol refers to something so deep and complex that consciousness, limited as it is, cannot grasp it all at once. In this way, the symbol always carries an element of the unknown and the inexplicable, that which is not amenable to words, and which often has a numinous quality. Yet the very fact that the symbol exists tells us that at some level we know or feel the meaning behind the symbol. In this tension between knowing and not-knowing, between conscious and unconscious, there is a great deal of psychic energy'.

(Furth 2002, p. 9)

## The art therapy studio approach

The stimulus for the use of the arts came directly from Jung, who said of psycho-therapy that it was 'less a question of treatment than of developing the creative possibilities within the patient' (1963, p. 16). The studios at Withymead were therefore regarded as a 'gymnasium of the soul' aimed at self-development and experimentation 'with one's own nature' through the use of art materials. This was thought to enable residents to 'enter into entirely new modes of experience' (Stevens, BBC Radio 1984, cited in Hogan 2001, p. 238). Jung saw engagement in art as something which could 'bring about a psychic state in which the patient begins to experiment with his own nature, a state of fluidity, change and growth where nothing is externally fixed and hopelessly petrified' (Jung 1954, cited in Champernowne 1963, p. 98). The empowering aspects of art making too were emphasised, promising that through work in the studios 'the painter has found himself as a person . . . his neurosis has disappeared; he has learned self-respect and self-reliance'. Furthermore, it was asserted that engagement in the arts allowed the patient to 'make his mark on life' (Champernowne and Lewis 1966, p. 6).

An assumption in this approach, an idea cherished by Champernowne, was that the unconscious could 'speak' through art work. She felt that art could circumvent the tendency to over-intellectualise in verbal therapy and put the ego in direct contact 'with the voice of the unconscious' (Champernowne, BBC Radio 1975, cited in Hogan 2001, p. 238). This view was espoused by Jung, who suggested that it was possible for an individual's ego to assimilate the content of symbolic content of a picture *without every detail of it becoming conscious*. Jung suggested that when a person does not understand the pictorial detail of their art work it may be because the painter's ego:

> does not have at its disposal those theoretical assumptions, views, and con-cepts which would make clear apprehension possible. In such cases one must be content with the *wordless but suggestive feelings which appear in their stead* and are more valuable than clever talk.
>
> (Jung 1916, cited in Hogan 2001, p. 238; my italics)

Art works might originate in dreams. Sometimes in a psychotherapeutic session Champernowne would say to a resident, 'go and paint as much of that as you can' or 'enlarge it by [making] a picture', or she'd suggest: 'Take parts of it and dream the dream onwards on paper in paint, in poetry, in dance, in mime, in models, in music' (Champernowne 1975, unpublished recording, cited in Hogan 2001, p. 239).

Champernowne saw self-expression using creative media as analogous to dreams, in which material may have significance evincing 'symbols of their life but very often the underside of life – the hidden unconscious aspects of the individual – the compensating, complementary aspects' (Hogan 2001, p. 239).

In this model, art work is a possible bridge between parts of the self. Symbols were regarded by Jung as 'the best possible expression for a complex fact not yet apprehended by consciousness' (Jung 1953, p. 75). Champernowne's idea of 'dreaming the dream onwards on paper' is very close to that described by Jung – indeed, she attributes the phrase to him (Champernowne 1973, p. 22). Jung wrote of the value of painting dreams thus:

> Often it is necessary to clarify a vague content by giving it a visible form. This can be done by drawing, painting, or modelling. Often the hands know how to solve a riddle with which the intellect has wrestled in vain. By shaping it, one goes on dreaming the dream in greater detail in the waking state, and the initially incomprehensible, isolated event is *integrated into the sphere of the total personality, even though it remains at first unconscious to the subject.* Aesthetic formulation leaves it at that and gives up on any idea of discovering meaning.
>
> (Jung 1953, p. 87; my italics)

Such a statement indicates that art making was regarded as potentially therapeutic even when not accompanied by a verbal analysis. Jung felt that giving an emotional disturbance 'visible shape' had a 'vitalising influence' because it reproduced the content of the disturbance in some way either concretely or symbolically (Jung 1953, p. 82). He wrote that:

> Patients who possess some talent for drawing and painting can give expression to their mood by means of a picture. It is not important for the picture to be technically or aesthetically satisfying, but merely for the whole thing to be done as well as possible . . . a product is created which is influenced by both [the] conscious and unconscious, embodying the striving of the unconscious for light and the striving of the unconscious for substance.
>
> (pp. 82–3)

The term 'active imagination' was used in 1935 by Jung for a process of dreaming with the eyes open. The patient concentrates on a specific mood, picture or event and follows a succession of associated fantasies. The content can be painted or written down: 'the images have a life of their own and develop according to their own logic' (Samuels *et al.* 1986. p. 9). In 1932, in an essay on the artist Picasso, Jung was to state his view thus:

> Behind consciousness there lies not the absolute void but the unconscious psyche, which affects consciousness from behind and from inside . . . As this 'inside' is invisible and cannot be imagined, even though it can affect consciousness in the most pronounced manner, I induce those of my patients who suffer mainly from the effects of this 'inside' to set them down in pictorial form as best they can. The aim of this method of expression is to make the unconscious contents accessible and to bring them closer to the patient's understanding. The therapeutic effect of this is to

prevent a dangerous splitting off of the unconscious processes from consciousness [which might then develop into symptoms].

(Jung 1964, p. 136)

He suggested that these pictorial representations of psychic processes, which are not to the fore, point 'in a rough and approximate way, to a meaning that for the time being is unknown' (Jung 1964, p. 136).

This translated in practice to a model of art therapy which was primarily non-directive, as art therapists felt that they were facilitating a *natural* healing process. Edwards described this as a policy of 'non-interference'. The job of the art therapist was regarded as 'facilitating a process' and if necessary 'being at risk of missing things' by standing back; in other words, it was better to fail to direct this process if being in control might hinder its natural progress. The underlying assumption was that the issue at hand would come to the fore, and in a safer way than had the art therapist interfered (Lyle 1995, cited Hogan 2001, p. 245). The art therapy studios were part of a facilitative environment; Jung recommended it be one in which there was 'the universal feeling of childhood innocence, the sense of security, of protection, of reciprocated love, of trust, of faith' (Jung 1930, p. 82, cited in Hogan 2001, p. 249). Champernowne, herself a Jungian analyst, saw her job as 'not to analyse the artistic productions so much as to participate in the artistic language and process thereby supporting its continuous expression. Conscious understanding must come gradually but the process is *healing in itself* (1963, p. 99; my italics). Richard Fritzsche, an art therapist at Withymead, shared this view. He regarded art therapy as 'a "natural" thing' and a 'natural form of language'. Art therapy was regarded as effective without fully conscious assimilation of the paintings' contents. He said of the process that 'the paintings speak to people . . . they are put in touch with the lost part of themselves' (Fritzsche 1995, cited in Hogan 2001, p. 258).

These techniques impressed Dorothy Elmhurst, who wrote of Withymead:

I can't help feeling it holds the key to a whole new development in the art of healing. It becomes so clear to me there, in the art studios, that not only the illness but the cure as well lies in the unconscious and that the arts provide a language whereby the individual spontaneously portrays the unrealised or repressed aspect of himself.

(1952, cited in Young 1982, p. 213)

Art therapist Elizabeth Colyer put her approach like this:

What you actually say about someone's painting doesn't matter as much as the *spirit* in which you receive it. I try not to forget that each painting is a unique expression of the individual who painted it – no one else could have done it. It has to be honoured as a unique creation.

(cited in Stevens 1986, pp. 4–5)

Norah Godfrey, another art therapist, described painting as 'part of the growth of the individual' and 'as a means of developing a more whole personality' (cited in Hogan 2001, p. 259). Michael Edwards stressed that art works were 'honoured' at Withymead. He said:

> Sometimes it doesn't matter that you don't talk about the picture; its presence is recognised. It sounds like New-Age nonsense, but it just doesn't feel like that . . . the fact that you are talking in the presence of a picture changes the way you are talking.
>
> (Edwards 1995, cited in Hogan 2001, p. 259)

Godfrey confirmed that she saw her role as supporting residents to 'gain contact with the inner healing process in themselves, which is self-regulating' and which 'would heal just as a cut is healed on the outside by nature', a process that cannot be rushed. The unconscious was seen as having 'tremendous force' (Godfrey 1995, cited in Hogan 2001, p. 261). Cunningham Dax, a psychiatrist who promoted the therapeutic use of the arts, suggested that the artist (art therapist) should maintain a 'passive' role (1948, p. 11). However, as I have indicated, the art therapists worked within a psychodynamic framework and were facilitative, and therefore not passive, but they were tentative and acutely sensitive to the sometimes very intense work taking place. The act of externalising images from the unconscious, or sub-conscious, in art media was seen as putting psychic material in symbolic forms where it could be:

> experienced more consciously and the creator can relate to them and live with them . . . no longer is there blind identification; what was inside is now out there . . . but one still hopes there is a sense of belonging to its creator.
>
> (Champernowne 1963, p. 98)

Thus material is externalised and this act of putting it down concretely outside creates a distancing; material which was having an effect without this being evident can now be sensed, if not clearly apprehended.

The images were also seen as providing a form of self-expression to material which could not be experienced in any other way. Irene's analyst wrote in 1951, 'I only hope you continue to paint as there is certainly no other form to express these experiences' (Wolff 1951, cited in Champernowne 1963, p. 19).

Godfrey felt that intuition and feeling functions were often rather neglected in general. Important also was acknowledging introversion and extraversion. Godfrey stated that introverts need 'knowledge of the outer world, but also of that strange world within, the world of the spirit which today has been largely abandoned' (1996, cited in Hogan 2001, p. 279). 'Recognition of type differences', recalled Fritzsche, 'was of value in relating to people and their needs' (Fritzsche 1996, cited in Hogan 2001, p. 276). A discourse about *balance* is prevalent. Painting was regarded as 'a self-healing, self-regulating mechanism at work within the individual' (Champernowne 1949, p. 14).

## Therapeutic interventions

Despite the fact that the 'natural process' of image making and the images themselves 'were treated with enormous respect', art therapists did intervene in subtle ways (Edwards 1995, cited in Hogan 2001, p. 259). The staff all had a broad understanding of Jung's idea of function types; the idea of compensatory function has been outlined above. A person's psychological type was thought to have a bearing on the kind of art he or she produced. The four function types, which refer to the functions of consciousness, are as follows: *thinking* (knowing what a thing is), *feeling* (a consideration of the value of something, a viewpoint or perspective), *sensation* (responsiveness to sensations which tells us what something is), and *intuition* (a sense of where something is going or of possibilities without conscious proof). Thus, there was an idea of 'a person's overall style of consciousness and his orientation towards inner and outer worlds' (Samuels *et al.* 1986, p. 153). The four function types often appear on a diagram in four quarters. In this model, it is not possible to 'dispense' with any of the four functions as:

> they are inherent to ego-consciousness. But the use of only one particular function may become habitual and exclude the others. The excluded functions will remain untrained, undeveloped, infantile or archaic and possibly completely unconscious and not integrated into the ego. But it is possible for each function to be differentiated and, within limits, integrated.
>
> (Samuels *et al.* 1986, p. 155)

This idea helped form an underlying premise to the art therapists' work. In other words, if skewed in the direction of a particular function type, art making might enable integration of the other functions into the total personality and therefore form a compensatory action.

There was also a psychodynamic emphasis at a community level. For example, an emphasis on practical tasks in the studio (such as ceramics – producing the cups and bowls used by the community) was considered very useful for patients who were experiencing a great deal of inner turmoil. In such cases, the art therapy might be viewed as complementing verbal analysis. In other words, the verbal analysis might be very intense, so art therapy might become geared towards a greater emphasis on apprehending 'outer' reality, and could include portraiture, still-life or landscape painting. In this way art therapy was considered as providing a balancing or complementary experience to the 'tremendous disturbance that was going on inside'.

Art therapists would also enter into a discourse with the client, by entering into the language of the painting, through a form of amplification (slightly differently defined to that of the analytic psychology establishment, because it is not particularly concerned with identifying archetypes): 'It is possible to accept the material in the state of the subject at the moment, and discuss it from the experimental point of view, rather than from the intellectual interpretation of the symbols used' (Champernowne 1949, p. 14). Here is an example of a 14-year-old boy who painted a sinking ship: 'He told us *through his picture* that he was a sinking ship although he was quite unable to convey his terrible situation in words'. Entering into the 'language' of the picture, and staying with the same mood tone, Irene suggested that 'lifeboats' might 'go to the rescue'. She saw this as entering into the boy's drama, and 'relieving the boy in fantasy' and in so doing 'sharing the problem at least emotionally' (Champernowne 1974, p. 22). This technique is called amplification and it is still advocated by analytically orientated art therapists today (McNiff 2004, p. 79).

Here is a detailed description of an art work from Fritzsche. As it is an evocative and detailed response to an image it is worth quoting at length. It gives a good indication of how early Jungian art therapists responded to images:

> The patient has represented herself bound and floating above the city in the darkness of the night. A golden cord winds round her body beginning at one hand and ending at the other. Not so plain to see is her hair which is strangely blue and spreads far from her head like a fan. It suggests a kind of rootedness in the atmosphere and this quality evidently keeps her in a state of suspense. She is carried away out of the human world below by a breath of wind. Wind and atmosphere have a natural association with the world of the spirit . . . her eyes are points of vivid red: emotional intensity and passion is concentrated there in the intellectual faculty. All this corresponds to the state in which the woman found herself. The body bound, it has become forgotten, its demands unrealised. And it was night time. We see the stars, the cosmos itself. The ordinary world of daily life had given place to the dark background of the spirit-world. The patient is cut off and other worldly.
>
> The picture suggests a return to a state before birth. The body is bound like the seed in the seed-case where life has drawn itself together into its smallest compass. Presently it will fall on the earth and initiate a new cycle of development. If this is so, we can see the power of 'Heaven' and 'Earth' both as regressional urges, the one to the world of the spirit, the other to that of instinct.
>
> (Fritzsche 1964, cited in Hogan 2001, pp. 271–2)

Dr Champernowne recalled saying to this woman, 'You cannot remain floating in space! You must come down to earth' (Fritzsche 1996, cited in Hogan 2001, p. 272).

One is aware, in reading Fritzsche's account, of the underlying religiosity of Withymead:

> It would be easy enough to interpret the image quite differently from a less spiritual perspective; for example, that she felt constrained in her feminine role and disenfranchised from the male-dominated city below her. The red in her eyes could denote suppressed rage etc., etc. It is hard not to read Fritzsche's analysis as being about spiritual rebirth.
>
> (Hogan 2001, p. 272)

It reflects the type of work done in the studios and reflects their 'spirit'. Clients were encouraged to contact a spiritual dimension of themselves as part of the healing process, or rather that spiritual dimension was seen as emerging from the unconscious during the process. The patient's art work was seen as evincing unconscious processes which were regarded as 'undeniably religious'; the pictures emanated from a 'spiritual source' (Fritzsche 1996, cited in Hogan 2001, p. 289). At Withymead the 'unconscious' was used as a synonym for the spirit or even for God.

This chapter, in summary, has sought to articulate key concepts used in the analytic model, such as 'compensation', 'active imagination', 'amplification', 'archetypes' and 'function types', and to explore theories of symbolism in relation to the notion of compensation. It illustrated how the first generation of analytic art therapists believed that paintings could yield information about the patient's unconscious which was specific and personal, and thus was slightly out of keeping with some of the analytic establishment. However, it would appear that Jung himself changed his view on this subject. Art therapy was viewed as part of a natural healing process, essentially one of spiritual death and rebirth. These processes were seen as self-regulating. The unconscious was both admired and feared at Withymead and interference with it viewed as potentially dangerous, but art therapists could intervene in subtle ways to help residents towards self-expression or intervene to help prevent them becoming overwhelmed. There is no doubt that analytic art therapy has quasi-religious overtones, and may be viewed as part of the counter-cultural movement towards alternative medicine.

There is some debate between those analytically inclined as to how conscious symbolic material would need to become in order for it to act therapeutically, with some art therapists suggesting that symbolic material can be assimilated without all aspects of it becoming fully conscious, whilst others argue that symbolic material should be brought into consciousness:

> How do we activate the healing power of the symbol? First of all, we need to bring it into consciousness and to allow its connected energy to flow. Spending time with a symbol invests energy into its flow. Drawing it, writing about it in a journal, or bringing its associations and amplifications to consciousness are means of accomplishing this.
>
> (Furth 2002, p. 11)

However, as previously noted, Furth does acknowledge that symbolic material may not be obvious in terms of its meaning, though is 'felt'.

The idea of healing through 'natural' processes can be seen as part of a cultural shift towards a more holistic method of healing that has now become more dominant; indeed, ideas of homeostasis and equilibrium are central to Jung's compensatory schema. 'Art heals' and 'creativity cures the soul' are the cries of modern analytic art therapists; even the more difficult manifestations of the psyche are still believed to have 'life-affirming purpose' (McNiff 2004, p. 97).

# Chapter 5

# Gestalt art therapy

Gestalt defies easy description, since it is constituted from a variety of approaches and practices that have drawn on many different sources. Zen Buddhism, with its focus on the moment, was one influence. The psycho-dramatic work of Moreno was another. Lore 'Laura' Perls (1905–90) and Frederick 'Fritz' Perls (1893–1970), who championed Gestalt therapy, also drew on an array of developing psychological and physiological research.

Fritz Perls had originally trained in medicine and then as a psychoanalyst in Vienna, completing in 1928. As a Jew he was forced to migrate to escape Nazi persecution, first to South Africa and then to the United States. He became interested in 'interpersonal psychoanalysis' and the work of a number of theorists who were adapting and challenging the work of Freud, including Adler, Fromm, Sullivan and Reich, the latter's work having an emphasis on catharsis. His subsequent interest in field theory (which looks at patterns of interaction between individuals and the environment) and in theories of perception is attributed to the influence of Laura Perls (née Lore Posner) whom he married in 1930. She had completed her doctorate in Gestalt Psychology at Frankfurt University. Indeed, much of the modern shape of Gestalt therapy may have come from her thinking (Sills *et al.* 2012). In particular, she is attributed with developing the 'dialogic' method, which is another distinctive characteristic of this approach: this is an attempt to say what is going on in the therapy situation, not in general terms, but reflecting on the immediate reality of the moment (Houston 2003, p. 20).

## Background theory: a tendency towards wholeness

Gestalt psychologists claim to be interested in the overall function of people, and the German word *Gestalt* (plural *Gestalten*) is translated variously as a 'complete pattern or configuration', 'an organized whole' or an 'overall shape'; there is no exact translation. The work developed in part out of twentieth-century research called field theory, which emphasised the importance of context in creating meaning (Lewin 1935, 1951). Korb *et al.* (1989, p. 1) suggest that three elements are crucial: 'a thing, its context or environment, and the relationship between them' – the context and the thing are indivisible. Sills *et al.* suggest that:

A person is a whole: body, emotions, thoughts, sensations, movements, perceptions and context. They all function interrelatedly to create this whole. This is antithetical to the Western emphasis on dualities such as mind–body, head–heart, individual–group, or person–environment.

(2012, p. 11)

We are born into a web of relationships or a 'field' (Ullman and Wheeler 2009) and these are interconnected; we are constantly engaged in 'co-creating experiences' from moment to moment. With reference to the pioneering work of Kurt Lewin, Sills *et al.* (2012) explain this further. The individual is seen 'both within and in relation to the environment. How we perceive and experience the environment will be dependent on our needs at a particular moment in time . . . A change in any aspect of the field changes the whole field' (p. 71).

Complexity theorists and others now 'suggest that we are engaged in ongoing processes of human interactions where people are forming patterns of relating whilst at the same time being formed by them' (Sills *et al.* 2012, p. 71).

Mackewn summarises the main principles of Gestalt field theory as follows:

1 People cannot be understood in isolation but only as integral and interactive wholes with their socio-cultural background and ecological environment.

2 The field consists of all the interactive phenomena of individuals and their environment and all aspects of that field are potentially significant and interconnected.

3 Human behaviour cannot be attributed to any single cause but arises from the interlocking forces of the field (or as a function of the organisation or constellation of the field as a whole).

4 The field and the forces operating in the field are in a continual state of flux. Individuals are constantly changing their perspective of the field as they organise and understand it differently, from moment to moment.

5 People actively organise and reorganise their perception of their circumstances (or field) by continually making some aspects of that field focus while others become [the] background, and vice versa. The need or interest organises the field.

6 People endow the events they experience with individual meaning.

7 In these ways they contribute to the creation of their own circumstances and lived experience (they co-create the field and have existential responsibility for their own lives or at least the meaning they give to their lives).

8 Human behaviour and experience happen in the present and a person's behaviour can only be explained in terms of the present field.

9 As all aspects of the field are interconnected, change in any part of the field is likely to affect the whole field.

(1997, p. 49)

Theories of perception were also important to the development of Gestalt psychology, particularly a postulated 'urge to complete': a phenomenon termed 'apophenia', the tendency to see patterns (Mackewn 1997, p. 15). Humans are argued to have an innate urge to 'make meaning out of perceptual stimuli' (Mackewn 1997, p. 15). When we see a series of dots distributed in a circular shape, our minds are active in seeing the circle. This tendency to want to 'fill in the gaps' is suggested as being indicative of an innate human dissatisfaction with incompleteness; Sills *et al.* describe this process thus:

> If we have only some of the elements of a situation or Gestalt, we will have a natural urge to provide the rest in our minds, in order to have completeness . . . For example, if we write 'elephan' here, you will probably automatically add a 't' in your mind. We are unsatisfied with incompleteness, and things that are not finished for us.
>
> (2012, p. 4)

The idea is extended by analogy to our emotional life; we are postulated to have 'a strong and inherent urge to complete or make meaning of our emotional life': we find unfinished emotional business unsettling (Mackewn 1997, p. 15). This is called the 'Zeigarnick effect', after the psychologist attributed as having first noticed the phenomenon:

> Whether they [the unfinished/incomplete things] are events, conversations, feelings or even our sense of ourselves, they seem to haunt us in our personal and professional lives and have the potential to stop us focusing wholeheartedly on what is happening in the present.
>
> (Sills *et al.* 2012, p. 4)

The idea is that we have an innate urge to complete our emotional matters, and part of the therapist's role will be to help enable the client to deal with unresolved material.

## The self-regulating organism

Dubbed 'sane psychoanalysis' by one reviewer, the early work of Fritz Perls, as a revision of Freud's theory and method, postulated that the human organism is striving for the maintenance of balance or equilibrium; this balance is interposed by our needs and regained through their gratification; the disturbance can be internally or externally generated: 'The central conception is the theory that the organism is striving for the maintenance of a balance which is continuously disturbed by its needs, and regained through their gratification or elimination' (Perls 1947, p. xvii).

This idea is based in part on the process of homeostasis, in which physiological readjustments constantly seek to stabilise organisms: for example, we sweat to keep cool, and we do this quite unconsciously. Humans are seen as self-regulating. Needs will arise. There may be competing values and desires, rather than one dominant need, modern Gestalt therapists acknowledge; Perls was insistent that one need is always dominant, though he concedes that there may be oscillation between more than one thing. These 'complex occurrences in the organism' are 'instincts' (but Perls warned against the notion of 'instinct' being viewed as a prima causa). This model is individualistic insofar as each organism will have different wants:

> In the working of the organism, some happening tends to disturb its balance at every moment, and simultaneously a countertendency arises to regain it. According to the intensity of this tendency we call it a desire, an urge, a need, a want, a passion, and if its effective realization is regularly repeated, we call it a habit.
>
> (Perls 1947, p. 29)

Perls gives an example of an 'internal' disturbance:

1　I am dozing on the couch. This is the organism at rest.
2　The wish to read something interesting penetrates my consciousness. This is the disturbing factor.
3　I remember a certain bookstore. Perls calls this the creation of an image.
4　I go there and buy a book. This is the 'answer' to the disturbance.
5　I am reading. This 'gratification' of the need creates a decrease in tension.
6　I have had enough. I set the book aside. This is seen as the return of the organism to balance.

> (Adapted from Perls 1947, p. 43)

From a therapeutic point of view, when a need is met it is seen as receding, then there is a sense of 'closure'. With closure come feelings of 'emotional satisfaction, integration, insight and completion' or 'grieving, insight, letting go' (Mackewn 1997, p. 16). Acknowledging that a need may not be met, and expressing emotions concerned with that, such as frustration and disappointment, can also offer closure. Korb et al. describe this process:

> Completed experiences, those that have been successfully resolved in the immediate present, fade into the background of a person's experience as something else comes to the foreground to be dealt with. When clear resolution of any experience occurs, the process of forming and completing gestalten functions very smoothly. Life becomes a series of emerging gestalten and the completion of those gestalten as the individual lives totally aware of the present and functions fully in the present.
>
> (1989, p. 5)

The Gestalt cycle, as popularised by Zinker (1977), is conceptualised as starting with some form of *sensory impact* from outside or within, which mounts in intensity, leading to *awareness*, and then leads on to *emotionality*, followed by the *search* for solutions or plans of *action*. This is the followed by the action or *contact* with the world. Lastly, there is assimilation or learning, which in-turn leads to quiescence and *completion* (adapted from Houston 2003, p. 16).

This principle of self-regulation is seen as extending to all human activity, such as the impulse to seek stimulation when bored, or withdraw if overstimulated. However, the process of seeking balance is dynamic; it is constantly in a state of movement:

> Changes in external events and new emerging needs create constant change and make it impossible to remain at a balanced point for long . . . balancing repertories develop through a balancing process, [sometimes] called equilibration, that regularly incorporates new ways of organising knowledge or behaviour into the old established cognitive organisation . . . approaches to homeostatic processes underline the fact that life is a constantly fluctuating process, not a matter of reaching completion or termination of activity.
>
> (Korb *et al.* 1989, pp. 12–13)

In Gestalt therapy the self is seen as 'in process'; we adapt and change in relation to our context. The Gestalt view of self is one's current experience of 'being-in-the-world-with-others', as Heidegger put it in 1927. However, our habitual habits of relating are thought to manifest themselves in the moment:

> The self we experience at any particular moment inevitably brings patterns of relating that have been established in the past, but it is then affected and shaped by our current needs and the response of the environment. Therefore, the self we are emerges of and from our context.
>
> (Sills *et al.* 2012, p. 10)

Put another way, Gestalt formulation is the 'organisation of a field, relating to the past, and future and the environment, to the internal and the external world' (Houston 2003, p. 15).

This Gestalt principle of holism is fundamentally very positive, as it assumes that people have the resources to maintain 'healthy self-regulative patterns and processes'. In this model of thought there is an assumption of an innate thrust towards personal health and balance which may be 'blocked' or even 'latent', but is inherent in the individual (Korb *et al.* 1989, p. 12).

## Gestalt therapy techniques

Drawing on the work of Fritz Perls, 'Gestalt' techniques focus on being in the here and now; he argued that we need to become aware of the obvious, not to 'dig' as in psychoanalysis (Perls 1969). There will be 'unfinished Gestalten'; what was important will emerge. What is most important is thought likely to emerge first (Perls 1969). Perls argued that it is possible to get rapidly in touch with the essence of a person and their plight (Perls 1969).

Perls felt that direct interpretations of the client's work were counterproductive, but also that voiced expressions were subject to self-censorship. Non-verbal expression was thought to be more authentic, so the technique might focus on a gesture that the client makes and elaborate it, perhaps even give voice to it; so, for example, the client's habit of shielding his face when talking about a particular issue might be explored. The person's hand might be asked to give voice, to 'speak': 'I'm hiding his face, because he doesn't want to be seen, even though he knows he is in front of an audience' (Hess 2007).

Gestalt therapists are encouraged to ask themselves phenomenological questions when they conduct an assessment. These are divided up into the following by Sills et al. (2012, pp. 80–1):

1   observable contact functions;
2   the contact boundary;
3   the cycle of experience;
4   self and environmental support;
5   the field.

First are 'observable contact functions', and these are some of the questions that a therapist might ask herself or himself:

1   With reference to movement and gestures, how does your client move – stiffly or in a relaxed way? Does he move a lot or remain still?
2   With reference to the client's voice, is it loud or soft, distant or present, fluent or tentative?
3   Does the client make eye contact? Is the gaze steady or darting?
4   Does the client hear what you say easily? Does he hear correctly or appear to mishear?

Regarding the 'contact boundary':

1   How does your client make contact with you?
2   What sort of contact?
3   Do you feel an immediate response from her or is she distracted and distant?
4   How and when does she modify contact?

Here are a few questions about the 'cycle of experience':

1   Does the client have clear sensations, which he recognises? Can the client mobilise energy to respond to his needs? Can he make a plan and take action? Does the person complete an action satisfactorily and then withdraw?
2   What modifications to contact of the cycle do you notice?

3   What unfinished business or fixed Gestalts do you notice or does the client talk about?
4   What patterns emerge from the client's account of himself with others? With you?

Regarding 'self and environmental support', they suggest the following questions:

1   What is the client's breathing like? Is it deep and relaxed, trusting both in the self and in the ability to see the world as able to offer nourishment?
2   Does the client seem able to sooth and regulate her experience? Does the client relax in the support of her chair?
3   Is the client dismissive of your feedback, or conversely overdependent on it?
4   Does the client report having a supportive network of friends and family?

Here are a few questions about 'the field' suggested to be core (slightly adapted from Sills *et al.* 2012, pp. 80–1):

1   What life circumstances are impinging on the client at the moment?
2   What are the cultural, social, organisational or sexual implications of his situation?
3   What feelings and images do you have in response to your client?
4   Do you (the therapist) like him? Why?
5   What do you (the therapist) notice in your body? Try to allow your observations to be tentative.

Houston summarises the assessment more succinctly as:

> Noting what the client seems to need, noting what interventions seem to work and what others do not, noting the minutiae of interaction, and modifying therapist behaviour in the light of all this, is the continuous assessment process that will be evinced in fluid gestalt formation.
>
> (Houston 2003, p. 27)

Houston's more holistic approach is arguably more in keeping with the Gestalt philosophy than the breakdown of components provided above by Sills *et al.* (2012), and this is an underlying tension in attempting to communicate to trainees this approach, which is interested in taking in *all* of the details of the whole person. Mackewn summarised the dilemma: 'You cannot divide a person into parts in order to study or treat that person without rendering meaningless the very entity you hope to get to know' (1997, p. 43). A criticism of the above schema by Sills *et al.* (2012) is that the Gestalt of the person may be lost in attempting to attend to the suggested details. Mackewn suggests that:

> To work holistically, you could try beholding clients with fresh curiosity and wonder, rather as you might gaze at a beautiful stream or seascape. For to

do therapy that is truly responsive to the needs of the other we need to allow ourselves to be touched by the mystery of their whole being. Working in such a profoundly holistic way can feel almost like a form of meditation in which you allow yourself to be fully receptive to clients and how they impact upon you. Although this sounds simple, developing this sort of openness to another person as a whole is not easy because most of us are trained to make suppositions and classifications . . . We are often so full of ideas about what is wrong or how to help that there is little room for just being with the other person as a whole person.

(1997, p. 43)

The three main elements of Gestalt therapy are:

- *connecting*, which includes the initial exploration, the development and agreement of themes and development of the therapeutic relationship.
- *exploring*, which includes relating the historical context to emerging figures in the here and now; co-exploration of themes; a heightening of self-awareness through experimentation.
- *integration*, through ongoing experimentation in the world, developing trust in one's [the client's] embodied experience; reviewing and acknowledging one's personal growth; leaving the therapeutic relationship and putting in place support for the future.

(Adapted from Sills *et al.* 2012, p. 84)

It is possible that a person may have developed 'fixed Gestalts' or have incomplete Gestalts; consequently, there is a 'need to surprise, to look afresh, to reverse, and play in many ways besides the verbal, with fixed perceptions' (Houston 2003, p. 19). Rhyne suggests that art making is very compatible with a Gestalt therapy approach, arguing that it is integrative:

Gestalt art experience, then, is the complex personal you making art forms, being involved in the forms you are creating as events, observing what you do, and hopefully perceiving through your graphic productions not only yourself as you are now, but also alternate ways that are available to you for creating yourself as you would like to be.

(Rhyne 1996, p. 9)

## Gestalt art therapy

There are different styles of using a Gestalt approach, from a fairly non-directive art therapy with an emphasis on 'being with' the client to more directive approaches, such as the one I shall now elaborate on, the technique developed by John Birtchnell, in which art therapy is used as an adjunct or aid to verbal psychotherapy.

He explains this model of working:

> The good thing about my style of doing art therapy is that the important peo-
> ple in a person's life get externalised on to the paper, so the person can look
> at them and speak to them . . . My aim was to get them to do very quick
> sketches. Lots of words got written around the drawings so there was a com-
> bination of the person they were talking about and the words that were spoken
> to or by them. It also seems to be the case that the quicker you draw the more
> accurate the drawing becomes. I still do quite a lot of pencil drawing of peo-
> ple and the quicker I do it the more like the person the drawing becomes. I use
> the term the 'inner me' to describe the automatic self that does the drawing
> for me as long as I don't interfere – by that which I call the 'outer me'.
>
> (Birtchnell, personal correspondence, 10 April 2013)

Birtchnell points out that talking and making an image involve two different
forms of cognitive processing:

> As a rule, the visual is registered in wholes and the verbal is registered in
> fragments. A picture of something is quite different from the words that are
> used to describe it. A picture of a pineapple is almost the same as an actual
> pineapple, but the word pineapple, although it conjures up in the brain a men-
> tal image of a pineapple, does not have the same impact as the sight of a pine-
> apple. If you did not know what a pineapple was, a picture of one would, at a
> glance, give you a clear idea of what one looked like, but a verbal description
> of one, even if it ran into several sentences, would always fall short of that
> direct, visual experience.
>
> You might ask, what about a crude sketch of a pineapple compared with bril-
> liant verbal description of one? I would still maintain that the crude sketch
> does something that the verbal description cannot do. It is something out
> there in the open that the eyes can focus upon. It is a thing. It is a single
> sensory input: You get the entire experience of the pineapple the moment
> you look at the sketch. With the verbal description, you have to follow the
> sequence of words and put them together in order to extract a meaning. Then,
> and only then, can you try to visualise what that meaning amounts to.
>
> (Birtchnell 2003, p. 1)

This is a model which works with the thoughts and feelings of a single individual,
although the therapeutic work is held within a group, as will be elaborated on. It
involves the therapist sitting with and talking to a person as he or she produces the
art works. Birtchnell states: 'Talking is encouraged and sustained throughout the
therapeutic process, and although the pictures that are produced are an important
component of the procedure, it is within the words that are spoken that the therapy
takes place' (1998, p. 144). However:

The picture, first and foremost, should be the focus of attention. Just a few scribbly lines or dabs of paint can easily come to represent that which the patient is talking about. A little square can become the patient's home. It rapidly becomes imbued with all the emotions that the person has about her actual home. It is no longer just a little square. As the session proceeds, and more scribbles or smears are produced, they all come to mean that which the patient was talking about when they were produced. In fact, in subsequent sessions, if they are retained, they continue to represent what they were when they were first produced; and all the thoughts and the feelings that were expressed at the time they were produced, continue to be associated with them. The lines and the shapes or the sploshes of paint become the visual embodiment of these feelings and the thoughts. They can no longer just be seen for what they are. They can only be seen as what they represent.

(Birtchnell 2003, p. 1)

The technique used is to spend about 10 to 15 minutes with each member of a circle of people:

making contact and getting a feel for the kinds of issues that are around, it may happen that one person triggers off another, so when finished with someone I ask if anyone can identify with them or is in a similar situation. The person who can, or is, I move on to next. This keeps the emotion going.

(Birtchnell 1998, p. 144)

He then makes a decision on whom to work with in greater depth based on his tour of the group and the group's issues. This is identified as an important part of the process:

It is important whom I start with, because if he or she brings out disturbing memories, it triggers off disturbing memories in others and the group really begins to work. If that person is defended, then others become defended and the group shuts down . . . If someone has begun to show emotion [in the reconnaissance round] I am inclined to start with them.

(p. 145)

This is an intense process:

Once settled down with someone, the session can last up to two hours . . . During this session, the two of us will be sitting close together, talking quietly; both with our eyes fixed on the paper in front of us. The rest of the group are watching and listening, usually intently, making themselves as comfortable as they can, propped against a wall or lying across some cushions . . . There is a general understanding that while I am working with someone, other group members do not speak. It is normally clear, as the session continues, that it would be both difficult and undesirable for anyone to break in.

(p. 145)

Pictures are made 'in the heat of the moment' (p. 146). Another distinctive feature is that words are written down and that the therapist may write down keywords too:

This is because we are not concerned with creating a work of art as such. Producing the picture is a means to bring about, enhance and reinforce a therapeutic process. The sheet of paper is purely and simply a workplace on which we work together.

(p. 146)

So this is art therapy as an adjunct or aid to verbal psychotherapy in which the image is used in the context of a primarily verbal exchange. Therapy is under way and a point may be reached in which the therapist feels the client is getting blocked or inhibited. But this is not cathartic paint splashing being advocated, it is a focused use of imagery we are talking about here.

In the Gestalt model, a parallel can be drawn with the use of drama therapy where it is not uncommon for a technique called the 'empty chair technique' to be used, which has been attributed to Moreno and Perls and popularised by the drama-therapist Landy (1994), among others. An empty chair is placed in front of the therapist and client. The therapist asks the client to imagine that his or her mother/father/abuser/sibling is sitting in the empty chair and invites the client to tell the person imagined in the chair what he or she would like to say: 'I always loved you', or 'I hate you', or 'you abused me as a child' – whatever the client needs to say. Then the client can change chairs and imagine he or she is the mother/father/abuser/sibling and talk directly to themselves as the other person. Such drama-therapy techniques are widely used.

Similarly, images can be used to stimulate such discourse. As John Birtchnell puts it: 'Talking to the picture, particularly in the here and now, is the most powerful device I know' (Birtchnell 1998, p. 149).

'Draw your mother/father/abuser/sibling', a therapist such as John Birtchnell might instruct. 'Now draw a phone. Now imagine you are picking up the receiver and tell them what you'd like to say . . .'. That's what is meant by art as an adjunct to verbal psychotherapy. It's essentially a psychotherapy that employs drama-therapy methods into which image making is then incorporated.

The art work in the Gestalt approach is usually a brief sketch rather than an involved piece aesthetically. As Birtchnell (2003) reflected:

There is a useful parallel between the therapy that I do (Birtchnell, 1998) and psychodrama (Moreno, 1972). What I do has little to do with art and requires no artistic ability, just as psychodrama has little to do with drama and requires no acting ability (Birtchnell, 2002b). When I do this kind of therapy with trained artists, as I sometimes do, their visual productions are no reflection of their artistic ability and they do not look like works of art. In fact they are not works of art. The relationship between what I do and conventional art therapy is similar to the relationship between psychodrama and drama therapy.

The emphasis is on the client expressing themselves, and the image provides a supplementary text, an alternative discourse to that which is spoken. This approach is not interested in the aesthetic aspects of art making:

> the patient depicts, or enacts, his or her own personal reality. It is not original, imaginative, fictitious or creative. That is not the point of it. The point is to complement [via the process of making art work] what she is saying, to convey in visual terms what it is like to be herself, what her relationships to certain relevant others feel like, to clarify these things for the therapist and for herself, to get in touch with them and to help her and the therapist make sense of them. I, just like the psycho-dramatist, do not want the patient to create anything. Creativity is not what therapy is about. Intentionally, I do not give the patient time to create a work of art.
>
> (Birtchnell 2003)

As we can see, this approach is rather different from those which are particularly interested in focusing on the aesthetic aspects of the art-making process. There is, as is evident, a fundamental difference in approach between this and the Jungian idea that psychotherapy is less a question of treatment than of developing the creative possibilities of the patient. The two approaches might be seen as antithetical.

As noted above, Birtchnell often works in a fairly intensive way with one individual in the group, with the other group members in a supportive role. He will encourage the person under focus to make a succession of images, but also to continue talking. In the Gestalt approach the client is seen as knowing what the trouble is:

> An important principle in this kind of work is that I should remain a step or two behind the person who is doing the work . . . she knows what the trouble is, I do not. Only she can take us to it. I sit quietly beside her, listening attentively, responding perhaps with amusement or shock to something that she says or draws. This is important because it makes her feel I am right in there for her. It also confirms that it *is* amusing or shocking. I must write 'MUM', 'KEVIN' or 'DAD', under the appropriate drawings. I might also write, beside the appropriate person, some phrase that has affected me, such as – 'He keeps to himself a lot.' I always write it exactly as it was said, because what she says, and how she says it, is an integral part of the picture. There is a need to catch it and preserve it for later. I may want to bring her back to it, but at this stage, I do not want to interrupt the flow.
>
> (1998, p. 147)

Towards the end of a period of intensive focus on one person, the facilitator may become very directive and this can provoke an intense emotional outpouring. Birtchnell explains this approach:

> An extremely valuable Gestalt technique is to invite the person to address his or her remarks to whomever they should actually be directed at. This is much more emotional than telling the therapist . . . Similarly, in art therapy, a woman may be drawing her husband, and saying as she draws, 'he's a bully.' I say, 'Tell him.' She looks at me strangely. I explain, 'Look at the drawing and imagine it really is him and just talk to him . . . Perhaps, as a way of escaping from this confrontation, she may revert to talking to me, and say, 'He used to lock me in our bedroom.' I correct her by saying, 'You used to'. She turns back to the drawing and says to it, 'You used to lock me in our bedroom', and then continues to talk to her husband about that . . . Adopting a here and now approach would involve my saying – 'Draw the bedroom from above. Put yourself inside and him outside. Imagine it is now, and tell him what you are feeling now.' She then begins to talk in the present tense. The whole scene feels horribly real. She is shaking and pleading with him to let her out.
>
> (Birtchnell 1998, pp. 148–9)

Talking to one particular person may continue for 30 or even 40 minutes. The facilitator is active during this process:

> The flow of this talking can be directed by quietly prompting with spoken or written words . . . Shorter or emotive phrases or words might be suggested that focus down upon the emotion, like 'You're an animal', or 'I hate you.' If the word or phrase is right, she will scream it over and over, and then dissolve into intense sobbing.
>
> (Birtchnell 1998, p. 149)

Because other group members may have resonated with aspects of the story which has just been told, the focus then returns to the group members as a whole, and members are then given an opportunity to express their feelings about the disclosure made and to explore their emotions triggered by it. Sometimes after feedback from the group, Birtchnell will invite the person who has spoken in depth to end with a positive picture in which she is 'free or triumphant' (Birtchnell 1998, p. 150). The focus of attention returns to the group as a whole, before the process of working intensively with an individual within the group may recommence.

In this method both the image making and the talking are important. To summarise, this chapter has outlined the key features of Gestalt therapy: the idea of holism, and the principle of the self-regulating organism. Field theory, which emphasises that the person and her or his context are indivisible, has been explored in some detail. The corollary of such theory is that we must actually reconceptualise what it means to be a person; even phrases such as 'co-creating experiences' do not do justice to this profound shift in thinking about what an individual is. Not only does it challenge Cartesian dualism, but also the dichotomy between self and other, self and environment, so entrenched in Western thinking.

The chapter outlined further ideas underlying Gestalt therapy techniques in general terms, and then moved on to present a detailed account of the Gestalt art therapy method. Gestalt art therapy is a distinctive approach. Some art therapists might usually use a different way of working but occasionally employ techniques, such as 'tell him what you feel'. This method of dialogue with the image is also used in an analytic art therapy approach.

# Chapter 6

# Person-centred art therapy

## The basic principles of the person-centred therapy approach

The concept of person-centred therapy (also called Rogerian therapy) stems from the work of American psychologist called Carl Ransom Rogers (1902–87). It arose as part of a critique of both behavioural psychology and classical psychoanalysis, that of humanistic psychology, which has sometimes been dubbed the 'third force' in psychology. The following is a summary of Bugental's (1964) basic postulates of humanistic psychology:

1 humans supersede the sum of their parts, so cannot be understood through a study of part functions;
2 humans have being in context, so interpersonal context is important;
3 humans have awareness, so cannot be understood without acknowledgement of their self-awareness;
4 humans have choice and create their own experience;
5 humans have intent: purpose, value and meaning.

The basic principles of person-centred therapy concern an attempt to create an environment of safety and trust in which personal growth can occur. A Rogerian approach assumes that individuals have the capacity to guide their own growth and development, without the necessity for complex strategies or guidance. In this way this 'non-directive' or 'client-centred' approach differs from the other more structured techniques already explored. It is an idealistic, libertarian model, interested in the notion of self-determination. Kirschenbaum and Land Henderson summarise Rogers' attitude towards healing as relying upon this idea of self-determination:

> All individuals have within themselves the ability to guide their own lives in a manner that is personally satisfying and socially constructive. In a particular type of helping relationship, we free the individuals to find their inner wisdom and confidence, and they will make increasingly healthier and more constructive choices.

(1990, p. xiv)

The method relies on the notion of 'self-actualising' tendencies within an organism: 'the tendency to grow, to develop, to realize its full potential. This way of being trusts the constructive directional flow of the human being towards more complex and complete development. It is this directional flow that we aim to release' (Rogers, cited in Kirschenbaum and Land Henderson 1990, p. 137). In his 'A Note on "The Nature of Man"' (1957) Rogers iterates that he sees humans as innately 'positive, forward-moving, constructive, realistic, trustworthy' (cited in Kirschenbaum and Land Henderson 1990, p. 403). He refutes the Freudian idea that the core of our being (unless repressed) is 'an uncontrolled and destructive id' (cited in Kirschenbaum and Land Henderson 1990, p. 405). Indeed, Freud's view 'that the satisfaction of instinct, such as the id demands, would often enough lead to perilous conflicts with the external world and to extinction' is specifically criticised (Freud 1949, p. 61). Rogers is affronted by the view that the human core is irrational, unsocialised or destructive. He prefers Maslow's thesis that 'anti-social emotions – hostility, jealousy, etc. – result from frustration of more basic impulses for love and security and belonging, which are themselves desirable' (Rogers 1961, p. 91). He also suggests that humans are fundamentally cooperative.

Rogers elaborates:

> in a relationship which is characterised by all that I can give of safety, absence of threat, and complete freedom to be and to choose. In such a relationship men express all kinds of bitter and murderous feelings, abnormal impulses, bizarre and antisocial desires. But as they live in such a relationship, expressing and being more of themselves . . . my experience is that he is a basically trustworthy member of the human species, whose deepest characteristics tend toward development, differentiation, co-operative relationships; whose life tends fundamentally to move from dependence to independence; whose impulses tend naturally to harmonise into a complex and changing pattern of self-regulation; whose total character is such as to tend to preserve and enhance himself and his species.
>
> (cited in Kirschenbaum and Land Henderson 1990, p. 405)

Again we see an emphasis on the quality of the relationship as crucially important; although Rogers acknowledges that previously denied or repressed feelings may come to the fore in therapy, he believed that full emotional acceptance of these was facilitated by the quality of the relationship: 'It is only in a caring relationship that these 'awful' feelings are first fully accepted by the therapist and then can be accepted by the client' (cited in Kirschenbaum and Land Henderson 1990, p. 407). Rogers believed that Freud's analysis did not contain this level of acceptance and that this prevented him from integrating the unwanted feelings that arose: 'More likely he continued to perceive them as unacceptable aspects of himself – enemies, whom knowing he could control – rather than as impulses which, when existing freely in balance with his other impulses, were constructive' (cited in Kirschenbaum and Land Henderson 1990, p. 407).

Rogerian theory rests upon the idea that a rift often develops between our immediate awareness and our deeper experiencing, a rift created by the demands placed upon us. Kirschenbaum and Land Henderson explain:

> In order to receive approval and love, we learn to suppress those feelings and expressions of ourselves that are deemed unacceptable to the important caretakers in our lives. Our need to be loved and accepted can impair our ability to be 'congruent', to be whole and genuine.
>
> (1990, p. 155)

The evaluations of others are internalised (introjected), until many of us can no longer recognise 'the difference between what is internal and what is external, so know who we really are' (p. 155).

The notion of an authentic self, ready to free itself from the shackles of society's demands, is somewhat naive and philosophically problematic in attempting to discern the authentic from the inauthentic; how can we make this differentiation? (This concept has been critiqued by field theorists, as we saw in Chapter 5 on Gestalt.) However, the idea of compromising beyond one's inner-nature is thought to lead to mental distress and dis-ease, and relies on the idea of a core of inner-self which is essential or true, with which we must become congruent, however theoretically problematic this is.

Furthermore, Rogers' assertion of a fundamental move from dependence to independence as a natural corollary of maturation is perhaps a very masculine twentieth-century model of psychology, as women still tend to be theorised as nurturing and supporting as a norm and an ideal; we stay embedded in contingent reciprocal relationships (elderly parents are more often cared for by a daughter than a son, for example, and many women promise to obey their husbands in a traditional marriage ceremony; women do the lion's share of housework and childcare and are more likely to make compromises in their careers to fulfil these roles, etc.). Arguably, reciprocity is always important in society, so this aspect of Rogers' work may also reflect the individualistic masculine capitalism of mid-twentieth-century North America.

His assertion of 'the urge which is evident in all organic and human life – to expand, extend, become autonomous, develop – the tendency to express and activate all the capacities of the organism, to the extent that such activation enhances the organism or the self' is also open to question, reflecting as it does popular notions of biological science of the period in which he wrote this, whereas specialism and niche adaptation are now more widely acknowledged. His idea that this is a 'natural' tendency of all organisms must therefore be open to question. He puts it thus:

> This tendency may become buried under layer after layer of encrusted psychological defences; it may be hidden behind elaborate facades which deny its existence; but it is my belief that it exists in every individual, and awaits only the proper conditions to be released and expressed.
>
> (Rogers 1961, p. 35)

However, his is a fundamentally positive view of humanity and of human potential. The Rogerian therapist is unlikely to hamper the therapeutic encounter with
unconstructive suppositions. Furthermore, there is something subversive in suggesting that the expertise of the patients to discern what is right for themselves
should be trusted. It is not surprising that the work of Rogers has aroused contro-
versy and vituperation from those supporting other viewpoints.

Wilkins suggests that Rogerian therapy aims to result in a 'psychological
homeostasis' developing 'where the balance is under dual control, with the drive
of the actualising tendency and the restraint of the social imperative both able to
exercise power' (2003, p. 34).

## Transference

Rogerian therapists do not generally work with the concept of transference at
all, but Carl Rogers did acknowledge it. In work written in 1986 and 1987, he
divides transference up into two types: feelings that are generated which 'are an
understandable response to some of the attitudes and behaviours of the therapist'
and client reactions arising from emotions 'that have little or no relationship to
the therapist's behaviour. These are truly "transferred" from their real origin to the
therapist' (cited in Kirschenbaum and Land Henderson 1990, pp. 129–30).

An explanation of why the former responses are called transference is not
given, since the 'negative client attitudes are simply a natural response to
their [the therapist's] statement or actions' (Rogers, cited in Kirschenbaum
and Land Henderson 1990, p. 129). He gives as examples the resentment of
clients towards 'superiority' in their therapist's demeanour, or possible anger
at therapeutic prescriptions. The converse would be loving feelings towards
the therapist, perhaps arising out of appreciation for the depth of understanding shown by the therapist. (Such attitudes might be seen as resonant of things
beyond the therapeutic relationship. In a fully psychodynamic model these
could be interrogated: what does my demeanour trigger in you beyond our
relationship?)

Transference proper is projection on to the therapist and the intensity of feeling coming from the client is *not* due to the behaviour of the therapist. Rogers
explains this in more detail:

> These projected feelings may be positive feelings of love, sexual desire, ado-
> ration, and the like. They may be negative – hatred, contempt, fear, mistrust.
> Their true object may be a parent or other significant person in the client's
> life. Or, and this is less often recognized, they may be negative attitudes
> toward the self, which the client cannot bear to face.
>
> (cited in Kirschenbaum and Land Henderson 1990, p. 130)

Either way, the transference does not become the focus of attention per se; therapy is seen as moving forward *through* these feelings. Transference feelings are

accepted and mirrored in the same way as other feelings expressed; here is an extract of Rogers responding to transference reactions:

> *Client:*  ... I think I'll throw you into a lake. I'll cut you up! ... I wish you were dead.
> *Rogers:*  You *detest* me and you'd really like to get rid of me!
> *Client:*  ... You think I want intercourse, but *I don't!*
> *Rogers:*  You feel I *absolutely misrepresent* all your thoughts.
>
> (cited in Kirschenbaum and Land Henderson 1990, p. 132)

Although showing awareness of transference, Rogers felt it should not become the focus of therapy. All feelings are treated in the same way. He elaborated on why he thought a focus on transference is problematic:

> To deal with transference feelings as a very special part of therapy, *making their handling the very core of therapy, is to my mind a grave mistake. Such an approach fosters dependency and lengthens therapy.* It creates a whole new problem, the only purpose of which appears to be the intellectual satisfaction of the therapist – showing the elaborateness of his or her expertise. I deplore it.
>
> (cited in Kirschenbaum and Land Henderson 1990, p. 134; my italics)

Shlien is candid on this matter, asserting that, '"Transference" is a fiction, invented and maintained by the therapist to protect himself from the consequences of his own behavior' (1984, p. 1). Shlien's argument is detailed, and cannot be expounded in its full complexity here. However, he suggests that what is mistaken for transference in the psychoanalytic model is the consequence of fundamental aspects of the therapeutic relationship, which is not an equal one:

> Intentionally he [the therapist] has been understanding, and this alone will, over time, activate in the patient some object-seeking components of trust, gratitude, and quite possibly affection or sexual desire. In this same context, misunderstanding is a form of hate-making. It works equally well since being misunderstood in a generally understanding relation[ship] is a shock, betrayal, [and a source of] frustration.
>
> (Shlien 1984, p. 13)

## Key therapeutic factors

Rogers identifies three factors which are crucial to providing this facilitative environment in his 1986 essay, 'A Client-centered/Person-centered Approach to Therapy'. First is *'genuineness, realness, or congruence'*. The second attitude is called *'unconditional positive regard'*. Rogers explains this also as acceptance, caring and prizing. The third crucial element for building a facilitative space is *empathy* (cited in Kirschenbaum and Land Henderson 1990, p. 135). These are attitudes which much be demonstrated by the *therapist* in order to create the necessary and sufficient conditions for positive psychological change to occur. Further attitudes must be demonstrated by the *client*, especially being able to discern and respond to the therapist's demeanour so that psychological contact can be enabled.

To elaborate further on these three important conditions of therapy, the first aspect – genuineness – is straightforward; it is that the therapist should put up no personal façade or front. The therapist freely experiences the feelings in the moment, not attempting to distance herself. There is a 'gut-level' correspondence between what the client is expressing and what the therapist is experiencing. The therapist is aware of her feelings and able to communicate them if appropriate; it is this sense of being with one's 'feelings and attitudes' in the moment that is called 'congruence' (Rogers 1961, p. 61).

The second important factor, that of unconditional positive regard, is elaborated on as 'a positive, non-judgemental, accepting attitude toward whatever the client *is* at that moment' (Rogers, cited in Kirschenbaum and Land Henderson 1990, p. 136). Rogers elaborates that this is a form of non-possessive caring and unconditional acceptance which makes change within the self more likely. The therapist accepts whatever emotions are to the fore – be they positive or negative – and does not reward one over the other. Unconditional positive regard by the therapist 'means an outgoing positive feeling without reservations, without evaluations' (Rogers 1961, p. 62). With facilitative conditions changes in attitudes and behaviour can occur.

The third crucial facilitative factor for growth and change is that of empathy. This is evident through an active listening process which Rogers regarded as very potent. Empathetic understanding 'means that the therapist senses accurately the feelings and personal meanings that the client is experiencing and communicates this acceptant understanding to the client' (Rogers, cited in Kirschenbaum and Land Henderson 1990, p. 136). He also called this 'empathetic understanding'. This is not the same as sympathetic understanding, or merely intellectual comprehension:

> When the therapist is sensing the feelings and personal meanings which the client is experiencing in each moment, when he can perceive these from 'inside', as they seem to the client, and when he can successfully communicate something of that understanding to his client, then the third condition is fulfilled.
>
> (Rogers 1961, p. 62)

When the therapist grasps 'the moment-to-moment experiencing which occurs in the inner world of the client as the client sees it and feels it, without losing the separateness of his own identity in this empathic process, then change is likely to occur' (Rogers 1961, p. 62). From the client perspective, Rogers asserts that, 'When someone understands how it feels and seems to be *me*, without wanting to analyse me or judge me, then I can blossom and grow in that climate' (p. 62).

The process is based on trust in the person and the empathetic responses given may be more intuitive that intellectual; it also involves a certain amount of 'checking out' with the client that the therapist's experience of the client's inner world is correct:

> Each response of mine contains the unspoken question, 'Is this the way it is for you? Am I catching just the color and texture and flavour of the personal meaning you are experiencing right now? If not, I wish to bring my perception in line with yours.' . . . we are holding up a mirror of his or her current experiencing. The feelings and the personal meanings seem sharper when seen through the eyes of another, when they are reflected.
>
> (Rogers, cited in Kirschenbaum and Land Henderson 1990, p. 128)

The therapist's action of checking her perceptions and understanding serves as a mirror, helping the client to perceive his or her experience. Rogers elaborates:

> I can continue . . . to test my understanding of my client by making tentative attempts to describe or portray his or her inner world. I can recognize that for my client these responses are, at their best, a clear mirror image of the meanings and perceptions that make up his or her world of the moment – an image that is clarifying and insight producing.
>
> (cited in Kirschenbaum and Land Henderson 1990, p. 129)

Rogers even describes a sense of the 'usual barricades' of 'me-ness' and 'you-ness' dissolving in group work resulting in a sense of the oneness of spirit of the group (cited in Kirschenbaum and Land Henderson 1990, pp. 137–8).

The quality of the relationship is crucial, in the Rogerian schema, for accounting for how change occurs; it is the therapist's active listening which is seen as enabling the client to listen to herself or himself:

> In the first place, as he finds someone listening acceptingly to his feelings, he little by little becomes able to listen to himself. He begins to receive the communications from within himself – to realize that he *is* angry, to recognize when he is frightened, even to realize when he is feeling courageous. As he becomes more open to what is going on within him he becomes able to listen to feelings which he has always denied and repressed. He can listen to feelings which have seemed to him so terrible, or so disorganizing, or so abnormal, or so shameful, that he has never been able to recognize their existence in himself . . . As he expresses more and more of the hidden awful aspects of himself, he finds the therapist showing a consistent and unconditional positive regard for him and his feelings. Slowly he moves forward taking the same attitude toward himself, accepting himself as he is, and therefore ready to move forward in the process of becoming . . . as he listens more accurately to the feelings within, and becomes less evaluative

and more acceptant toward himself, he also moves toward greater congruence. He finds it possible to move out from behind the facades he has used,
to drop his defensive behaviours, and more openly to be what he truly is. As
these changes occur, as he becomes more self-aware, more self-acceptant,
less defensive and more open, he finds that he is at last free to change and
grow.

(Rogers 1961, pp. 63–4)

The fluidity which develops allows enhanced 'internal experiencing' and communication, and less rigidity in general: behaviour is increasingly determined by
immediate experience. There is enhanced recognition of the role of the self in the
construction of problems as well as a sense of 'self-responsibility' for them (Rogers 1961, pp. 157–8).

## Person-centred art therapy

Carl Rogers' daughter Natalie has written on a person-centred understanding of
creativity and points out the 'inner conditions' that are most often associated with
creative acts. Drawing on her father's ideas, she states that these are:

(i)   Having an openness to experience – or 'extensionality,' the opposite of
psychological defensiveness.

[Carl] Rogers described this explicitly as being aware of *this* existential
moment *as it is*.

(ii)  Having an internal locus (or place) of evaluation.

. . . The value of his product is, for the creative person, established not by the
praise or criticism of others, but by himself. Have I created something satisfy-
ing to me? Does it express part of me? . . .

(iii)  Having an ability to toy or play with elements and concepts.

[This is described as] . . . the ability to play spontaneously with ideas, colors,
shapes, relationships – to juggle elements into impossible juxtapositions, to
shape wild hypotheses, to make the given problematic, to express the ridic-
ulous, to translate from one form to another, to transform into improbable
equivalents. It is from this spontaneous toying with life that there arises the
hunch, the creative seeing of life in a new and significant way.

(Rogers *et al.* 2012, p. 34)

Natalie Rogers is keen to add to the core conditions of therapy, already outlined
above, a further important component, that of 'offering stimulating and challenging experiences' via the use of expressive arts (Rogers *et al.* 2012, p. 35). Quoting
her own earlier work, she suggests:

> We need to get people up and out of their chairs and actively engaged in the creative process to experience it. We do not become creative by talking about it. I may suggest to a client who is experiencing grief or fear to express her feelings in color or clay or movement. These suggestions are meant to facilitate expression rather than to direct a client's experience. Also, the product becomes part of the language between client and therapist.
>
> (Rogers 1993, cited in Rogers *et al.* 2012, p. 35)

Crucially, 'these ideas place creativity at the heart of what it is to be human: to be fully functioning is to be creative; and to be uncreative or to have a creative block is to be in some way alienated from ourselves – and others' (Rogers *et al.* 2012, p. 35).

Rogers *et al.* elaborate:

> Expressive art refers to using the emotional, intuitive aspect of ourselves in various media. It is a process of discovering ourselves through any art form that comes from an emotional fullness. It is not about creating a beautiful picture, a perfect poem or a choreographed dance. To use art expressively means to go into our inner realm to discover feelings for expression through visual art, movement, sound, writing or improvisational drama. We emphasize the process more than the product although the product may give us a depth of personal insight.
>
> (Rogers *et al.* 2012, p. 35)

Natalie Rogers is adamant that the therapist should maintain a non-directive attitude and not offer interpretations of art work. She noted that the arts are 'a language for self-expression . . . which [offer] an open-ended structure so that people can have a creative experience . . . We are setting up a structure to allow people to have an experience; we're not directing the experience' (Rogers *et al.* 2012, pp. 40–1).

> When I invite clients or students to use the arts for self-expression I want them to know their products or images will be respected and not interpreted or analyzed. I help them uncover the meaning the image or movement has for them. If these images stir deep emotions, I listen and respond empathically and without judgment or interpretation. I am a companion on their path doing my best to understand the world as they perceive it. This creates a very safe environment in which people can explore and express further.
>
> (Rogers *et al.* 2012, p. 36)

Rogers is using expressive arts (plural) but arguably aspects of all of the elements are included in art therapy, as an image may be supplemented by a word or a sculptural form, or a poem as an accompaniment; movement is inherent in the process. For example, it is possible to sit almost motionless, or to produce a large art work which requires a performance around the room: fetching materials or making bold marks involving much bending and stretching, perhaps accompanied by noises such as groaning or grunting. Some art therapy participants use the entire room, as in installation art. Although people seldom sing in art therapy, this would be accepted if it were to occur. The multi-dimensionality of art therapy will be elaborated on further in Chapter 8 on group-interactive art therapy, but it can be argued that it involves very many different elements. Natalie Rogers speaks eloquently as to the merits of using the arts:

> The expressive arts are profound in helping people become aware of all their feelings and particularly help them accept their dark or shadow side. The arts are a way to channel that energy constructively. You can dance your rage, paint your fear, or despair. Then several things happen: you discover how to find inner balance, inner peace. You are not so likely to view people who disagree with you as the 'other' or the enemy; in other words, you are likely to have more compassion. The result is becoming empowered to go out and take action. It is different for each individual, of course. However, when each one of us comes from a very clear emotional place we are a light, a candle, a force in the world. When we come from such a spiritual place, we will radiate that out in concentric circles. The Buddhist paradigm says that the inner light is it; the way to peace is for each one of us to find inner peace.
>
> (Rogers *et al.* 2012, p. 43)

## Implications for practice

Liesl Silverstone (1997), in her work in training art therapists, is helpful in elaborating an understanding of a person-centred approach to working therapeutically with art:

(1)  The mirror is held up not only to words, but to the picture. The counsellor may reflect the whole process of image making, not only the end product:

'You took a piece of paper and folded it in half'.
'You started, turned the paper over, started again'.
'You tore a piece off'.

The size/colour of the paper or material used may be reflected:
'You took a large white sheet'.
'This is the only part you did in red'.

Position, size:
'You put yourself on the edge of the page'.
'What about the size of this shape'.

What is missing can be significant:
'I notice there are no hands'.
'You have left this part blank'.

Wider reflections can be fruitful:
'You drew mother in red paint, you in grey chalk'.
'Last week you used only black, this week there was no black'.

All of these elements . . . can be of importance.

(Silverstone 1997, pp. 6–7)

An observation at this point could be that such interventions are not just confined to a Rogerian approach. Furthermore, those with complex personality disorders may perceive themselves as being criticised by even the most simple of remarks such as, 'I notice there are no hands'; an explanation of the approach would be imperative with such a client group.

Silverstone continues:

(2) The picture is an extension of the self in symbolic form made visible. Therefore, the facilitator needs to help the client towards recognition of such projected material by making 'bridges' from the picture to the client. However well you work with the picture, if you treat it as something separate from the person you are not working to full effect.

'I need to define the shape of this cat'.
'Does that speak to you? Defining the shape of the cat?'
'Oh yes! I need to define *my* shape! *Me*!'
'I'm puzzled. I'm terrified of the violence of these men'.
The bridge here took the client to a denied childhood memory.

(3) In 'eye-to-eye' counselling, not everything the client says needs to be reflected. When talking about an image, the client becomes less self-conscious, and the words he/she uses become ever more spontaneous and uncensored. Words . . . of potential significance. These the client needs to hear. Thus it can be that more words need to be reflected [upon] when working with images.

'I couldn't bear to draw the image, it disturbed me so much; these three black roses'. These spontaneous words lead to denied feelings about the three children who have left home, and the client's changing role as a mother.

Sometimes the whole process needs to be reflected, as a re-enacted symbolic microcosm:

'It took you a long time to get into the water: you're very afraid of it; you need to make sure your oxygen cylinder is in position. Then you swim to the bottom of the sea and discover a treasure in the cave' . . . Sometimes noting what is missing leads to a shift, . . . 'No Kitchen', I say. Pam cries: 'That's where mum used to be cooking, talking to me . . .'. The dam has burst. She could grieve, let go. To conclude, 'At every level of development, the therapeutic use of art releases and enables shifts in awareness and development'.

(Silverstone 1997, pp. 7–8)

Silverstone often starts with a direct exercise and then follows through in the person-centred manner. Here are some examples:

- 'I suggest the students close their eyes, focus on how they are feeling. "Without thinking, let an image emerge, a symbol, of you, now. When you're ready, open your eyes, and convey this image". Then each student says her name and talks about her image' (p. 15).
- 'We play a "name game". We stand in a circle. I say my name – pause – and throw a ball to a student. She says her name – pauses, so that her name can be heard – throws the ball on. When everyone has said her name at least twice, the rule changes: the student throwing the ball calls out the name of the person to whom she is throwing the ball. We stop, after two turns each' (p. 19).
- 'I suggest an exercise, in pairs, each person to listen for five minutes to the other. "Notice your body language. Is your body saying: 'I am paying you my fullest attention?'" Some adjust their position. I say that the speaker should share something about herself, take responsibility for the level of sharing – today, and in all ensuing exercises. The listener tells her partner how she felt. The partner may want to respond. They swap over, and share again. Then they share with the group' (p. 21).
- 'Listening. I say something like: "Close your eyes. Focus on the exercise, we've just done on you listening, perhaps on what you noticed about you not listening fully. (Pause) See if an image comes up for you. A scene. (Pause) Maybe from now, or an earlier time, about listening, perhaps about being listened to – or not. (Pause) Now convey that image to paper". They do. Then each person says something about the image' (p. 21).
- 'Reflecting the visual: In pairs, two minutes each way, with feedback in between. As "counsellor", simply reflect what you see, as if you were the mirror – client stays silent – for example, "your head is turned to the left side, your right hand is holding your left hand" . . . As we get more familiar with the process of real listening, making wider reflections is helpful: "You say you are worried, and you are laughing". "Every time you talk about your father, you shut your eyes"' (p. 27).
- Silverstone also uses more analytical techniques such as this one: it looks at blaming, placating, generalising, distracting and what she calls 'level' which is the 'I think; I feel; I want; I don't want' position. This 'level' position is regarded as the congruent person-centred one. These are elaborated on:

  1  It's your fault is blaming.
  2  It'll turn out alright is placating.
  3  Everyone feels like this is generalising.
  4  Look! There's an aeroplane is distraction.
  5  I think/feel/want/don't want is the congruent position.

- 'Close your eyes. Reflect on these five behaviours: blame, placate, generalise, distract, level. (Pause) Maybe you were drawn more to one? (Pause) Maybe you resisted one? (Pause) Now let a picture, a scene, float up, perhaps about such behaviours. (Pause) Maybe from an earlier time? (Pause) When you're ready, open your eyes. Portray this scene. Each student talks about their picture in the group' (p. 37).

Silverstone reproduces many such exercises and the above give a little illustration. She also uses guided fantasies in which a story is told and then used as the starting point for an art work. This is one example:

- 'Now close your eyes – and now you're in the costume room of a theatre – looking about you, you may be drawn to one costume in particular – have a good look at it – note all the details. What are you doing – feeling? When you're ready, open your eyes and make visible, however you need to do it, your time in the costume room' (p. 137).

Above is an example of a rather directive frame, but one which gives freedom of movement within it. Mearns and Thorne argue that it is important that the therapist work with his or her client's symbolism. As pointed out above, the skill of the person-centred therapist is to help the client 'unravel the uniqueness of his own structures and dynamics', which are reflected back – 'unveiled' even (2000, p. 127). They argue that:

Not changing the client's symbolisation of parts of his Self is respectful but it is also functional. The symbolisation, however poorly it is formed, expresses the closest the client can get to its meaning in his existential world at that time. The skill of the person-centered therapist is to work *without* offering external constructions – that is not an easy matter, for such external constructions help therapists to feel both secure and smart . . . Where a client has declared the existence of a configuration, this information becomes a significant part of the person-centered counsellor's record keeping . . . the way the client has talked about parts of themselves in the past . . . As well as recalling names and descriptive terms it is important to remember interrelationships and dynamics among configurations and be ready for these to change.

(pp. 130–1)

Unlike in other approaches:

Nothing is done with this record during supervision between sessions. The person-centered counsellor is not concerned to use supervision as a means of further analysing the client and his configurations . . . Supervision in the person-centered approach is not about 'detective work' on client material but, instead, it focuses upon the counsellor's 'congruence'.

(p. 131)

Mearns and Thorne note that there is a lack of consensus about addressing configurations directly, but the therapist is aware and reflects back the symbolisation.

It is hoped that, in the therapeutic encounter, 'related, but previously unattended memories, thoughts, feelings and images emerge and transform themselves into more clearly understandable forms' (2000, p. 146).

To conclude, this is a deceptively simple-sounding model which relies on three core conditions to be met: *'congruence'*; *'unconditional positive regard'* and *empathy* (Rogers, cited in Kirschenbaum and Land Henderson 1990, p. 135). Person-centred art therapists may wish to add a fourth core condition suggested by Natalie Rogers, *the capacity to offer stimulating and challenging experiences* via the use of the arts (Rogers *et al.* 2012, p. 35).

# Chapter 7

# Mindfulness art therapy

May I be well and happy.
May I be at ease in my body and in my mind.
May my heart be filled with loving-kindness – with love and kindness.
May I let go and be free.
May I live in peace.

May you be well and happy.
May you be at ease in my body and in my mind.
May your heart be filled with loving-kindness – with love and kindness.
May you let go and be free.
May you live in peace

May all beings be well and happy.
May all beings be at ease in my body and in my mind.
May all beings' hearts be filled with loving-kindness – with love and kindness.
May all beings let go and be free.
May all beings live in peace.
May there be peace. May there be peace. May there be peace.
(*Metta* Loving Kindness Exercise, Rappaport 2014a, p. 318)

## The foundations of mindfulness

Buddhism is a philosophy and world religion founded on the teachings of Siddhartha Gautama in northern India in the fifth century which has some features in common with Hinduism, notably the idea of *karma*. This is the idea that moral actions are consequential, even to the extent that future lives will be determined by past actions in a process of rebirth, which could be seen as rather deterministic, but through right conduct, an ascetic regime of moral rectitude, one is able to change one's fate. It is often referred to as a philosophy because the ideas involve 'claims concerning the nature of persons, as well as how we acquire knowledge about the world and our place in it'; in other words, the concerns of metaphysics and epistemology (*Stanford Encyclopedia of Philosophy* 2015). The aim of a Buddhist is to become 'awakened' and to move towards *nirvana*, that is, beyond misery and existential pain, the frustration, disaffection and hopelessness that afflicts us because of the transitory nature of all things.

An essential underlying aspect of Buddhism is an understanding that desire causes human suffering. In the Tibetan tradition, complex mandalas (images representing a harmonious universe) are made with different-coloured sand and then swept away, emphasising the transitory nature of all things and beings: the fundamental truth of impermanence.

Meditation is central to Buddhism. This is a form of contemplation and awareness. Meditation is an opportunity to be utterly in the moment without desire. It is a practice of 'non-attachment' in which the ideas of 'mine' and 'I' are challenged experientially. Self-inflicted suffering, brought about by grasping at things with one's mind, slips away, or at least the thoughts that arise can be viewed at a certain distance dispassionately. There are many types of meditation and some involve repetitive chanting of incantations (*mantras*), such as the *Metta* above, or the simple repetition of 'Om'. Chanting serves to clear the mind of other thoughts and to transmit positive moral messages about correct demeanour.

Mindfulness art therapy is a fusion of the principles and practices of art therapy with some of the ideas found in Buddhism (Monti *et al.* 2006). There are several traditions of Buddhism, but the practice of *meditation* is central to all of them; a common practice is to sit and still the mind, then to note the kind of thoughts that arise: to take note of them, but not to follow or elaborate them. This takes a bit of practice, but using this basic meditation technique can enable the practitioner to begin to observe what the mind is doing, and to identify patterns of mind, including the sort of negative inner speech that CBT also identifies. Being mindful is about experiencing the moment *non-judgementally*.

Meditating has been compared to tuning a musical instrument; if the strings are either too loose or too tight the sound will not be pleasant: likewise meditation cannot be forced. If too relaxed the mind will run away with elaborations of thoughts and one will no longer be meditating: one will have lapsed into thinking. Some people use a focus on the sensation of the breath, to help provide something definite to focus on: it isn't an analysis of the breath, it is simply an arbitrarily chosen focus for the mind. The gentle heaving of the chest can be noted, as can the sensation of the air leaving one's nostrils. If the mind wanders it is gently brought back to the focus on the breath.

Mindfulness is a technique of self-analysis that has core aspects in common with a behavioural approach, but also occurs within other psychotherapeutic approaches:

> Mindfulness is about being in the moment, using the senses to become aware of what is happening right now. Intrusive thoughts might pop into the head on a regular basis but the task is to notice them and then turn the attention back to the task in hand which is to be in the moment . . . It is about labelling the thoughts as 'intrusive thoughts' (some people even visualise the thoughts being scooped into the back of a lorry and being driven off) and then turning the attention back to the task of the moment.
>
> (Simmons and Griffiths 2009, p. 144)

Other techniques for the disposal of unwanted thoughts might include visualising a blue sky and attaching unwanted thoughts to passing clouds. Another simple technique is to note the event of thinking, to label the event with the word 'thinking', and then to simply return the mind's focus to the here and now. Or if the meditation practice is focused on an image, any intrusive thought or image can be replaced by that original image. The symbol of the lotus flower is a popular focus for meditation, because it grows in muddy places yet can be pristine and beautiful. It is seen as a metaphor for the human ability to rise above our ignominies and suffering. The lotus flower can be imagined in our mind's eye, or we can try to imagine it as our body, so that the practitioner becomes the lotus flower. The white lotus flower also symbolises purity of mind and body. The open flower also represents enlightenment, which is the goal of Buddhist practice. Painting the lotus can also function as a meditative exercise.

## Mindfulness as part of a CBT-orientated art therapy

A core value of Buddhism is compassion to all beings. Whilst CBT, for example, doesn't encompass this philosophy, there are parallels in that CBT focuses on developing compassion towards the self, in rejecting damaging self-appraisal. Willis defines mindfulness as 'using awareness and thoughts to bring consciousness fully into the present moment' and he notes the common aim of Buddhism and CBT 'of eliminating mental afflictions through mental training' (2009, p. 69).

Simmons and Griffiths suggest that mindfulness can be used as a part of CBT and that exercises can be used such as handling a particular textured material, listening to sounds or observing colours in a room. Mindfulness is noted as useful early on in therapy as it is helpful 'to enable the client to 'notice' and 'let go' of unwanted intrusive thoughts instead of focusing on them'. They suggest that learning to practise mindfulness is particularly useful for those experiencing obsessional problems, as intrusive thoughts are a key aspect of obsessive-compulsive disorder and the cause of much distress (Simmons and Griffiths 2009, p. 100).

Willis (2009, p. 70) suggests that mindfulness-based cognitive therapy has also been advocated to prevent relapse among those who have been treated for depression. Mindfulness can combat worry that leads to depression through practising distancing. The idea of distancing is intended to break obsessional preoccupations:

> Many people seem to have negative thoughts . . . but are able to 'shrug them off' without engaging in them. What distinguishes sufferers is that they engage with these negative thoughts in a fixated way. Such problem areas typically include obsession, compulsions and worries, and they are characterised by intrusive and perseverative ruminations – thinking too much and paying too much attention to thoughts.
>
> (Willis 2009, pp. 57–8)

Beck noted that, 'The severely depressed patients often experienced uninterrupted sequences of depressed associations, completely independent of the external situation' (1963, p. 326). Rappaport concurs, using the term FOAT (focusing-oriented art therapy). She adds that focusing in art therapy 'grounds the experience in the body, accesses the client's inner knowing, cultivates greater compassion, and enhances skills to stay attuned to the moment-to-moment unfolding and the client's experiential process' (2014b, p. 193).

One technique developed by Leahy (2005; cited in Willis 2009, p. 146) involves the subject using this simple formula: 'I am simply having the thought that . . .' and 'I am simply noticing the feeling . . .'. He advocates the use of five 'thinking steps', which use an amalgam of CBT and mindfulness:

1   Gain distance from your thoughts ('I am simply having the thought that . . .').
2   Describe what is in front of you.
3   Suspend or postpone evaluating or judging your experience.
4   Take yourself out or away from the centre of things.
5   Disappear to see reality: once you are out of it, you can 'see' it.

Other interventions combine mindful attention with direct cognitive work. Mindfulness techniques could be integrated into a cognitive behavioural art therapy session, or simple art making such as mandala making could form part of a mindfulness exercise.

## Focusing-oriented art therapy

### Foundational principles of FOAT

Rappaport (2014b) theorises the mindfulness technique of focusing-oriented art therapy and identifies stages in the therapy process and how they connect to mindfulness concepts. She suggests parallels between FOAT and mindfulness, especially that a 'Focusing Attitude is crucial for adding a mindfulness component and deepening self-compassion, and for helping to stay in the eye of the storm' (p. 206).

First are *foundational principles* aimed at establishing mindfulness and deep listening. Rappaport elaborates on these 'grounding' 'focusing' techniques. She identifies 'presence' like this:

> Mindful awareness begins with the therapist's sense of presence: Are you here and ready to receive the client? Are you present in your own body, heart, mind, and spirit? Are you ready to listen compassionately? Are you aware of your own issues – and can you set them aside to be present? Presence in FOAT is similar to mindfulness practices of being aware and compassionate acceptance in the present moment.
>
> (2014b, p. 194)

Next she identifies the *Focusing Attitude*, which is more than simply being attentive. She describes it like this:

> The Focusing Attitude is characterized by qualities of 'being friendly,' accepting, nonjudgmental, and welcoming toward one's inner felt sense – and it cultivates self-compassion. Rome (2004) describing the Focusing Attitude as 'akin to the Buddhist virtue called maître – lovingkindness or friendliness directed toward oneself. It is a potent and at times quite magical way of making friends with oneself' (p. 63).
>
> (p. 194)

Another important aspect that Rappaport identifies is what she calls 'grounding'. This is a technique also used in some martial arts, and is a form of bodily awareness, a moment of being in the body and stopping mind-chatter before practice begins. Rappaport elaborates on this:

> During Focusing, unexpected feelings and issues may surface. It is helpful for therapists to teach clients grounding or centering practices – such as, mindful breathing, body awareness of feet on the ground – before Focusing. A monk, Thich Nhat Hanh (1991, 2001, 2012), describes the importance of mindful breathing to calm the body and mind prior to working with strong feelings.
>
> (p. 195)

These techniques can be done with open or closed eyes, depending on the preference of the client. Rappaport urges clinical sensitivity and warns against instructing that eyes be shut.

### The FOAT check-in

The second principle Rappaport describes as the 'FOAT check-in', which is aimed at cultivating mindful awareness. In practice, it involves asking clients to, 'bring mindful awareness and the Focusing Attitude of being "friendly" to their felt sense of their experience' (Rappaport 2014b, p. 195). She suggests that the FOAT check-in corresponds to Nhat Hanh's (1991) suggestion that 'Meditation has two aspects: stopping and calming is first, and looking deeply is the second' (cited in Rappaport 2014b, p. 195). The attention is on 'a felt sense of one's inner bodily sense of an experience, feeling, or issue, then, in an unrushed way, the client is asked if she is able to formulate a word, phrase, image, gesture, or sound – that matches the felt sense' (Rappaport 2014b, p. 195). Rappaport calls this felt sense a 'symbol/handle' from Genglin's work (1981, p. 44, cited in Rappaport 2014b, p. 195). Rappaport says, 'From a felt sense, a word or phrase naturally unfolds into writing or poetry; an image into art; a gesture into movement or dance; and a sound into music, voice, or sound exploration' (p. 195). Her own technique is to echo or mirror the initial felt sense gesture (symbol/handle) and then to invite the focuser (client) to express this felt sense through expressive arts (p. 195).

## Clearing a space with the arts

The third aspect of FOAT described is clearing a space with the arts. The client is prompted not to think about all the difficulties and stresses in her life, but to name what is present in that moment that is in the way of feeling fine with the present moment. In other words, an inventory is taken of what is in the way of being okay. Between three and six points are identified as having an impact in the present moment. When each in-turn is sensed, it is put at a distance, either imaginatively via one's mind's eye, or it is depicted using art materials and thus externalised. Rappaport says:

> Setting the stressor [source of stress] outside of the body, either through the imagination or use of the arts, helps the Focuser to dis-identify with it. The Focuser senses a *me* that is separate from those stressors. Once the issues are set aside, the Focuser is guided to sense the place inside that all is 'All Fine' or clear – and to find a handle/symbol that matches this 'All Fine Place'. This helps the Focuser to access and ground an aspect of self that is intrinsically whole.
>
> (2014b, p. 196)

## Theme-directed FOAT

Rappaport gives examples of 'compassion', 'gratitude', 'forgiveness' and 'generosity' as useful themes which she suggests cultivate mindfulness, compassion and wisdom. She explains how this could be used in practice:

> the Focuser can become aware of something in their life that has been a teacher of compassion – perhaps a person, pet, spiritual sources, or something from nature. The Focuser is guided to bring mindful awareness into the body along with an attitude of friendly curiosity, and to get a felt sense of the teacher of compassion. Next, the Focuser is guided to see if there is a symbol that matches the felt sense – a word, phrase, image, gesture, or sound – followed by artistic expression.
>
> (2014b, p. 196)

# Focusing-oriented arts psychotherapy

Focusing-oriented art therapy is based on five mindfulness steps: (1) recognise feelings; (2) be one with the feeling; (3) calm the feeling; (4) release the feeling; and (5) look deeply (Rappaport 2014b, p. 197). Thich Nhat Hanh (1991) suggests that:

> Mindful observation is based on the principle of 'non-duality': . . . our feeling *is* us, and for the moment we *are* that feeling. We are neither drowned in nor terrorized by the feeling, nor do we reject it' . . . It is best

not to say, 'Go away Fear. I don't like you. You are not me'. It is much more effective to say, 'Hello Fear. How are you today?' Then you can invite the two aspects of yourself, mindfulness and fear, to shake hands as friends and become one.

(pp. 52–4, cited in Rappaport 2014b, p. 318)

## Integrating mindfulness into art therapy

Shapiro *et al.* (2006) have suggested that some characteristics of mindfulness are evident in studio approaches, especially intention, attention and attitude. Allen (2014, p. 55) elaborates on this where she feels there are aspects in common. First, she identifies 'witnessing', which she says is the process of being aware of the contents of our own mind and our art. *Witness writing* is a technique which involves participants noting and recording their experience; they are encouraged to do this without editing or explanation. Expression may be prosaic or poetic. Allen suggests that this technique is helpful in allowing participants to traverse a liminal space in art therapy: the experience of merger with images and materials. Another element identified by Allen is what she calls *witness consciousness* in group work: 'Our mutual sitting, being present with an attitude of non-judgement, paying attention without comment creates a spaciousness that allows the speaker to hear their own words as coming from a deep self without interference' (p. 55).

Shapiro *et al.* (2006) emphasise being in the here and now as an important aspect of some forms of art therapy, which is also an important aspect of mindfulness:

> In the context of mindfulness practice, paying attention involves the operations of one's moment-to-moment, internal and external experience. This is what Husserl refers to as a 'return to things themselves,' that is, suspending all the ways of interpreting experience and attending to experience itself, as it presents itself in the here and now. In this way, one learns to attend to the contents of consciousness; moment by moment.
>
> (p. 376)

Peterson (2014) has developed some simple exercises that are intended to enable participants to have a mindful exploration of art materials. Here is an example:

> Holding the paper, what is the experience of touch? Holding it to the light, what touches the eye? Bringing the pencil to your nose, what are you aware of as smell? Now that you have opened the box of coloured pencils, what are you aware of in thoughts or feeling? As you are moving the ink brush color across the marker on the paper, what is the feeling in the body? What is the experience of sound touching your ear as the group works at the art table?
>
> (p. 68)

She also uses techniques to enable focusing and grounding:

> Beginning, bringing attention to the full cycle of your breathing. Now bringing attention to the awareness of your feet on the ground slowly observing your body experience; noticing any sensations, perhaps tingling, pulsation, tension, or tightness, openness, coolness, or warmth; sensing in to any of these or other experiences. Now, bringing attention to the awareness of your head area, noting your mind experience; perhaps busy or slow, closed, open, agitated, calm, tense, or other experiences in your awareness.
>
> (p. 69)

Peterson (2014, p. 76) also uses mindful walking with digital photography. Pictures which touch the senses are taken, with a maximum of ten then printed out for collage making.

Chang (2014) points out that mindfulness techniques are also very compatible with a person-centred framework. She argues that person-centred expressive arts therapy (a model she attributes to Natalie Rogers, discussed earlier in Chapter 6) cultivates similar qualities, 'including being present, deep listening and non-judgemental awareness' (p. 219).

Chang herself also uses tea meditation as an opening ritual to her sessions:

> Practicing 'tea meditation' is being truly present with our tea and friends to dwell happily in the present moment, despite sorrows and worries. The expressive arts help to enrich the meditation experience. In return, the tea meditation refreshes awareness and grounds the soul to mindfully experience the creative process.
>
> (p. 223)

Chang (2014, p. 229) also uses a 'Buddha Board'. She cites Yongey Mingyur Rinpoche as having said that mindfulness is 'the key, the how of Buddhist practice [that] lies in learning to simply rest in a bare awareness of thoughts, feelings and perceptions as they occur'. An important tenet of Buddhism is an awareness of the impermanence of all things and beings. Clinging on to things which will slip away is seen as a cause of suffering, but an attitude of non-attachment, advocated in Buddhism, should not be confused with nihilism, because engagement with others is suffused with compassion. However, it does challenge some Western notions of self, suggesting that we have no fixed essence. A Buddha Board allows an image (using water) to be made, which then fades away.

> A 'Buddha Board' (see www.buddhaboard.com) is a product where you simply paint water on the surface of the board; the images come to life in a darker color and then gradually fade away. It is a wonderful vessel for us to stay still with our moment-to-moment awareness. We can paint, enjoy and observe the moment. It is based on the Zen concepts of living in the present moment and impermanence. It is a healing process of being in the moment, appreciating

each precious moment, letting go, and clearing our mind. It is a wonderful teacher that things change and are not permanent.

(Chang 2014, p. 229)

Reflecting on the use of mindfulness techniques with children, Weiner and Rappaport (2014) advocate simple mindfulness practices such as sitting and walking meditation, noting arts activities also:

the arts often provide an enjoyable, tangible route to access and express mindfulness practices. For example, a child can choose a color and draw a line coordinated with their in-breath followed by creating another line with their out-breath. Children can notice how it feels in their body after mindful breathing, and then draw the feeling into a body outline or cut-out figure.

(Weiner and Rappaport 2014, p. 248)

FOAT (discussed above) is also advocated as an arts-based method for children and adolescents to learn the fundamentals of mindfulness techniques, to allow them to become 'more accepting of their inner-experience, developing a healthy relationship with their emotions, accessing a place of wholeness, and cultivating both self-compassion and compassion towards others' (Weiner and Rappaport 2014, p. 248). FOAT can combine art with other techniques such as 'self-kindness journals' in which children can be asked write on a daily basis three things they are grateful for about themselves and/or ways they can show kindness to themselves (p. 254). Weiner and Rappaport (2014) suggest that mindfulness fits in easily with programmes of stress reduction, and note that the art aspect enhances mindfulness for children (p. 249). Isis (2014) also advocates mindfulness-based stress reduction (MBSR) in hospital settings. She blends mindfulness with the use of expressive arts in a community outreach programme which attracts a wide range of presenting issues. She suggests that MBSR results in decreases in stress, depression and anxiety, resulting in improved mood and resilience. She uses a number of structured exercises to enable participants to reflect on their bodily experiences. She starts off with simple work, mindful sitting with the emphasis on the breath, followed by an instruction to depict the breath, for example. Another exercise, as part of mindfulness sitting, is to notice pleasant, unpleasant and neutral events inside and outside their bodies. Each is felt in-turn. Here is the prompt she gives:

You are invited to visualise a situation in your life right now that is pleasant. Utilise your senses and allow a clear picture to arise in your mind's eye. Notice your breathing. When you feel ready, render your experience of the breath with line, shape, and colour (oil pastels, markers, coloured pencils). On the other side of the paper, first, visualise a situation in your life now that is unpleasant. Feel it completely in your body. When you are ready, give form to it through the experience of your breath.

(Isis 2014, p. 161)

Participants are asked to notice their responses as part of the practice of non-judgemental acceptance. Another exercise focuses on the whole body and places all these sensations on to a whole body outline which she provides pre-drawn. She then moves towards more complex exercises which explore coping styles and stress reactions more explicitly. This example is an adaptation of an assessment tool:

> Drawing 1: You are going on a journey, down a path that leads into a forest. You come to a rushing river. You must get across the river to resume your journey. On page 1, draw how you get across the river.
>
> Drawing 2: Now, imagine yourself returning to the trail and leaving the forest. You begin to climb up a mountain. The trail switches back and forth due to the steepness of the slope. You stop for a moment to catch your breath . . . you notice a wild animal coming towards you. On page 2, show how you get past the animal.
>
> Drawing 3: Imagine you are back on the mountain trail and encounter a massive hail storm. You need to find shelter . . . you see a cave close by. There is a monster on both sides of the entrance. On page 3, draw how you manage to get into the cave.
>
> Drawing 4: Once in the cave, you are tired and need to rest. Before you close your eyes to rest, you hear something and realise that you are no longer alone in the cave. Page 4 reflects your experience in the cave however you choose to end the story.
>
> (Isis 2014, p. 164)

Participants share their experiences in pairs and then with the larger group. The exercise gives scope to participants to explore their sense of passivity or aggression in the face of obstacles, or other possible reactions such as helplessness.

A further exercise, which Isis calls 'The Social Atom', enables participants to explore their relationships:

> Reflect on your life right now and the most significant relationships in it. You are going to create an artistic map of your most significant relationships, including you. Use circles to represent females and triangles to represent males. Place the circle or triangle that symbolises you on the paper to indicate where you see yourself in your life now (i.e. in the centre, off centre, below centre, above centre etc.). consider how big or small you feel in your life at this time. Use colours that resonate with your perspective of your relationship to yourself currently. Write 'Me' under the symbol. Continue to use the circles, triangles and selected colours to demonstrate how close or far, big or small, wide or narrow each prominent relationship is for you right now . . . Pets can be part of this picture as can deceased individuals. Use a slanted line through the circle or triangle to show that person is deceased.
>
> (2014, p. 165)

Analysis includes the following questions: Do you feel crowded or lonely? If you could have it exactly the way you wanted it, what would it look like?

Franklin (2014) advocates that art therapy trainees learn mindfulness because mindfulness, the ability to be fully present, is essential for skilful therapy or counselling. Zimmerman calls this 'unconditional presence':

> One of the most important contributions that this kind of practice offers is warmth and acceptance of our own self-judgement. We call this *maître*, which is friendliness to one's own complex subject matter. When we meditate we begin to see and develop a relationship to our self-judging mind. Over time, it is this relationship to seeing what *is* and letting it *be*, that sets the stage for acceptance of our own unwanted material . . . When we are new to our art therapy practice, it can be challenging to sit with another's pain. We may find ourselves strategizing, problem-solving, lost in our associations. Our mindfulness practice brings us back to the present moment in our therapeutic relationship.
>
> (2014, p. 269)

Franklin (2014) asserts that perception and sensitivity are enhanced by meditation. He argues that 'Practitioners of meditation become adept at observing rather than reacting to thoughts, a skill known as *disidentification* (Walsh and Shapiro 2006)' (2014, p. 272). He goes on to argue that just as the meditator becomes the skilful observer of the mind's thoughts, the artist externalising his or her thoughts goes through a similar process. The symbolic forms in art are a form of thought. He goes on to suggest that, 'Seeing and actually holding thoughts fixed in tangible forms offer additional access to inner contemplative awareness, especially when thoughts and feelings are ambiguous and confusing' (2014, p. 272). This is a different way of conceptualising the art therapy process which does not rely on psychoanalytic theories.

## Working with compassion

A key tenet of Buddhism is that of developing a compassionate attitude towards oneself and others. Hanh (2001, p. 2) also advocates 'compassionate listening', which is a form of 'deep listening' with an attuned attentiveness. Gilbert describes the use of compassionate imagery as a useful part of compassionate mind training. Imagery is used which is (a) unique to the individual; (b) soothing; and (c) incorporates compassion. When using traditional cognitive techniques of identifying negative thoughts, and identifying alternatives, it is possible to add a prompt that the generated alternative be compassionate, that individuals 'hear and sense' it with warmth: 'In essence, the aim is to have an inner conversation with parts of the self through the use of imagery' (Gilbert 2009, p. 216). A compassionate ideal is imagined, 'what the compassionate image would say to the self and how s/he would say it' (Gilbert 2009, 216). (This is actually very similar to guided-fantasy techniques, which are discussed in detail elsewhere.) 'Compassionate imagery can be a practice in its own right (as in meditations or active imagination), and used in activities such as generating alternative thoughts and compassionate letter writing' (Gilbert 2009, p. 226). Obviously these images can be made as well as spoken about. In theme-directed FOAT, discussed above, Rappaport gives examples of 'compassion', 'gratitude', 'forgiveness' and 'generosity' as useful themes. Here is an example of a self-compassion guided mediation:

> Imagine someone living, who you see regularly in your life right now; some-one who it is easy for you to have loving thoughts and feelings about, and someone who helps you feel loved. Feel in your body how it feels when you think about and/or imagine this person standing in front of you. Imagine this person telling you loving things and giving you a huge hug/smiling at you (pause for about 30 seconds). Now imagine loving yourself the way this person loves you. See if you can tell yourself these same kinds of loving things. See if you can give yourself a loving hug and smile. Many people often find it hard to give love to themselves, as compared to[ward] others. It can take time to cultivate this sense of love toward yourself. Be patient, be gentle. Even when you are not able to be loving toward yourself, see if you can find a way to be loving toward this part that is finding it difficult and learning how to love! Even if you don't feel compassionate toward yourself right now, that is ok. Whatever you feel is ok . . . just notice and be accepting. Sense inside what it feels like in your body right now, and see if there is an image, word, or phrase that matches your felt sense.
>
> (Weiner and Rappaport 2014, p. 254)

Finally, Monti *et al.* (2006) suggest that the quality of life for people with cancer can be improved using mindfulness-based art therapy (MBAT). Their small randomised-controlled trial reported significant reductions in psychological distress. Peterson integrates art-based practice into a range of mindfulness techniques for use with cancer patients which 'include awareness of breathing, body scan meditation, sitting meditation, gentle yoga practice, mindfulness eating, walking meditation, mindful awareness of the art materials, and creative expression as a meditative form' (2014, p. 66).

The relaxation response elicited by mindfulness practices of meditation and chanting are regarded as 'an effective therapeutic intervention that counteracts the adverse clinical effects of stress in disorders including hypertension, anxiety, insomnia and [stress related to] aging' (Bhasin *et al.* 2013, p. 1). Benefits regarding long-term resilience with respect to other physical disorders are under investigation. Mindfulness is associational with an 'enhanced expression of genes associated with energy metabolism . . . and reduced expression of genes linked to inflammatory response and stress-related pathways' (Bhasin *et al.* 2013, p. 1). In other words, mindfulness techniques would appear to be able to switch on and off some genes linked to immune and stress functions.

To summarise, this chapter has explained the fundamental ideas contained within Buddhism and described a range of non-religious mindfulness exercises which are based on basic Buddhist practices, especially the development of a compassionate sensibility and the cultivation of 'non-attachment' through meditation. It articulated the philosophical and theoretical underpinnings of mindfulness art therapy, which can form a part of a CBT or other art therapy approach or is a distinctive approach in its own right. Various examples have been provided of how art therapists are developing mindful art therapy practices.

# Chapter 8

# Integrative art therapy

## The group-interactive art therapy model

This is an integrative model in that it brings together a number of theoretical ideas into one mode of practice. Group-interactive art therapy has aspects and vocabulary imported from psychoanalytic and analytic art therapy; it incorporates ideas from systems theory. In particular, it draws on 'interactive' or 'interpersonal group psychotherapy', which in-turn uses an uneasy amalgam of psychoanalysis, social psychology and existential philosophy. There is an interesting tension inherent between these conceptualisations of humanity (quite different in psychoanalytic theory, analytic psychology, social psychology and existential philosophy) and the differing explanatory frameworks for psychopathology.

The distinctive aspect of the group-interactive model of art therapy today is that, as the name suggests, it is interested in looking at how people *interact* in the group with a view towards *interpersonal learning*:

> Group interactive psychotherapy [from which interactive art therapy has derived] focuses on the actions, reactions and characteristic patterns of inter-action which constrain people in their everyday lives and for which help in modifying is sought in the group . . . A fundamental of this approach is that each person constructs an individual inner world which is continuously being reconstructed through interactions with others and which determines that person's view of himself and others and affects the expectations of others.
>
> (Waller 1993, p. 22)

It is immediately obvious that this is a rather particular way of conceptualising what people are and how they are constituted in comparison with a more tradition-ally psychoanalytic view, which insists that our personality traits (or neuroses) are developed early in childhood. This model of thought, in sharp contrast, proposes that we are continuously shaped and reshaped, and that, to some extent, our iden-tities are in a state of continual flux and reconstruction. Philosophically, this is potentially at odds with the orthodox psychoanalytic model, though interactive art therapists incorporate some psychoanalytic features into their work (commonly the feelings of members about others, or the group as a whole, which are not generated by their here-and-now experience, but triggered by habitual reactions which are then stimulated in the session). Consequently, childhood experiences, while not overlooked, are not the main focus of the group's attention.

Of the overarching approach, Waller says:

> Group interactive art therapy draws on the fundamental principles of art therapy. These are that the image- (or object-) making is an important aspect of the human learning process; that image making (and this includes painting, drawing, clay-work, constructions, etc.) in the presence of a therapist may enable a client to get in touch with early, repressed feelings as well as with feelings related to the here-and-now; that the ensuing art object may act as a container for powerful emotions that cannot be easily expressed; and that the object provides a means of communication between therapist and patient. It can also serve to illuminate the transference (that is, feelings from the past which are brought in to the here-and-now and influence the way that we experience others) between the therapist and patients.
>
> (1993, p. 3)

## Background and theory: interpersonal group theory and existentialism

The term 'group-interactive art therapy' refers in particular to the model developed by Diane Waller, which is what will be elaborated on and discussed here in further detail. This chapter will also refer to the theorists whom Waller acknowledges as underpinning this model. However, the term 'integrative art therapy' could be (and probably is) applied to a range of group-interactive art therapy methods which have slight differences of emphasis (and are more or less psychoanalytically psychodynamic, for example). Nevertheless, this approach does have important differences from a conventional psychoanalytic orientation because of the centrality of the social construction of self as well as the existential orientation, so there are tensions inherent in the model. A pragmatist might say that the model attempts to hang on to the useful bits of psychodynamic theory and discard the rest.

The shift away from an absolute focus on inter-psychic processes is attributed to Martin Heidegger's phenomenological philosophy and the concept of *dasein* (literally 'there' and 'being'), which is often described as 'being in the world' and is concerned with humans' self-definition and the process of making meaning in their lives. Yalom, in his 1931 text *Existential Psychotherapy*, explains that the existential position confronts the Cartesian dualism of subject–object; human consciousness participates in the very construction of reality. Each *dasein*, Yalom notes, 'constitutes its own world; to study all beings with some standard instrument as though they inhabited the same objective world is to introduce monumental error into one's observations' (1980, p. 23). Revolutionary sentiments indeed!

Yalom swiftly summarises some of the main differences between psychoanalytic psychotherapy, neo-Freudian psychodynamics and existential psychotherapy. He points out (and I'd also refer the reader to Chapter 3 on psychoanalytic art therapy) that the child is seen, in psychoanalysis, as governed by instinctual forces:

> There are conflicts on several fronts: dual instincts . . . [which] oppose one another; the instincts collide with the demands of the environment and, later, with the demands of the internalized environment – the super-ego; the child is required to negotiate between the inner press for immediate gratification and the reality principle which demands delay of gratification. The instinctively driven individual is thus at war with the world that prevents satisfaction of innate aggressive and sexual appetites.
>
> (1980, p. 7)

Neo-Freudian psychodynamic theory (including the work of Harry Stack Sullivan, Karen Horney and Eric Fromm) puts more emphasis on the interpersonal environment. Yalom notes that the demands of significant adults impinge on natural attributes of the developing child:

> The child . . . has great innate energy, curiosity, an innocence of the body, an inherent potential for growth, and a wish for exclusive possession of loved adults. These attributes are not always consonant with the demands of surrounding significant adults, and the core conflict is between these natural growth inclinations and the child's need for security and approval. If a child is unfortunate enough to have parents so caught up in their own neurotic struggles that they can neither provide security nor encourage autonomous growth, then severe conflict ensues. In such a struggle, growth is always compromised for the sake of security.
>
> (1980, pp. 7–8)

In existential psychotherapy there is a different sort of struggle:

> neither a conflict with suppressed instinctual strivings nor one with internalized significant adults, but *instead a conflict that flows from the individual's confrontation with the givens of existence* . . . those intrinsic properties that are part, and an inescapable part, of the human being's existence in the world.
>
> (Yalom 1980, pp. 8–9)

These are divined through 'deep personal reflection', but include an inevitable acknowledgement of death, freedom, isolation and meaninglessness (Yalom 1980, p. 9). An existential psychodynamic orientation is not interested in exploring the past; it acknowledges the past as informing current existence, but rather it is interested in the present existential situation. Stresses *inherent* in the 'human condition' are seen as the root cause of psychopathology. Yalom uses the analogy of bacterial infection, pointing out that bacteria are always present in the environment, but that our immunity and resistance fluctuate.

Existential analysts approach the patient phenomenologically: 'that is, he or she must enter the patient's experiential world and listen to the phenomena of that world without the presuppositions that distort understanding' (Yalom 1980, p. 17). Existential psychotherapists are interested in the uniqueness of identity. Consequently, they object to psychoanalytic reductionism (in tracing all human behaviour to a few basic drives) and also to its determinism ('the belief that all mental functioning is caused by identifiable factors already in existence') (Yalom 1980, p. 17).

However, apart from its phenomenological approach in therapy, and its objections to the deterministic and mechanistic model of psychoanalysis, existentialism is *not* a 'coherent ideological school' (Yalom 1980, p. 17). Since it is the phenomenological approach which is the core element, it is worth clarifying and elaborating it. A phenomenological stance is to focus on:

> the phenomena themselves, to encounter the other without 'standardized' instruments and presuppositions. So far as possible one must 'bracket' one's own world perspective and enter the experiential world of another. Such an approach to knowing another person is eminently feasible in psychotherapy: every good therapist tries to relate to the patient in this manner. That is what is meant by empathy, presence, genuine listening, non-judgemental acceptance, or an attitude of 'disciplined naivety' – to use May's felicitous phrase. Existential therapists have always urged that the therapist attempt to understand the private world of the patient rather than focus on the way the patient has deviated from the 'norms'.
>
> (Yalom 1980, p. 25)

Rather than mental illness being conceptualised as a confusion of intrapsychic conflicts, the emphasis in interpersonal method and theory is very much on personal freedom and personal responsibility. Indeed, there are some points of tension between social psychology and existentialism – *freedom of choice* is a much abused clarion call, given how circumscribed real choices might be both materially and conceptually (a point emphasised in the feminist and social-art-therapy models to be discussed in later chapters). Ratigan and Aveline (1988) suggest that existentialism was attractive to a North American audience because of the ethos of autonomy, industry and self-reliance.

Waller attributes the genesis of the group-interactive art therapy model to the post-war rehabilitation movement, of which group psychotherapy was a part. She highlights as significant the Northfield Military Hospital experiment, started in 1942 by two psychiatrists, Wilfred Bion and John Rickman, who 'used "group dynamics" to encourage men to learn a way of coping and adapting to inter-group tensions' (Waller 1993, p. 5). A 'second' Northfield experiment was tried some years later, this time involving Sigmund Heinrich Foulkes, who had been psychoanalytically trained with Helene Deutsch in Vienna. In 1945 Foulkes was given a brief to develop group techniques, including psychodrama and art therapy. A pilot 'art class' with 'group discussion' was started on 19 October 1945 and this took the form of free painting followed by group discussion of some of the work produced; though the art works tended to be a catalyst for discussion of wider issues, there was some attention to responses to the works in the here and now (Hogan 2001, pp. 209–10).

Waller also notes the importance of ideas from social psychology. She goes on to argue that many people referred to, or who self-refer to psychotherapy, 'have problems which turn out to be mainly societal in origin' (1993, p. 6); social disadvantage, alienating conditions and social isolation combine to disturb our equanimity. However, this model does not deny the veracity of mental illness, but rests on a theoretical foundation that is different from that of both the psychoanalytic and analytic orientations.

Waller sees the work of Harry Stack Sullivan as of particular importance in the development of a group-interactive mode:

> Sullivan believed that an individual's history influences every moment of his life, because it provides a dynamic structure and definition of his experiences. He saw anxiety as arising from threats arising to an individual's self-esteem. The individual uses well-tried defences to deal with these threats. Sullivan did not agree with Freud's idea that the basic personality structure was laid down in childhood: *rather he felt it developed, through interaction with significant others*, right through to adulthood and was therefore open to change. A person's psychological growth, then, depends on a concept of the self which is largely based on how a person experiences himself in relation to others.
>
> (1993, p. 19; my italics)

Ratigan and Aveline simplify Sullivan's main point of theory about reciprocal emotional states being inherent in transactions between members of the group as follows:

> (1) each person encourages others into certain role relationships, and (2) relationships are strengthened when needs are met and disintegrate when they are not. (3) The interpersonal group shows to members how they are the architects of their interpersonal 'fate'.
>
> (Ratigan and Aveline 1988, pp. 47–8)

It is suggested that the group in interpersonal group therapy can become a 'laboratory where the form of interactions reveals the nature of the members' difficulties and a workshop where new resolutions may be achieved and practiced' (Ratigan and Aveline 1988, p. 43).

The move away from an emphasis on analysing childhood as pivotal to understanding personality is a profound shift away from psychoanalytic tenets. This has important implications for how humans are theorised as malleable and mutable: wrought by constant change in relation to others. It also has implications for the focus of therapy. Here Waller elaborates her original proposition:

Group interactive psychotherapy focuses on the actions, reactions and characteristic patterns of interaction which constrain people in their everyday lives and for which help in modifying is sought in the group . . . A fundamental of this approach is that each person constructs an individual inner world which is being continuously reconstructed through interactions with others and which determines that person's view of himself and others and affects expectations of others. In group therapy, the individual gradually realises how inner assumptions may determine the patterns of interaction that develop. Exploration of these patterns and willingness to modify them in the safety of the group enables the person to try out new ways of relating in the 'outside world'. *Clearly, then, the model places the main source of change in the interaction between group members and depends upon the participants learning from each other.*

(1993, p. 19; my italics)

Although the term field theory is not used, we can see that the individual and her or his context are seen as inseparable: we are in flux; this is a theorisation of the self which is fundamentally 'socially constructivist'. However, our sense of ourselves can have an impact on how people respond to us, and we may indulge in certain habitual ways of being which can be thought about in relation to others. Indeed, this is not just a self-reflective process, but depends on analysis of the interactions in the group – it is *the self in social interaction which is the object of scrutiny*. Though aspects of our inner worlds may be very enduring, because the self is seen as continuously reconstructed through interactions with others, it is not necessary to delve into the past, in order to affect personal transformation. This is an orientation which can be more present-focused and forward-looking, thinking about tangible changes for the future and steps which can be made towards them.

## The group as a learning environment

There are five concepts that are central to an interpersonal approach noted by Ratigan and Aveline (1988), and Waller suggests that these tenets are what distinguish interpersonal from psychoanalytically oriented group psychotherapy. The defining characteristics of the interpersonal approach are existential in orientation:

1   Human actions are not predetermined; freedom is part of human action.
2   The corollary of this is the importance of choice in human life.
3   It is essential to take responsibility for one's actions.
4   Death is inevitable; but the fact that we shall die can paradoxically give meaning to life.
5   We are each engaged in a creative search for individual patterns that will give meaning to our existence.

(Ratigan and Aveline 1988, p. 45)

Waller notes that individual responsibility, freedom and choice are central to a 'group-interactive' method (Waller 1993, p. 20). She cites Ratigan and Aveline, who suggest that this method can provide a context in which:

> members can move from being trapped in a personal world view in which they are passive victims . . . to one where they can take more responsibility for their lives, relationships, symptoms and difficulties. The central therapeutic effect is not just an intellectual appreciation of an active world view but a lived experience in the group of enlarged freedom through experiences of new personal acts or refraining from maladaptive acts. This is not an absolute freedom but a tension [and move] towards greater freedom within the context of a person's circumstances . . . The group can help show members the nature of their choices and identify characteristic maladaptive interpersonal patterns; the group invites reflection on the desirability of the choices now made explicit and 'owned' by the individual, a process which prepares the ground for changing maladaptive choice patterns.
>
> (1988, p. 46)

This model has an emphasis on the capacity for change, and an assumption that human actions are not predetermined and that we have both choice and responsibility. It also assumes that we are looking for existential meaning in our lives (Ratigan and Aveline 1988, p .45). However, our habitual ways of being may not be very evident to us, which is why the group is important. The anthropologist Pierre Bourdieu has highlighted this tendency and called it *habitus*. This is an 'embodied history, internalised as a second nature and so forgotten as history – is the active presence of the whole past' (Bourdieu 1990, p. 56). An important aspect of the group work is to increase personal self-awareness of this habitus; this is done through active participation in group processes: 'Members do not simply talk about their difficulties in the group but actually *reveal them through their here-and-now behaviour*. In this model, the "here-and-now" is where the therapy takes place' (Waller 1993, p. 23).

The focus is more on the here and now of the group and how the past informs the present. Participants are encouraged to gain a sense of their influence on events in the group. The aim is that group members will move from unproductive ways of being and relating to being able to take on more responsibility for their lives, including their symptoms and difficulties (Ratigan and Aveline 1988, p. 45). This is achieved by giving participants constant feedback, which can come from other participants, and the therapist may also assist in this role. Hence the therapist is analytically investigative in the sense of synthesising group dynamics and reporting them for group discussion, and although this may be conceptualised as a form of interpretation, I would suggest it is a tentative one which is actively 'checked out' with the group for its veracity: 'Taking responsibility for one's participation in the learning experience of the group, having a sense of one's influence on events, and learning to give feedback are prerequisites' (Waller 1993, p. 314).

Enacted patterns of being are scrutinised. This can also take place on a more conscious and self-conscious level in the group. Waller advances the following as an example: 'Participants are encouraged to explore irrational belief systems (i.e., if I don't get married, pass an exam, get promotion by 30, then I am a complete failure)' (1993, p. 314).

Both Ratigan and Aveline (1988) and Yalom (1980) emphasise the usefulness of a sense of *solidarity*, and suggest that this will combat feelings of fragmentation, individualism, isolation and alienation, which may have previously been felt by participants. An important component, noted by Ratigan and Aveline, is the sense of *being of assistance* to others in the group:

> this process is a vital element of the interpersonal group. Often members will report that what helped them in the group was not the contribution of the leader, however well intentioned, but the realization of all being in the same boat and that they had something to give to another human being.
>
> (1988, p. 51)

The model also attempts to respond to 'social, political, and economic realities including discrimination and racism and how internalisation of these realities can lead to feelings of despair and powerlessness' (Waller 1993, p. 314):

> If we accept that patterns of behaviour are learned and that it is possible to unlearn or relearn more effective or rewarding ways of being, then there is much to be learned from interpersonal interaction within the boundaries of a group.
>
> (Waller 1993, p. 25)

Waller (1993) endorses Bloch and Crouch (1985), who suggest that there is an important therapeutic factor created through interaction, which they call 'interpersonal learning' or 'learning from interpersonal action'. Interactive groups offer two important aspects, according to Yalom (1995, p. 77), which are, first, that the group functions as a 'social microcosm' and, second, that it offers the opportunity for a 'corrective emotional experience'. Waller expands on this concept:

> 'Social microcosm' refers to a group process which resembles customary everyday functioning, in which patients tend to behave in their usual maladaptive way. It is by observing and drawing attention to these behaviour patterns in the group that the therapist and other group members can have a 'corrective emotional experience', thus helping each other to change.
>
> (1993, p. 26)

So, in other words, the group becomes a place where participants can learn about patterns of behaviour which are causing them distress, and result in disturbed interpersonal relations. Group members may *see* these for the first time in a revelatory way, or perhaps dimly perceived aspects will come more slowly into focus.

Increased self-awareness permits the possibility of change, and changed ways of relating can be rehearsed or 'tried out' in the group; as Waller emphasises, feedback from the therapist and other participants, in addition to self-observation, enables an expansion of self-awareness:

> Feedback from members of the group and the therapist, illuminating aspects of the self which have become obvious to others, but which are not recognised by oneself, is essential. To be effective it must be well timed and delivered with sensitivity. In this respect the therapist is an important role model, demonstrating a positive clinical approach as opposed to a negative and judgemental one, observing and commenting on behaviour and images and their effects on the process of the group.
>
> (Waller 1993, pp. 314–15)

Ratigan and Aveline summarise the role of the facilitator in the interpersonal model, as to:

1 establish and sustain the group boundaries (selection and preparation of members, preparing the group room, receiving apologies, etc.);
2 model and maintain a therapeutic culture;
3 provide an understanding of events in the session;
4 note and reward members' gains;
5 encourage members taking responsibility for their actions;
6 predict (and possibly prevent) undesirable developments;
7 involve silent members;
8 increase cohesiveness (by underlining similarities and caring in the group); and
9 provide hope for members (it helps members to realize that the group is an orderly process and that the leader has some coherent sense of the group's long-term development).

> (1988, pp. 54–5)

The facilitator is a participant in the group's process, not maintaining an opaque screen, and is active, though as the group matures group members will be able to facilitate and challenge each other unaided, and the therapist can take on a more background role, giving an important sense of safety. Whilst the facilitator reflects on group processes, it is done in such a way that the account is co-constructed with the group's members, or failing that, a hypothesis is put tentatively. It is possible for the facilitator to say, 'please add to this or tell me if you feel I have missed something' or 'do you think I've got the emphasis right here, that these two events have had an equal impact this week?' or 'is there a general feeling that . . . '; 'Please help me to understand what just happened here . . .'.

The facilitator also models helpful behaviour such as attentive listening, tactful facilitation and questioning, or mild challenging of 'projection' behaviour, sometimes by invoking feedback from the group ('how does the group feel about what X has just said about Y?'), as getting feedback from several group members is more powerful than just hearing it from the facilitator. The facilitator in modelling constructive behaviour engages in giving authentic responses to images and situations within the group – not in arcane technical language, but put plainly. However, the therapist also keeps an eye out for meta-narratives and reverberations across sessions and may make observations which 'join up' events over time, or recall a repeating dynamic. Supporting Yalom's (1975) idea, Ratigan and Aveline also advocate sending a written group summary to all members after each meeting:

> The summary, a personal non-authoritative account by the leader, gives a second opportunity to live the session and enhances its therapeutic impact; group norms are further shaped and it is possible for the leader to add afterthoughts or highlight change. Finally, the summary fills the gaps for the absent member [if there has been one].
>
> (1988, p. 55)

This model can be directive or non-directive. Using this model, I have used a verbal (rather than written) account to open so that the verbal account can be assimilated whilst revisiting the images produced the previous week. The verbal account works well because having the images or objects on view is important in art therapy.

The group-interactive model is one taught to art therapy trainees. In well-established training groups, I have asked for the account to be written and presented by a different trainee each week. This has the disadvantage that the trainee taking the record may feel less able to participate in the session she is recording (as the participant-observer role is hard). However, it is a very useful learning experience.

The role of helping to create a caring space is also distinctive; it is partly by giving a model of genuine, gentle concern, but also a modelling of non-punitive reactions, even to challenging behaviour. Challenging behaviour is heard and acknowledged, rather than negatively *reacted* to, although an authentic emotional response might be appropriate if it is offered helpfully.

In the therapeutic arena, the ways of being that are being rehearsed in the group are taken outside the group process by participants, who can then 'report back' to the group on how aspects of their lives are changing; indeed, art therapy students also often report changes in their own lives. Bloch and Crouch (1985, p. 78) suggest that an 'adaptive spiral' is developed. Waller (1993, pp. 35–7) identifies a number of interrelated features of group work, which she suggests are generally regarded as 'curative features'. These are in summary:

1   the giving and sharing of information;
2   what she calls 'the installation of hope' regarding the process of participation;
3   mutual aid;
4   the discovery that other participants have the same kind of anxieties, problems or fears, and that the individual is not alone in having this problem

(there may be someone who has overcome this particular issue and who can provide inspiration);

5    the group can work as a reconstruction of the family, allowing potential family dynamics to be recognised and worked out;

6    catharsis is an important aspect whereby a person admits to feelings and thoughts (of which he or she is often deeply ashamed), or re-experiences a traumatic experience with the group, and can then experience a strong sense of relief or even release; such intimate disclosures often precipitate similar 'confessions' from other participants, which, in-turn, allows the group to become more intimate. The containment of these feelings also makes the group feel safer;

7    participants learn more about how they interact with others and get feedback in response to which they can try out different ways of being;

8    the group is a safe place where deep feelings can be shared without fear of reprisal, allowing group cohesiveness to develop;

9    through interpersonal learning, old ways of relating can be examined and changed.

## Group-interactive art therapy

There is both visual and verbal expression in interactive art therapy; the focus can move from the art to an interaction, in a back-and-forth manner. Certain themes can be held by the art and art works can be brought out over and over again and reworked. This pictorial process could take place over weeks or months. Making a picture can feel less threatening to some people than having to talk in a group, and playful aspects of art making can come to the fore. Many people 'did art' at school, so there is sometimes a regressive dimension to using art materials, especially in initial sessions. The actual physical art object is in some sense a record of what has taken place, but is also a future stimulus for reflection and disclosure. Although the image is a disclosure in pictorial form, the maker of the image may decide when to share content with the group, so, depending on the nature of the image (which may be more or less pictorially revealing), the pace of disclosure can be controlled by the participant. This gives power to the art therapy participant (Hogan 2004a, 2004b).

The art work can become the focus of attention in group work, so that conversations between participants may become indirect and via art works. Also, the art work can become the focus for projected material, and can be destroyed and repaired. Members can show empathy towards each other by adopting a similar pictorial style or particular symbols or motifs, and this has been called 'group resonance' by Gerry McNeilly (1983). The phenomenon of two or more clocks next to each other becoming synchronised is an example of this concept in the psychical sense. McNeilly used it metaphorically to describe the way images can seemingly influence each other and 'resonate' or reverberate together. Group processes can be intensified through the use of group painting, and group conflicts can be articulated and explored. The pictorial struggle itself (the mess made, or the effort in articulating a concept) can be tremendously revealing, so thinking about the process as well as the product is useful:

> Whether or not we agree that art-making necessarily gives easier access to 'irrational' material, it is certainly non-verbal and non-linear, and presents a fundamentally different, but very rich, way of communicating to others and with oneself. One aspect of art work which is importantly different from verbal language . . . is that art works can contain multiple and conflicting discourses simultaneously, exemplifying irreconcilable ideas or impulses.
>
> (Hogan and Coulter 2014, p. 169)

Sally Skaife is articulate in describing what the art work brings, allowing:

> feelings to be expressed in an alternative way and metaphorical and symbolic language to stay on in the group in a concrete form. As well as this, feelings that are not easily expressed in words can be played with in their symbolic form, for instance colour and shape, and thus worked on in a way that can make them more accessible to language and thus to consciousness. As in other art therapy settings group members are encouraged to use the art materials to express themselves freely; this work is then looked at as both belonging to the history of the individual and [potentially] as an expression of the dynamic of the group.
>
> (1990, p. 237)

From these two quotations, it is evident that the art work itself can function on many different levels within a group.

Waller does not see the use of themes as in any way antithetical to a group-interactive approach (1993, p. 29), so it may be directive or non-directive in emphasis. She points out that image making can be akin to 'free association' or 'dreaming into paper' (p. 38). Here Waller is using language derived from the Jungian analytic tradition in describing art therapy.

Waller argues that some fundamental processes of an interactive group are enhanced by the addition of art making:

> These include projection, mirroring, scapegoating, parataxic distortion, and projective identification. Projection involves group members having feelings and making assumptions about other members which are not based on their here-and-now experience. For example, one member might experience another as his critical mother and make assumptions about that person's feelings toward him. Mirroring entails a member having strong feelings and emotions about another's behaviour, which is in fact an aspect of the member's behaviour. Projection and mirroring are often accompanied by splitting – by experiencing a group member, the facilitator, or the whole group as all good or

all bad. Scapegoating occurs when the group tries to put all its difficulties onto one member and to get rid of them. The members' tendency to distort their perceptions of others (parataxic distortions) provides valuable material for the group to consider. An important and often disturbing phenomenon is projective identification, which can result in one member projecting his or her own (but actually disowned) attributes onto another toward whom they may feel 'an uncanny attraction-repulsion' (Yalom 1985, p. 354). These attributes may be projected so strongly that the other person's behaviour begins to change.

(Waller 1993, p. 315)

## Discussion and conclusion

An integrative model is ambitious, given that there are real frictions inherent in the ideas which feed it: psychodynamic theory, existentialism and social psychology. Agazarian and Peters (1981) (whom Waller cites extensively) provide a spirited rationale for the combination of methods regarding verbal group-interactive therapy; however, a caveat must be made, that a predominant focus must be inevitable, as there will be too many things happening at once for all aspects to receive equal note and emphasis:

in any group performing complex behaviours relevant to a group goal, everyone does something different: leadership and other roles and functions are differentially allocated. Why does A perform task functions and B perform social maintenance? If A is incapacitated or absent, why does C rather than anyone else perform A's functions and then surrender those functions when A returns, or not surrender them? Group dynamics will describe the necessary roles and functions of the group, and the pressures relevant to understanding and predicting the phenomena associated with those functions. Psychoanalysis must provide the information we need if we are to understand *who* will perform the functions and *why* those who do not, will not or cannot . . . We must understand the individual, i.e., [the] psychoanalytic dynamics that he brought with him into the group.

(Agazarian and Peters 1981, pp. 16–17)

How explicitly psychoanalytic this understanding of the self needs to be is open to question and debate (and this book provides other explanatory schemas for understanding the self); key psychodynamic ideas can be employed, as Waller suggests, *with a social psychological and existential emphasis, rather than a narrowly psychoanalytical one* (a bit like mindfulness without Buddhism; it's possible to gain the benefits of meditation practice without believing in Buddha or reincarnation). A number of core psychodynamic concepts useful in conjunction with a systems approach have been outlined above. This is a model which is necessarily open to interpretation by practitioners in how far it is 'weighted' towards these key elements. For example, some practitioners might work with a 'narrative' emphasis;

the participants analyse their own dynamics, without a narrowly psychoanalytic-interpretative framework, and the group leans more towards a social psychological or existential orientation. It is still possible to integrate some psychodynamic insights to help understand groups and individuals (projective processes etc.).

Agazarian and Peters add: 'In short, we need a two-theory system for understanding and performing group psychotherapy; we need [a theory for] the group's dynamics and the individuals' dynamics' (1981, p. 17).

For group-interactive art therapy, we need a three-theory system, in order to encompass the unique properties of the image, and image-making process. An emphasis on group dynamics combined with analysis of the images made provides a rich therapeutic environment. An argument in favour of the integrative model is that it is more holistic. There are difficulties in adopting the here-and-now norm of the group, as we often like to share stories about ourselves, but these are not insurmountable:

> In this model, the 'here-and-now' is where the therapy takes place and 'reporting' on past experiences is discouraged. Disclosure does, however, take place: that is, revelation of 'secrets' or significant events from the past and present outside the group and this may be important in understanding the behaviour of that individual in the group.
>
> (Waller 1993, p. 23)

There may be an inner compulsion to reveal past traumas and revealing them and being accepted by the group is potentially curative. Traumatised individuals often hold the irrational belief that they will be rejected, or that people will be repelled by them if they tell . . . . Exorcising deeply internalised feelings of guilt and shame can be helpful, especially when such disclosure is met with loving support and compassionate acknowledgement; groups can 'hold' despair and distress powerfully. However, as noted above, there will be a 'steer' towards staying in the present in this model.

Acknowledging group dynamics, reporting on them coherently, noticing what is happening for individuals, whilst also showing cognisance of art work, is complex and multi-faceted. A lot can be happening all at once and the pace can be fast moving. One reason why this model has been at the core of a number of art therapy training courses, is that it's best learnt through direct experience (experientially). It is also a model which can benefit from having two facilitators, as it can be genuinely difficult, especially with more disturbed individuals, as Waller points out:

> Clearly conducting interactive art therapy groups with patients whose grasp of reality is, at least at times, very tenuous, requires much skill and confidence and support from other staff in the institution – not least for the conductor, who is likely to be extremely stirred up by the material of these intensive groups.
>
> (1993, p. 80)

It is also the case that the 'personalities' of these groups vary depending on their unique composition; they can have a predominant disposition – perhaps immensely reticent, desolate, combative or compassionate – a different set of facilitation skills is needed for each of these temperaments. Also mood changes can occur quite rapidly, again demanding a sure-footed facilitation. Whilst acknowledging the challenges involved, it must be emphasised that such groups are very powerful and truly transformative.

For further reading, see Diane Waller (2015) *Group Interactive Art Therapy: Its Use in Training and Practice*, Second edition. London: Routledge.

# Chapter 9

# Feminist approaches to art therapy

A feminist approach is implicit rather than explicit for many art therapy practitioners. Sensitivity towards 'gender issues' in general is regarded as good practice, though what precisely is meant by this varies (Hogan and Cornish 2014). In terms of publications which explicitly discuss feminism, this approach is most associated with Hogan's edited volumes (1997, 2003, 2012a) and a special edition of *The Arts In Psychotherapy* on Gender Issues (2013). The edited volumes are *Feminist Approaches to Art Therapy* (1997), *Gender Issues in Art Therapy* (2003) and *Revisiting Feminist Approaches to Art Therapy* (2012). Hogan has in-turn been principally influenced by the work of Simone de Beauvoir (1908–86) especially in adopting a perspective that sees gender as socially mediated and in flux. Feminist art therapy practice could sit under the umbrella term 'social art therapy', which is discussed in the next chapter. Both approaches are interested in how individuals are shaped by their social context and how illness is generated by and within social structures and relationships. But feminist art therapy is an important philosophy in its own right as women are subject to different pressures and constraints to those influencing men. For this reason, it is a topic worthy of separate consideration.

In *The Second Sex* de Beauvoir asked the question, *What is a woman?* She argued that in the Christian tradition woman is defined in relation to man, as for instance in the biblical story of Genesis, 'in which Eve appears as if drawn from Adam's supernumerary bone' (often translated as rib). She cited Michelet's view that woman is a 'relative being' – the 'other' to the masculine norm who 'determines and differentiates herself in relation to man' (de Beauvoir 2011, p. 6). What the Genesis story suggests to her is that:

> Humanity is male, and man defines woman, not in herself, but in relation to himself; she is not considered as an autonomous being . . . A man's body has meaning by itself, disregarding the body of the woman, whereas the woman's body seems devoid of meaning without reference to the male. Man thinks himself without woman. Woman does not think herself without man.
>
> (p. 6)

Thus she is the second sex.

She notes the way female physiology is so often dominant in discussions of womankind:

> Woman has ovaries and a uterus; such are the particular conditions that lock her in her subjectivity; some even say she thinks with her hormones. Man vainly forgets that his anatomy also includes hormones and testicles. He grasps his body as a direct and normal link with the world that he believes he apprehends in all objectivity, whereas he considers woman's body an obstacle, a prison, burdened by everything that particularises it.
>
> (p. 5)

'One is not born, but rather *becomes*, a woman', Simone de Beauvoir is most celebrated for writing in 1949 (2011, p. 293). The idea that women are fashioned by civilisation, not biologically determined, sought to overthrow a significant body of theory and practice, which oppressively situated women as inferior to men. She argued that no biological, psychological or economic fate determines the figure that woman presents to society; it is *civilisation as a whole* that produces this creature – woman (2011, p. 293).

Prior to this change in attitude, much research and polemic was orientated towards proving that women are not just biologically determined but biologically determined as inferior in every respect to men. Explanations varied, from Darwin's idea in *The Descent of Man* that hunting was more stimulating than foraging and childcare – primitive women's work (Darwin 1871, p. 901), to suppositions relating to the shape and size of the head (Galton) or the actual weight of male versus female brains (Broca). Underlying the disparate theories was a confidence in female inferiority. Gould, a historian of science, argues that 'ranking' has been used as a tool to draw conclusions, suggesting that 'metaphors of progress and gradualism have been among the most pervasive in Western thought' (Gould 1981, p. 56). Ranking uses one or more criteria for assigning individuals to their proper place in a series. Stocking points out that in evolution, as popularised in the nineteenth century, a number of social groups were classified together. For example, labourers, children, women and the insane were thought to share certain 'mental characteristics' which placed them on a 'lower point on the unitary scale of intelligence and moral development: governed more by impulse, deficient in foresight, they were in varying degrees unable to get beyond this' (Stocking 1987, p. 230).

De Beauvoir's ideas have been immensely influential in feminist thought. The way that ranking and biological determinism are embedded in disciplinary norms has been critiqued (Bleier 1984; Fausto-Sterling 1985; Harraway 1992; Hubbard 1990; Lewontin *et al.* 1984; Oudshoorn 1994; Sayers 1982; Shiebinger 1993; Tarvis 1992). Some wrong-headed ideas underlie a number of current psychological theories. The implications of these embedded ways of thinking for women's mental health has received attention (Chesler 1972; Hare-Mustin and Marecek 1990; Howell and Baynes 1981; Hubbard 1990; Ussher 2011). A feminist consciousness has been developing within the arts therapies in general, in an attempt to cultivate and maintain non-abusive practices. Pragmatically, feminism is seen as just good practice by many. Analysis of psychology by feminist writers has provided a justification for a reappraisal of some of the underpinning theory, especially biological determinism, which can be seen masquerading as a rationale for the imposition of outmoded customs and ideals. Biological determinist frameworks have been used to tell women how they are *supposed* to behave, and to thereby validate inequality. Biological determinism has served to justify the status quo as an extension of nature (Gould 1981, p. 21) and has been used to actively resist women's advancement. One strand of this theory was used as a justification to exclude women from higher education on the grounds that the mental strain would damage their reproductive organs and possibly render women infertile (Showalter 1985). Women were exhorted to think of their overriding duty in perpetuating Mankind (Hogan 2006a; Showalter 1985). Ironically, there *is* a negative correlation between formal education and reproduction, with educated women having fewer children globally than those less highly educated. However, this a deliberate decision to limit family size using contraception; women have not been rendered infertile by mental strain, as feared! Nevertheless, there are still many cultures today in which males, but not females, are sent to school and the birth of a male is celebrated, but not the birth of a female. In some cultures women may only be initiated into society following the birth of a male (Duvvury 1991). The World Health Organisation (2010) notes that educational equality has many benefits:

> Educational attainment in women and girls has been correlated with decreased fertility and smoking rates, increased age of marriage, adequate birth spacing and overall [health] treatment adherence. Yet, multiple household responsibilities, including water collection, combined with household poverty and social norms that privilege boys for education deny many girls and young women the chance to attend and complete primary and secondary levels of education. These girls and young women are further deprived of the health benefits education provides. Lower levels of education in many contexts have also been found to increase the risk of sexual and gender-based violence.

De Beauvoir was very critical of the indoctrination of passivity among certain groups of Western women, which she notes as often commencing at the onset of menstruation. Even my own generation, influenced by 1950s' cultural mores, was taught it was wrong to be too forward, especially sexually: we were trained in a femininity which was modest, deferential and self-effacing. Indeed, de Beauvoir is also very frank about women's sexuality and its insistence and a woman's need for sexual gratification (Seymour-Jones 2008). Written at a time when many myths circulated about women's lack of desire, her work was seen as an affront by those unwilling to address such subjects.

There are two main distinct, but interconnecting, strands to feminism. They are not mutually exclusive but interwoven; sometimes there is an emphasis more on one or the other. One ongoing strand is based on concerns about equality, which have arisen in the context of the political and ideological struggle towards equal rights for women. This is part of feminism's long march, with its antecedents with those women in history who questioned inequality, including the Suffrage movement.

Another strand is a tradition of intellectual investigation of the ideological and political nature of knowledge (the backbone of 'consciousness raising'). This scholarly strand has latterly included a critique of feminism itself (sometimes misleadingly called 'third wave' feminism, which is really an ongoing filament of intellectual enquiry within feminism and a struggle for power and voice).

## Feminism and structural inequality: the fight for equal rights

I am still occasionally asked why we still need to talk about women's issues. Feminism proposes that the social, political and other rights of women should be equal to those of men. Feminism is necessarily interested in the question of equality. The idea of structural inequality is an acknowledgement that a 'level playing field' does not exist and that the ideology of meritocracy is just that – empty ideology; in other words, that there is an embedded bias in social networks and organisations which privileges men over women. The lack of equal pay for women in most sectors in the West (despite an equal pay act, in place in the UK since 1970) is a good demonstration of this. Equality doesn't mean sameness necessarily, but a hope for equality of opportunity. Rather than attributing the root cause of the poverty or mental illness of women to their intrinsic biological inferiority, moral weakness or bad behaviours, a more global perspective is brought to bear on the subject (Royce 2009).

Links are made from structural inequality to mental health. For example, it has been pointed out that:

> globally, many women do not have equal access to resources, and in many cultures have little autonomy outside of male control, or are regarded as of lesser value than males, or face male resistance to independent action. Women still do not have adequate access to safe and legal reproductive-health services locally or globally.
>
> (Hogan 2006b)

The World Health Organisation (WHO 2012) acknowledges that:

> Gender determines the differential power and control men and women have over the socioeconomic determinants of their mental health and lives, their social position, status and treatment in society and their susceptibility and exposure to specific mental health risks.

However, this determination is varied, with varied effects. Given women's unequal access to structural resources, it is hardly surprising to learn that we are particularly prone to depression, anxiety and somatic (bodily) complaints. WHO estimates that these 'disorders, in which women predominate, affect approximately 1 in 3 people in the community and constitute a serious public health problem' (WHO 2012). This is a complex subject and it may be the case that the diseases which are noted as of medical significance are both culturally and gender prescribed. For example, men tend to act out distress through illegal or antisocial activity and are consequently condemned as criminal or delinquent, while women in the UK comprise a relatively small percentage of the prison population. Women, however, tend to be defined as depressed, anxious or as exhibiting somatic complaints. Drawing on the work of anthropologists, we might begin to view illnesses as both biological *and* social phenomena, which may usefully be understood in terms of personal and cultural narratives: as enactments – perhaps, sometimes, a refusal to 'cope' (Scheper-Hughes 1991, p. 8). Scheper-Hughes gives the example of Brazilian cane-cutters, paid little more than starvation wages, who developed distinctive collective maladies. Humans everywhere 'employ their bodies in expressing complicated, contradictory, or hostile sentiments, especially when other avenues of expression are blocked or extremely dangerous' (1991, p. 6). Hogan (2012b, p. 79) applies these ideas to childbirth, so that art therapists won't view new mothers referred to them as merely postnatally depressed, but as perhaps wrestling with emotions which are deemed socially unacceptable, with a profound fear that if they speak out (or fully acknowledge their feelings) their baby may be taken away. As Scheper-Hughes suggests, both nervous and physical disorders may be viewed as 'bodily idioms for registering protest and for negotiating power relations' (1991, p. 6).

A detailed investigation of obstetric regimes and practices followed in the wake of Oakley's *From Here to Maternity* (1981), which led to a large body of feminist literature dedicated to questioning the protocols used by hospitals. Martin's (1987) *The Woman in the Body: A Cultural Analysis of Reproduction* is a good example of the kind of astute anthropologically informed material being written. This resulted in a reappraisal of how art therapists might work with new mothers (Hogan 1997, 2003, 2012a, 2012b, 2015; Hogan *et al.* 2015). This work attempts to develop a holistic picture of the transition to motherhood as an important rite of passage, and produces a discussion of the traumatised or depressed mother in relation to a range of factors: from a disrupted sense of self-identity, compounded by sudden social isolation or discriminatory workplace practices, to societal reactions which may include restrictive expectations relating to behavioural change – 'you're a mother now so . . .', to idealised expectations of motherhood and mothering which are oppressive in themselves, to an analysis of iatrogenic hospital practices (those practices which are illness-inducing, for instance supine birthing postures in obstetrics). Rather than situating the new mother as inadequate, a feminist analysis is gentler in its judgement (Hogan 2015; Hogan *et al.* 2015).

Furthermore, feminist scholarship looks further still at the underlying discourses, and critiques the inadequate models which underpin some dominant psychiatric theories about motherhood (Hogan 2012b). The misuse of theory is also a structural issue, insofar as it has an impact on services and on women's lives. For instance, a generation of women have grown up worrying about leaving their infants in the care of another believing that the baby could become traumatised or develop 'attachment' problems; this has led to much unnecessary maternal misery and guilt. Sound research supports the idea that babies are resilient and will tolerate numerous regular care givers (Hogan 2003, 2012b). An edifice of practice has been built on faulty theory resulting in much maternal suffering and under-socialised offspring.

Structural inequality also leads to women staying in violent relationships and oppressive employment situations; cultural norms (such as the ostracisation of women who leave their husbands) compound this. Furthermore, many women who are referred for drug rehabilitation have experienced abuse, or have been led into addiction through prostitution (Jones 2012; McGee 2012). Prostitutes as a group of women are highly likely to have experienced abuse in childhood, as well as when they prostitute themselves. At the very least this is self-abuse, though they are often controlled by ruthless men, as is well documented (Hogan 2012a; Jones 2012; Ross 1997, 2012; Slater 2003).

Body image issues are sometimes addressed as a structural matter, emanating from concern at the ubiquity of 'airbrushed', impossibly perfected images of impossible female beauty with which women are continually bombarded, and with which they inevitably compare themselves (Redfern and Aune 2010). Also ubiquitous is the presence of pornography, which is genuinely difficult to avoid, from the so-called 'lad mags' in the supermarket (magazines which contain nude photography of women often with highly misogynistic text), to the harder-core porn which leaps on to the computer screen unbidden during Internet use. In such material women are often depicted as passive and brutalised; their subservience is frequently eroticised – the 'You know you want it' lyric of a recent pop song featured women in submissive poses, and in hard-core pornography force and submission are eroticised.

Ministerial concern has recently been prompted by the prevalence of eating disorders in young children. In 2012 the British Home Office launched a 'Body Confidence Campaign'. The campaign's aim was to 'reduce the burdens that popular culture places on people's wellbeing and self-esteem' (Home Office 2012). It included the production of a 'body confidence pack', which comprises before-and-after pictures of male and female celebrities. This is intended for use with children aged between 6 and 11 years, to show them what digital manipulation can do. The pack is also concerned with an overemphasis on thinness and dieting by young children, expressing concern that 75 per cent of girls aged between 11 and 21 diet in order to look more attractive (body image 'parent pack', Home Office 2012, p. 5). As I have noted (Hogan 2013), so-called 'free-market sensibilities' would appear to prevent any real action being taken (and a feminist's answer to the free-market economists might be: if I were pimping *your* daughter would that still be legitimate capitalism?). Though body image and the harm done by prostitution and pornography are issues now to the fore in new feminist writing, as well as being in the headlines, art therapy was quick to see the power of images on the psyche, producing powerful early critiques (Hogan 1997). Feminist art therapists are aware that the body is the 'ground' on which sociopolitical determinants take hold and are realised – it is contested space (Hogan 1997, 2012a). Bodily ambivalence is hardly surprising as women are not only bombarded with contradictory discourses about how bodies should be, but also how they should perform (Hogan 2014). The body as the 'ground' is a metaphor, but with the ubiquity of digital manipulation of images ('airbrushing') it is becoming a literal canvas upon which feminine ideals are projected.

Structural inequality in so-called developed countries is still rife, and 'women are more likely than men to suffer from late-in-life poverty, lack of opportunity and unequal access to public resources' (Hogan and Warren 2013, p. 6). Furthermore, in many places, because of the emphasis on their appearance, women, as they age, may feel particularly devalued (Hogan and Warren 2012). Issues of structural inequality have also been applied to art therapy with respect to the position of older women who face these particular difficulties; feminists have also sought to challenge the cliché of the sexless crone, giving voice to the experiences of older women and later-in-life sexuality to challenge this predominant and incorrect stereotype (Hogan and Warren 2012, 2013; Huet 1997, 2012; Martin 1997, 2012).

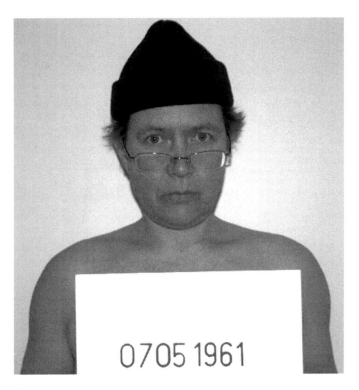

*Figure 9.1* I Feel Like a Prisoner of the Numbers by Claudia B. Kuntze. From a project with sociologists in which older women explored their experience of ageing in relation to societal expectations (Hogan and Warren 2012, 2013).

*Figures 9.2a and 9.2b* Jude, Age 60. From the Representing Self: Representing Ageing Project (Look at Me! Phototherapy Workshops). Jude Grundy in collaboration with Sue Hale. 2010.

The photographer Rosy Martin said of her 'Outrageous Agers' series:

> It was turning 50 that made me want to explore how the dominant representations of older women showed only stereotypes of decline and redundancy. I wanted to challenge this, and find ways of representing my ageing self through my photographic practice in a subversive, playful and resistant way.
>
> (University of Sheffield 2010)

*Figure 9.3* Trying It On. From the Outrageous Agers series by Rosy Martin and Kay Goodridge. 2000. This is from a series of photographs which challenge negative stereotypes about ageing.

I have argued that art therapy must maintain a critical relationship to the discipline of psychology in order to avoid oppressing women with the misogynistic discourses which are embedded and accepted in its theories and practices (Hogan 1997, 2006a, 2012a). Furthermore, I have suggested that we are morally complicit unless we question and attempt to transform them; hence, I have advocated a 'social art therapy' which moves beyond a narrow focus on individual psychopathology and includes an understanding of structural inequality in society and how it relates to mental health issues which could be mistaken as being merely individual (Hogan 2012a).

## The importance of feminist scholarship: the intellectual investigation of the ideological and political nature of knowledge

One important strand of thought evident in feminist art therapy, to have arisen out of feminist scholarship, is work interested in analysing how inequality is perpetuated through scholarly (and sometimes polemical) investigation of texts, both

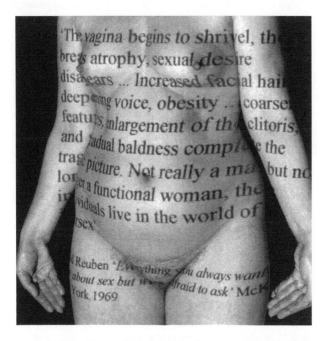

Figure 9.4 The Vagina Begins to Shrivel . . . . From the Outrageous Agers series by Rosy Martin and Kay Goodridge. 2000.

visual and written. This work has produced a critique of both theory and practice via an analysis of power differentials and other mechanisms by which sexual inequality is perpetuated.

This strand of intellectual analysis includes an interest in the visual representation of women, and art therapists are well placed to understand and respond to these ideas. Semiotic analysis has explored how expectations about gender are embodied in the pictorial representations that surround us. People often give expression to their experience in metaphorical discourse, which can better conceptualise and articulate their situation. In ideological struggles, metaphors are commonly used around a contested site of meaning. This can take the form of pictorial or linguistic strategies to establish one meaning over another. Pictures can be seen as providing women with a tool for carving out a self-identity which might challenge dominant exemplifications or those representations connected with their gender or particular socio-economic status (Hogan 1997, 2012a). It is no surprise to art therapists that images both suggest and delimit conceptual possibilities.

Hogan's edited volumes looked broadly at women's issues and art therapy, and especially at the negative discourses surrounding definitions of femininity, and claims about female instability, with reference to the negative positioning of women within psychiatric discourses. Feminist scholars have been particularly helpful in showing how psychiatrists and psychologists have perpetuated negative expectations about women's mental health. Showalter points out the contribution of feminist scholarship:

> Contemporary feminist philosophers, literary critics, and social theorists have been the first to call attention to the existence of a fundamental alliance between 'woman' and 'madness'. They have shown how women, within our dualistic systems of language and representation, are typically situated on the side of irrationality, silence, nature, and body, while men are situated on the side of reason, discourse, culture, and mind.
>
> (1985, p. 4)

It is the intellectual contribution of feminists which will break down these dichotomies. Feminist critiques suggest:

> Women outnumber men in diagnoses of madness . . . Women are also more likely to receive psychiatric 'treatment', ranging from hospitalisation in an asylum, accompanied by restraint, electro-convulsive therapy (ECT) and psycho-surgery, to psychological therapy and psychotropic drug treatments today. Why is this so? Some would say that women *are* more mad than men, with psychiatric treatment a beneficent force that sets out to cure the disordered female mind. I proffer an alternative explanation – that women are subjected to misdiagnosis and mistreatment by experts whose own pecuniary interests can be questioned, as can their use (or abuse) of power. This is not to deny the reality of women's experience of prolonged misery or distress, which undoubtedly exists. However, if we examine the roots of this distress, in the context of women's lives, it can be conceptualised as a reasonable response, not a reflection of pathology within.
>
> (Ussher 2011, pp. 1–2)

Feminist scholarship has included critiques of psychiatry, especially certain psychiatric presumptions about femininity and how it is often equated with pathology (Appignanesi 2008; Howell and Baynes 1981; Russell 1995; Showalter 1985; Ussher 1991, 2011), and this interest is reflected in the writing and practice of some feminist art therapists (Burt 2012a; Eastwood 2012; Joyce 2008; Manuel 2008; Wright and Wright 2013) and many of the writers in Hogan's edited volumes (1997, 2012a) explore these issues. As highlighted in the introduction to this chapter, biological determinism in psychiatry has been highlighted and critiqued. For example, analysis of psychiatric classificatory manuals is also of relevance in thinking about how femininity relates to ideas about illness (Rehavia-Hanauer 2012). Cultural misogyny and violence against women have also been emphasised (especially by Burt 2012b; Huet 2012; Jones 2012; Joyce 2012; McGee 2012; and Ross 2012). Issues of sexuality and sexual orientation and art therapy were explored by Hogan (2012a), Jones (2012) and Martin (2012) and also in a further edited volume, which focused on gender and sexuality more closely, including transexuality (Hogan 2003). The books also contain an exploration of ethnicity and gender in the art therapeutic encounter (especially Campbell and Gaga 1997, 2012; Landes 2012).

Women's bodies, especially the experience of pregnancy and childbirth, received attention. Ongoing work on women's issues and art therapy includes an examination of women's changed sense of self-identity and sexuality as a result of pregnancy and childbirth (Hogan 1997, 2003, 2012a, 2013a, 2015; Hogan *et al.* 2015), and a trenchant critique of the reductive application of object-relations theory, as well as a critical appraisal of frankly misogynist theories about 'too good' mothering. Maternal guilt, depression and anger are reappraised in the light of negative theories about mothers (Hogan 2012b).

In *Feminist Approaches to Art Therapy* (1997) and *Revisiting Feminist Approaches to Art Therapy* (2012), Hogan suggested that, for several decades, disciplinary boundaries have been shifting, particularly in the social sciences and the humanities. In psychology increasing attention has been paid to the social construction of illness, with psychologists straying further into territory previously occupied by sociologists and cultural theorists and vice versa. Theorists, such as those highlighted above, have pointed out that women are 'pathologised' in our culture: in other words, that the defining characteristics of femininity are considered unhealthy. The effect of this upon women's mental health has been the subject of much feminist enquiry. Critiques of psychiatry exist which argue that it is quite possible for a psychiatrist to give a diagnosis of mental illness when there may be simply a clash of values between the patient and psychiatrist; and, further, that the position of women rejecting dominant patriarchal 'norms' is likely to be seen as 'dysfunctional', rather than as evincing a constructive conflict between the individual and society (Russell 1995, pp. 33–7). Also, because women are now more likely to be defined as in need of 'treatment' rather than 'punishment', they may as a consequence end up for a longer time in psychiatric custody, than if they had been jailed, as there is a tendency to jail men and give women psychiatric treatment for exhibiting very similar behaviours. Of those women who do end up in prison in Britain, over half report having been the victims of childhood sexual abuse, pointing to an endemic abuse of power (Prison Reform Trust 2014, p. 4). This is a shameful statistic.

In disciplines such as psychology, psychoanalysis, cultural studies and literary studies more attention is being paid to language and images as part of discursive practices in the production and maintenance of subjectivity (Lupton 1994). In an optimistic mood, I suggested that, whereas art therapy had been a peripheral practice of little consequence, it has now become, or at least has the potential to become, much more relevant because of these theoretical shifts. (In the next chapter the contribution of art therapy to social science research is considered.) A feminist approach to art therapy can be viewed as constituting part of this general movement. These ideas are likely to halt the drift within British art therapy towards the use of reductive and universally applied dogmatic psychological models which do not represent women's heterogeneous lived experience or sufficiently acknowledge the socially constructed nature of individual distress (Hogan 1997, 2012a). This is still my hope as a feminist art therapist. The three books (Hogan 1997, 2003, 2012a) remain the essential corpus on feminism and art therapy.

## Women-only art therapy

Creating a deep understanding of women's conditions and women's experiences is one rationale for a focus on this subject, as well as for women-only groups specifically addressing women's issues. Many feminists would argue that being a woman is a shared experience and therefore women's groups per se are valid, because women are all subject to the same overarching oppressive, idealistic and misogynistic discourses. This is the 'separatist' position. It also supports a call for solidarity among women.

Separatist feminism is a powerful idea. If women cooperated we would be a force to be reckoned with. If all women worked together who could stop us? We could feminise society: workplace crèches not guns! Playgrounds not cruise missiles! Education not forced marriage! Think what a feminised society might look like.

Of course, structural inequality and women's experiences of being in the world are interlinked, but other feminists might counter-argue that, because women are

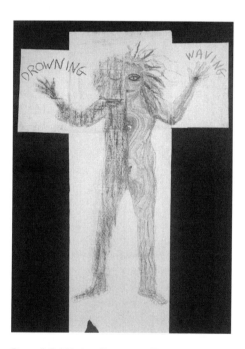

*Figure 9.5* Waving Drowning. From the Representing Self: Representing Ageing Project (Look at Me! Art Elicitation Workshops). 2010.

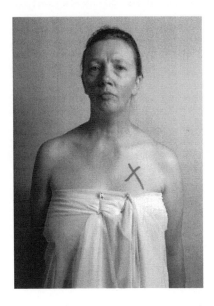 

*Figures 9.6a and 9.6b* Infantilization. Jo Spence and Rosy Martin, Phototherapy (Mind/
Body). 1984. 'One morning, whilst reading, I was confronted
by the awesome reality of a young white-coated doctor, with
student retinue, standing by my bedside. As he referred to his
notes, without introduction, he bent over me and began to ink
a cross onto the area of flesh above my left breast. As he did a
whole chaotic series of images flashed through my head. Rather
like drowning. I heard this doctor, whom I had never met before,
this potential mugger, tell me that my left breast would have to be
removed . . .'.

a heterogeneous lot, with cross-cutting allegiances, women actually experience
the world very *differently* depending on their cultural context, and that includes
differing experiences of structural inequality. Women's experience cannot be
generalised; we are all dissimilar from each other, and we experience the forces
at play in the world differently. This is perhaps a worrying perspective from a
feminist point of view, as it suggests that women may not be interested in working
with other women because our predominant allegiances will be to other causes.
Women's first allegiances are not necessarily to other women. However, the focus
on difference helps to give voice to those traditionally more marginalised (including by feminism/s).

Other feminists say they are unable to focus on women's issues alone, but
must work with all those who lack power and who face oppression, such as ethnic
minority groups, gay men, the geographically disadvantaged or the poorly paid.

Furthermore, some worry that educated, able-bodied, white women's voices
may often speak for all women, obscuring other voices. Consequently, feminist

scholarship has become very sensitised to issues of representation and voice. Nevertheless, even those who emphasise heterogeneity may advocate a focus on 'women's issues' therapeutically. These may still be addressed, but in a more tailored way, through groups which address specific aspects of women's lived experiences such as birth trauma, the transition to motherhood, and dealing with breast cancer or endometriosis.

## What does a feminist art therapist look like?

Below, a leading feminist art therapist acknowledges the political and ideological nature of her enterprise; the quote suggests that enquiry into subjugation must always play a part in the therapeutic encounter. Another key aspect of the quote is that the therapeutic process must create space for *multiple perspectives* and *diversity*:

> As a feminist I believe that . . . [art] psychotherapy is a political act . . . one is integrating the analysis of oppression as well as the recognition of the multiple perspectives that comes with the diversity in the human race.
>
> (Burt 2012b, p. 30)

The importance of greater acknowledgement of 'issues of culture' more broadly has been highlighted as crucially important, if we are not to inadvertently oppress others in art therapy practices (Holloway 2009; Talwar *et al.* 2004). Therapeutically, this has led to work focused on the idea of 'internalised sexism' and 'internalised racism' – art therapy which has a 'consciousness-raising' agenda as part of the therapeutic practice, including an enhanced awareness of 'intersectionality' (those other aspects of identity that are also of importance, which have been highlighted in more recent feminist thinking, especially ethnicity, class and sexuality). Oppression may be widespread, but how it *intersects* with sex, sexuality, ethnicity and other factors is particular, is located in time and place, so cannot be absolutely generalised. Oppression is experienced variously. Consequently, identity 'is not a fixed category' (Talwar 2010, p. 15); whilst not all feminist art therapists are social constructionists, a view which sees the self-in-process in relation to fields of force concords well with a feminist practice.

In many groups which have a diverse makeup, issues of identity will arise naturally in practice:

> When running a varied group myself recently, *diversity* is precisely what came to the fore, with the British Caribbean women dissimilar to each other in their experience of being black women, and others, such as a British Yemeni Muslim woman, having had a very different life-experience, especially with reference to community expectations and restraints. Explication of different cultural perspectives was intrinsic to the group process.
>
> (Hogan 2014, p. 114)

As Lala (2011) usefully reminds us, our clients 'are the experts on their own lives'. It is those we work with who 'must be seen as self-determining unique beings who are constantly composing and reconfiguring their own identity, experiences and struggles' (2011, p. 33). An enhanced receptivity to these issues is central to a feminist art therapy.

Laura Brown's view is that a feminist therapy is primarily concerned with issues of 'empowerment':

> Feminist therapists are interested in creating 'feminist consciousness', that is, the understanding that one's difficulties in life are not a reflection of personal deficits or failures to sufficiently strive, but rather derive from systematic forms of culturally based oppression. Developing personal power, defined in a very broad manner, is an overarching goal of feminist therapy.
>
> (2010, p. 337)

Similarly, Waldman (1999) explicitly attempts to create a synthesis of 'social art therapy' and 'feminist psychotherapy' which is informed by postmodernist social theory, with a view to enhancing thinking about social context in clinical practice; Waldman's distinctive position is around women's sense of powerlessness being institutionally produced, by a combination of factors which she outlines, such as social isolation, lack of control over resources and an unsympathetic legal system. In particular, she considers the way in which established demands on women to nurture others while repressing their own emotions can lead to their own emotional distress. The motivation for this emphasis is stated as Waldman's experience of observing that women frequently feel reluctant to challenge others when they feel disempowered or misunderstood. She produces a useful illustrative case study using clay. Her client's work emulated her feelings of being bullied, abused and dominated by men. She related herself to the clay saying, 'I'm whatever people make of me' (1999, p. 15).

Jane Ussher does not dismiss the idea of mental illness per se, nor does she reject diagnostic labels, but she worries that the label can mask the sources of distress, especially with respect to violence against women:

> Diagnostic labels such as the term 'depression' may function to communicate the extent of a woman's distress, and validate her subjective experience; however, they can also serve to obscure the conditions that lead to distress in the first place, and simply dismiss a woman as 'mad'.
>
> (Ussher 2011, pp. 212–13)

Some feminist therapists recommend 'consciousness-raising' exercises as part of therapy, which can enable an analysis and deconstruction of the images and texts that surround us and bolster gender norms (Hogan 2012a; Martin 2012). For instance, bringing in found images from magazines, newspapers or art can play a part. Looking at liked and disliked images can be revealing. This can include aspects akin to semiotic investigation. What is it about this image that disquiets me? Where there is knowledge there is power, or the potential of it. It is a form of cultural analysis and critique which moves beyond a narrow focus on individual psychopathology (Hogan and Coulter 2014).

To conclude, representations of gender difference are crucial in determining the repertoire of 'ways of being' for each gender. They represent conceptual possibilities. It would therefore seem appropriate for art therapists to engage with cultural representations and interrogate them as part of our practice. Of course, we all engage with these cultural mores, whether we are particularly aware of doing so or not, and we are not passive in exploring and enacting them, though with different levels of self-knowing (Butler 1990); performative exploration allows for the possibility of transcendence, or for the development of enhanced self-awareness (Martin 2012). How we internalise these messages that surround us is individual, even though the messages themselves are ubiquitous. *There is no simple determinism here.* There are no simple answers, but feminist scholarship helps us think about structural inequality and what it might mean; it develops an analytical consciousness and changed ways of being. We can literally picture things differently and experiment with seeing. This wasn't invented in the twenty-first century.

*Figure 9.7* Edith Garrud demonstrating her ju-jitsu skills.

Feminism is implicit in most art therapy practice by both female and male practitioners, but has been explicitly discussed and investigated in a relatively small body of art therapy literature to date. There are three main aspects to a feminist-orientated art therapy. First is the cultivation of an acute critical awareness of issues of inequality. Second, linked to this, is a critical investigation of the construction of knowledge, including an analysis of the power dynamics within institutional practices, use of language and pictorial representation which sustain inequality. There is an interest in tearing down false suppositions (deconstruction) in order to expose and to challenge the theoretical foundations of prejudice and oppressive practices. Third, through these engagements is consciousness-raising and empowerment. Feminist art therapy, whilst it does not deny the reality of human suffering, wishes to engage women in thinking about their subjectivity in their social context as affected by particular social norms which create distress and dis-ease. It is acknowledged that any generalisation made about gender differences must take into account a myriad of factors, including class, culture, age, health issues, sexuality and geographical location, as important contributory factors in how women are perceived and treated. Many feminist writers adhere to a model of selfhood which sees it in flux in relation to multiple forces.

Feminism is interested in a critical engagement with dominant theories which are unhelpful to women's well-being and flourishing. Feminist art therapy has been important in its challenge to the reductive and potentially damaging use of psychological ideas in art therapy practice and has worried about the inflexible application of often misogynistic ideas about 'psychic' development; at worst, the imposition of reductive psychodynamic interpretation and rigid application of theory results in psychic abuse. In particular, the essay 'Problems of Identity: Deconstructing Gender in Art Therapy' (chapter 2 in Hogan 2012a) contains an illustration of the kind of reductive theorising that we should all be keen to resist. A feminist art therapy is interested in challenging dominant stereotypes and creating more empowering narratives for women's lives, new repertoires and vistas.

# Chapter 10

# Social art therapy

## Art therapy as social action and art therapy as research tool

### Theorising a social turn

Junge *et al.* (1993), in an important and radical essay, queried the fundamental role of the art therapist in relation to maintaining the status quo. A rhetorical question was posited: are we as art therapists 'helping people adjust to a destructive society' within a 'fatally injured mental health system?' (p. 150). What are the implications for art therapy, if the answer is yes? The essay went on to challenge the dichotomy between the patient with a psychopathology and the expert healer; indeed, mutuality is emphasised and mutual recovery advocated.

Some of the earlier art therapy pioneers, such as Adrian Hill and Edward Adamson, had also asked such questions. Hill had been critical of the sterility of many rehabilitation settings and had not seen them as intrinsically curative, advocating an arts-in-hospitals movement. Adamson, in contrast, had seen the art therapist as an 'outsider' to the psychiatric hospital regime: the fact of the studio being set apart from the main wards was important; it was a refuge. It's still a tiny niche profession, but art therapy developed as a more widely used treatment in the aftermath of the Second World War, often as part of therapeutic-community endeavours, which were notable for attempting to reconfigure the patient–curer divide (Hogan 2001).

Hocoy suggests that implicit in the concept of art therapy as social action 'is an understanding of selfhood in which multiple levels of experience are inter-dependent – that is, in which the psychological-political, ecological-economic, cultural-social, corporeal, and spiritual are entwined and interpenetrating' (2007, pp. 33–4). Such an emphasis is interested in social justice, he suggests (p. 36).

Social art therapy is concerned, like feminist art therapy, with acknowledging power differences between groups of people and between the therapist and the client, or the facilitator and the participants. (A different language might be adopted by some working with 'participants' and groups – the word 'client' eschewed; however, this should be more than a lexical nicety with power relations being considered during all the phases of engagement.) Furthermore, recognising the impact of dominant cultural norms and exploring these is likely to be a factor in all approaches. Although there isn't just one way of theorising the self, as is evident in this book, all social-art-therapy approaches are interested in breaking down the dichotomy between self and society: interconnectedness, reciprocity and the construction of the self *in relation to others* tends to be emphasised.

As Hocoy (2007) asserts, 'Within the illusory boundaries of the Western construction of a flesh-enveloped Self, the intrinsic interrelatedness of the work of [art] therapy and social action is easily obscured' (p. 29). Feminists have articulated this view for some time: *the personal is political.*

Theories vary, but some art therapists have turned to the idea of symbolic interactionism, which stresses that we are constantly in a state of flux and reconstruction, through our interactions with others. We are constituted in and by these interactions. Our selfhood is not static. These theories challenge the idea that certain key events in childhood, or developmental processes, irrevocably mould and shape us; indeed, that they mark us at the deepest layers of our psyches in ways which are productive of psychopathology. Although early profound neglect can damage, generally human beings are viewed, in this more social model, as resilient with capacity for change. All is mutable.

Hogan and Pink (2010) explored the problem of the dualism of self and society in Western thought, suggesting that the entrenched dichotomy between self and society is embedded in language in a way that makes it hard for us to think otherwise about it: there appear to be *no words* to describe the way we come into being through social action:

> The French have a word which Henriques et al. (1984: 1) suggest encapsulates an active and complex subjectivity that acknowledges the individual as an active agent in the production of their subjectivity through a process of *assujettissement*. There is no English equivalent; however, the reflexive verb which means 'to make subject' or to 'produce subjectivity' as well as to 'submit' or 'subjugate' is perhaps rather negative with respect to subjugation. Arguably a more neutral term is needed to encapsulate our coming into being – being made and making simultaneously. The lack of a suitable word for this process illustrates an entrenched dichotomy between self and society and a conceptual 'hole' in post-structuralist theory.
>
> (Hogan and Pink 2010, p. 171)

Society can be conceptualised in many ways, but social context is inevitably seen as important. Some feminist and other writers have utilised the concept of *habitus*. This is an idea from the French sociologist Pierre Bourdieu. Habitus is concerned with the way that social classifications can appear 'natural' and 'given', but habitus is more than an unconscious assimilation of classificatory norms and ways of being; it is 'a set of dispositions which generates practices and perception' (Johnson 1992, p. 5). As discussed in Chapter 8, habitus is described by Bourdieu as an 'embodied history, internalised as a second nature and so forgotten as history – is the active presence of the whole past of which it is the product' (1990, p. 56). All of our understandings about the world are in this sense cultural.

What is considered abnormal or disturbed is constantly shifting (with a few notable exceptions – murder and incest taboos being relatively widespread cross-culturally). Deviancy is socially and historically located, rather than biologically determined. Explanations vary across cultures, including concepts about what is actually occurring and what is required to alleviate lack of conformity to social rules, including mental aberration. For example, in some cultures a more community-based response is involved in alleviating mental distress. Anthropologist and cultural theorist, Mary Douglas, suggests that:

> One day, not too far away, we in the west will meet on equal terms what was once called 'primitive medicine' . . . to look at these distant philosophies of healing which never had a Cartesian revolution, so never thought of separating either mind or body from social context . . . Often it involves showing pictures or drawing designs for the sick person, or requiring the patient to dramatically enact the diagnosis. The body is directly involved, and so also are the kin and neighbours of the patient who must also join the enactment which in various ways dramatises the underlying trouble. By these physical enactments lost identity is caught, and publicly affirmed. Guilt, remorse and fear are summoned, rebuked and dispersed. The patient, on the way to recovery, re-enters a responsible community which the enactments have made vividly aware of its contribution to the former disordered condition.
>
> (Douglas 2001, pp. 10–11)

Western medical norms may be increasingly penetrating all corners of the globe, but there are inherent tensions between different 'thought styles' regarding conceptualisations of health and illness (Douglas 1996). Art therapists working in an unfamiliar cultural context may find themselves out of their depth, both in terms of understanding the cultural norms expressed and in being able to decipher the symbolism employed in the art work (Landes 2012; Lofgren 1981). Moreover, culture invariably mediates the expression of distress. For example, what is considered to be 'normal' and 'natural' grieving is culturally determined and specific (Hogan 2012b, p. 80). A woman beating her chest and wailing aloud in one context is demonstrating her sorrow about the death of a loved one, whereas exactly the same behaviour in Britain might result in the woman being sedated or, worse, being labelled as psychotic. We need to be sensitive to these differences (Hogan 2013b).

It has always been the case that modern art therapy has looked to cultural anthropology and social psychology as well as the more turgid *DSM* (*Diagnostic and Statistical Manual*)-dominated psychiatric mainstream. Cultural complexity is exemplified by Clifford Geertz's story of the winking boy (he is actually illustrating Gilbert Ryle's notion of 'thick description'):

> Consider . . . two boys rapidly contracting the eyelids of their right eyes. In one, this is an involuntary twitch; in the other, a conspiratorial signal to a friend. The two movements are, as movements, identical; from an

I-am-camera, 'phenomenalistic' observation of them alone, one could not tell which was twitch and which was wink, or indeed whether both or either was twitch or wink. Yet the difference, however unphotographable, between a twitch and a wink is vast; as anyone unfortunate enough to have had the first taken for the second knows. The winker is communicating, and indeed communicating in a precise and special way: (1) deliberately, (2) to someone in particular, (3) to impart a particular message, (4) according to a socially established code, and (5) without cognizance of the rest of the company . . . Contracting your eyelids on purpose when there exists a public code in which so doing counts as a conspiratorial signal is winking. That's all there is to it: a speck of behaviour, a fleck of culture, and – voila! – a gesture.

(Geertz 1973, p. 6)

This example is further elaborated on:

Suppose there is a third boy, who, to give malicious amusement to his cronies, parodies the first boy's wink, as amateurish, clumsy, obvious and so on. He, of course, does this in the same way the second boy winked and the first twitched: by contracting his right eyelid. Only this boy is neither winking nor twitching, he is parodying.

(1973, p. 6)

This interpretation of discourse is situated as a 'semiotic' endeavour which is interested in viewing culture as 'an interworked system of construable signs . . . what I would call symbols' (Geertz 1973, p. 14). Human behaviour thus is largely symbolic action, 'action which, like phonation in speech, pigment in painting, line in writing, or sonance in music, signifies meaning' (p. 6). The thing to ask, Geertz asserts, is 'what their import is: what is it, ridicule or challenge or pride, that, in their occurrence and through their agency, is getting said?' (p. 6).

Such an acknowledgement of complexity of symbolic action renders an immediate momentary 'reading' of culture problematic. A photograph might capture the moment, but can it capture the meaning? Might it capture quite the wrong meaning – a moment rather out of keeping with the general mood tone? It also illustrates the dilemma of the art therapist in working with unfamiliar cultural norms, but even the art therapist working in a familiar cultural contest, with a well-known language, faces a degree of this complexity . . .

What about my influence as the therapist or photographer on the field of action? What about the presence of the camera on the field of action? Are these different? What about making a video instead? Then can I perhaps capture these nuances of winking and parody? However, as Wittgenstein and others have pointed out, one human being can be a complete enigma to another – we may understand the language, but we 'do not understand the people' (Wittgenstein 1958, p. 223). There is still the potential problem of comprehension. McNiff has suggested that we might 'view all therapeutic relationships as meetings between cultures' (1984, p. 128); I have argued that the circumspect position generated by this stance is a useful one for art therapists to adopt (Hogan 2012a, 2013a).

More than cultural sensitivity is advocated by some socially motivated art therapists who want to see art employed as community action towards tangible social change. This shift in emphasis towards social art therapy has not arisen just out of social theory and critiques of psychology (discussed in extra detail in Chapter 9 on feminist approaches), but also out of politicised art practice. In Britain art therapists still tend to come from a fine-arts orientation and many have come to their training aware of radical arts activities: the Guerrilla Girls was just one of many groups exploding gender stereotypes and pointing out discriminatory practices in the 1970s and 1980s. They produced posters, of female nudes in the postures of classical paintings, wearing gorilla masks, pointing out in text that fewer than 5 per cent of art works in the modern art sections of the Metropolitan Art Museum in New York were by women, but that 85 per cent of the nudes were female – asking, 'Do women have to be naked to get into the Met. Museum?' (1989).

The systematic erasure of women from history is a peculiar phenomenon: the hefty history of art book I was given for my 'A Level' Art History revision had *no women artists in it at all*. This is the era in which the all-male histories of art were challenged, and progressive art historians championed a panoply of technically accomplished women artists (Artemisia Gentileschi (1593–1652), Judith Leyster (1609–60), Marie-Guillemine Benoist (1768–1826) and Elisabeth Vigée Le Brun (1755–1842) to name but a few), in answer to the challenge that the history books were devoid of female artists because there weren't any good ones. My generation came to art therapy training admiring the work of Gwen John or Kathe Kollwitz, but also realising that something was profoundly wrong with the way art history was conceptualised and understood. Where were the disparate voices of our diverse culture? Where were the women? Why were there no great women artists in our history books? Why was there no discussion about female geniuses?

The Dinner Party is still proclaimed as an icon of 1970s' feminist installation art; it is a monumental symbolic work, the 39 place settings commemorating Goddesses or women from history; each place setting is rendered in a style appropriate to the woman or women in question; so, for example, the artist Geor-

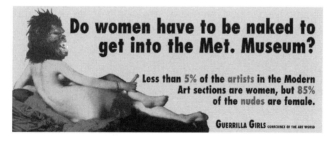

*Figure 10.1* Guerrilla Girls. Do Women Have to be Naked to Get into the Metropolitan Museum? 1985. Screenprint. © Guerrilla Girls. Reproduced by kind permission of the Guerrilla Girls.

gia O'Keeffe's setting is in the style of her painting. Vulva motifs predominate, leading to claims that the work was pornographic. The Dinner Party is a robust challenge to what Chicago calls 'gender-based apartheid': a profound negation of women's contribution by major cultural institutions. A further 999 women's names are inscribed on the floor tiles. Works such as this helped to create a consciousness which was carried into art therapy at a time when it was being dominated by reductive, misogynistic psychological theories that labelled women as inherently unstable, dissimulating and subject to depression: mad, bad and sad.

## Practice

Increasingly, art therapy is being used as part of social action (Hogan 1997, 2003, 2012a; Kaplan 2007) and social change (Levine and Levine 2011). Individuals may wish to speak out using art. Art may be made for both personal and political purposes, for example, the highlighting of social issues, such as the AIDS pandemic, with art being displayed to raise global awareness (Crimp and Rolston 1990; Junge 1999). Similarly, work with traumatised women who were victims of domestic abuse has been exhibited to help de-stigmatise being the recipient of violence. Sontag suggested that images can help as beacons around which beliefs can coalesce, arguing that 'sentiment is more likely to crystallise around a photograph than around a verbal slogan' (2003, p. 76). Art therapy has also been used to aid conflict resolution (Liebmann 1996).

*Figure 10.2* Judy Chicago, The Dinner Party 1979. Mixed media, 48' × 48' × 3'. Collection of the Brooklyn Museum, Brooklyn, NY. © Judy Chicago, Photo © Donald Woodman.

Figure 10.3 Judy Chicago, The Dinner Party 1979. Mary Wollstonecraft place setting. Collection of the Brooklyn Museum, Brooklyn, NY. © Judy Chicago, Photo © Donald Woodman.

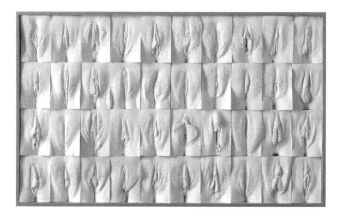

Figure 10.4 Panel 1 of 10 from the Great Wall of Vagina by Jamie McCartney. c.2011. 'For many women their genital appearance is a source of anxiety and I was in a unique position to do something about that.'

Some social art therapy traverses the line between art therapy and participatory arts, employing art therapy techniques to facilitate art-elicitation groups (Hogan and Warren 2012). Art therapy is also being used as a social science research method (Hogan 2012c; Hogan and Pink 2010; Hogan and Warren 2013; McNiff 1998; Pink *et al.* 2011). The following section will outline some examples of contemporary work in this area.

Participatory ideals are those which situate the locus of power more fully with the recipients of services; though there is a spectrum of activity, consumers of services may fully set the agenda. Participatory-art approaches have evolved out of attempts by communities to represent themselves through the production of art. These can be actual populations, such as the indigenous populations in developed and colonised countries, communities of shared experience, such as breast cancer survivors, or communities of shared identity, such as the homosexual community (especially when solidarity and protest were particularly required pre-legalisation and homophobia was rife). Participatory ideals can also inform community-based and community-led art-therapeutic processes. Whilst therapeutic communities have egalitarian features and attempt to minimise the therapist–patient divide, participatory arts-based social action goes much further in that the community in question should be setting the agenda and controlling processes of engagement as far as possible.

Wright and Wright call for a socially invigorated practice and point out that art therapy lends itself to social action (and a feminist orientation):

> as it is about the vulnerable, marginalised and traumatised in society, and about the liberal thinking values of empowerment and of gaining social justice for the socially disenfranchised . . . it is important for such practitioners to consider critically how their own position and thinking impacts on the therapeutic relationships in which they are engaged . . . Maintaining fundamental values and actions towards empowerment and social change, while also challenging the socially privileged, is what could significantly re-orientate art therapy.
>
> (2013, p. 3)

Quite a number of art therapists have been working in a socially orientated manner, especially feminist art therapists, but also those working with particular groups and communities. Hogan, for example, has been running art therapy support groups for pregnant women and new mothers, to enable them to explore their changed sense of self-identity and sexuality (1997, 2003, 2012a, 2012b). Although the groups started from an exploration of personal experience, they also critiqued and challenged iatrogenic aspects of the hospital regimes (that is, those medical and institutional practices and norms which are counterproductive and oppressive, though often well established). As such, this is art as social action and critique, which moves beyond a narrow focus on individual psychopathology, though art therapists are trained to 'hold' intense and difficult material and personal distress which may arise, and are skilled in managing interpersonal conflict.

The specialised practice of re-enactment phototherapy, developed in Britain by Jo Spence and others, is also interested in social critique, about a variety of issues: Spence's work especially comments on the production-line quality of her engagement with health services, following a diagnosis of breast cancer in her Picture of Health series. Spence described her practice as a form of cultural 'sniping':

> Taking aim at certain personal and political myths – the family snapshot, the domestic goddess, the cancer victim – her work asks unflinching questions about the power structures of visibility, of who can be seen under whose terms and in what light.
>
> (Sherlock 2012, p. 1)

Often, re-enactment phototherapy is interested in challenging dominant stereotypes and creating new, more empowering narratives which are told in a pictorial sequence and are frequently publicly exhibited – indeed, the work is displayed as a proclamation (Martin 2012). This work straddles the line between social science research, political activism and art: Martin refers to herself as an 'artist-researcher', for example.

## Art therapy and participatory arts as a social science research method

Participatory approaches are also used in research and broadly recognise the 'particular expertise' of people within particular circumstances (Bennett and Roberts 2004); this could be because of local geographical or particular experiential knowledge (Breitbart 2003). Some theorists conceptualise this as 'active co-research' between researchers and participants (Wadsworth 1998) who are active in defining research problems (Anyanwu 1988) and that, furthermore, participatory research 'must be sharply distinguished from conventional elitist research which treats people as objects of the research process' (Tilakaratna 1990, p. 1). It asks the question, whose knowledge counts? (O'Neill 2012, p. 154). Birch and Miller assert that those participating must be clear about the project's research aims (2002, p. 103) and open about the research process (p. 99). Banks and Armstrong advocate that there be clarity about power and responsibility:

> It is important to be clear about where power and responsibility lie in relation to different aspects of a research project. If there are parts that require specific academic skills or certain outputs for funders then this should be acknowledged. Equally, thought should be given as to whether some academic processes can be demystified or adapted for use by community participants (e.g. a participatory literature review).
>
> (2012, p. 12)

One form of this is called participatory action research (PAR), which involves 'a commitment to research that: develops partnership responses to facilitate learning and social change' (O'Neill 2012, p. 157). This is an approach that strives towards 'inclusion', which is described as:

> working with participants as co-researchers – community members as experts through democratic processes and decision-making. This involves mutual recognition, what Paulo Fréire calls dialogic techniques. PAR uses innovative ways of consulting and working with local people, for example, through arts workshops, forum theatre methods and stakeholder events. PAR is transformative and it is also rigorous and ethical. PAR is a process and a practice directed towards social change *with* the participants.
>
> (O'Neill 2012, p. 157)

Maggie O'Neill, a criminologist, states that she wishes to explore the sensuousness of ethnography in the immersion in the life-worlds of participants: 'I always looked for ways of exploring and representing the complexity of psychic and social lived relations by combining art and ethnography' (2012, p. 154).

If art-elicitation groups intend to delve deep into emotionally difficult subject matter, there is a strong case to be made that a highly skilled art therapy practitioner is employed for this work, as artists may quickly find themselves out of their depth (Hogan and Pink 2011). Trained art therapists also have a good understanding of ethical issues, which can be useful in working in multi-faceted situations.

Research exploring women's experience of ageing is another example of work which straddles the line between social science research and political activism (Hogan and Warren 2012, 2013); these particular projects were interested in enabling a variety of women in different circumstances, broadly representing different demographics (independent and ageing, newly retired, older and in supported accommodation), to explore their feelings about the ageing process using a variety of art media. Two of the projects provided professional artists for the women to engage with, a phototherapy group produced intense and exciting images of ageing, and an art-elicitation group, based on group-interactive art therapy, yielded some of the more intimate images produced. The art-elicitation group employed a model of working which acknowledged group members' feelings in the here and now. The group started off with a structured activity based on a simple instruction about bringing in images of older women from any genre which participants disliked or found discomforting, and those they found inspiring or uplifting. The women produced a range of multi-media work which reflected on their embodied experience of the ageing process, and societal responses to older women in general.

Phototherapeutic techniques, facilitated by Martin, were also used to enable the women to analyse and then reframe and articulate their own narratives of ageing and age. Martin used a range of techniques drawn from her own pioneering practice (Martin 1997). The women worked with found images, as well as a selection made from their own family albums; these were used to enable participants to explore and reconsider how each felt about her own representations of ageing. As

Martin put it, through a series of carefully structured sessions, each woman found the aspects about herself and her relationship to ageing that she wanted to make visible (1997). The re-enactment phototherapy technique involved women working in pairs and deciding on specific scenarios to explore, enact and reinterpret. The women took turns being the client/performer and the photographer. Using props to help the performance of her story, each woman was given the opportunity to explore a storyline, which was photographed at various junctures. The control rested primarily with the person doing the telling, with the photographer acting very much under her instruction. Martin explains the process:

> Working in pairs, each woman performed her stories, using her chosen clothes and props, and determined how she wanted to be represented. The woman being photographed asked for what she wanted, and the photographer was supportive, encouraging and was 'there for' her partner as witness, advocate, and nurturer, whilst photographing the process as it unfolded . . . It is a collaborative process both sitter/protagonist and photographer work together to make the images.
>
> (Martin, cited in Hogan and Warren 2012, pp. 340–1)

Martin stresses the psychotherapeutic dimension of her work, and emphasises that the woman in the role of photographer offered a 'gaze of nurturance and permission' to the sitter. Each narrative ended with images of transformation: the process as a whole enabling each woman to find ways to transform aspects of her lived experience.

Reflecting on her work, Martin added:

> The re-enactment-phototherapy sessions produce an atmosphere of playful creativity. The roles are exchanged, so both have the opportunity to be in the picture, and to be the photographer. The resulting images challenge stereotypes of ageing. The whole process enabled each participant to find ways to transform her views of herself. It is therefore important not just to look at the phototherapy image in isolation, but as part of a developing narrative.
>
> (cited in Hogan and Warren 2012, p. 341)

O'Neill brought together people to respond to stories of migration and settlement. The work was concerned to explore experiences of exile and displacement, as well as to 'facilitate processes and practices of inclusion and belonging' through creating opportunities for dialogue and collective working (2010, p. 7). As well as wishing to stimulate opportunities for making art, the work has an overtly political aspect to it in wishing to generate material which can 'contribute to public awareness of the issues facing new arrivals' and a desire to have an impact on public policy in this area (2010, p. 10). She says of the work, 'Our collaborations . . . examine how the arts – defined in their broadest sense – might help mediate and represent the experience of arriving in a new country and what it means to feel a sense of belonging', as well as how best 'to deliver cultural, social, and economic benefits to new arrivals in the East Midlands region' (2010, p. 13).

Events were staged in which an exchange of ideas could take place between arts practitioners, new migrants and refugees, academics and policy makers. She suggests that her methodology constitutes an approach to knowledge production which regards it as collaboratively made, not found. O'Neill proposes that the 'knowledge/power axis' involved in knowledge production and expertise is loosened. She works collaboratively with performance artists, poets, writers, visual artists 'and participants' (her terminology: perhaps a semantic slip – they are all participants). O'Neill describes this work as ethnography which is also social action: the combination of biographical narrative and art combining to create a 'potential space' and 'transformative possibilities'; she has dubbed this space between ethnography and art 'auto-mimesis' (2008, p. 3). This notion of the 'creation of potential space . . . the relational space between subject and object, between the here, now and the past, action and image' which she describes is actually very evocative of art therapy processes (p. 15).

*Figure 10.5* Paul Ghent. Dreamers Group Panel. I Want to Go Back Even if I Die. Work by Ghent based on his interviews and conversations with the refugees. 2010.

*Figure 10.6* Paul Ghent. Dreamers Group Panel. Time Means Nothing to a Child
Soldier. Work by Ghent based on his interviews and conversations with the
refugees. 2010.

Hogan and Pink discuss the validity of using the arts in research:

> the act of art making can be a moment of ontological uncertainty, and poten-
> tially liberating. Consequently art making can become a route through which
> interiority might be considered not simply as something that comes to the
> surface and is recorded as a static event, or crystallized and made static, but
> rather, and importantly, it offers ways of understanding interiority through an
> anthropological paradigm that views inner states as being in progress, rather
> than ever static . . . Art in art therapy is of significance not only as a repre-
> sentation of the feelings of the individual at a particular moment in time – an
> inner 'snapshot', if you like . . . The self of art therapy does not become crys-
> tallized anywhere . . . A feminist art therapy sees images as producing and
> being produced through a 'self in process'.
>
> (2010, p. 160)

O'Neill suggests that in the interpretive role for social research, ethnography,
biography and performance-based arts-based work can be important. She suggests

they can make 'the unfamiliar familiar as well as fostering mutual understanding of diverse communities, cultural traditions, subcultures and ultimately [contribute to] tolerance of diversity' (2008, p. 6). The art making explores the migrant's experiences of home, of place, and what it is like to be dislocated. Journeys also featured strongly:

> the perilous journeys people make to seek freedom and safety. The emotional and physical impact of these journeys, and the experiences of 'double consciousness' and being 'home away from home' are represented alongside the rich cultural contributions and skills migrants bring.
>
> (O'Neill 2010, p. 8)

The particular quality of the work produced is important: 'Knowledge is produced forcing us to abandon instrumental rationality and reach towards a more sensuous understanding that incorporates feeling involvement as well as cognitive reflection' (O'Neill 2010, p. 9).

Jamie Bird, who collaborated with O'Neill on some of the *Beyond Borders* work, is an art therapist whose work is interested in representing, documenting and disseminating information about women's experience of domestic violence, particularly that of South Asian women; he argues for a 'strong reflexivity'; drawing on the work of Harding (2004), he suggests that starting research with the detail of women's lives is important, especially when it concerns people marginalised in relation to dominant groups.

'Standpoint' theories have been dryly critiqued:

> theories based on the idea that oppression or deprivation results in a privileged standpoint are especially implausible; if they were right, the most disadvantaged groups would produce the best scientists. In fact, the oppressed and socially marginalized often have little access to the information and education needed to excel in science, which on the whole puts them at a serious 'epistemic *dis*advantage'.
>
> (Somers 1994, p. 75)

A number of things can be said in reply to this. Bird is not suggesting that there is a distinctively female way of knowing, but rather he is situating his endeavour in the context of participatory research which, as noted above, is often conceived as 'active co-research' (Wadsworth 1998) between researchers and participants who are active in defining research problems (Anyanwu 1988). This is a perfectly cogent approach to tapping into the particular knowledge that different communities or individuals might contribute: if I were redesigning a shopping centre, then I might want to ask users of the space how they experienced it, for example. Bird also argues that only when the researcher acknowledges her or his own standpoint and situated position, and that of the participants, can a stronger form of representation emerge. Such an approach recognises the historical and situated nature of

*Figure 10.7* Installation Piece. Photo Aria Ahmed. Sense of Belonging Exhibition. 2010.

the object of enquiry and the inescapable subjectivity of the researcher (2010, p. 4). Furthermore, Bird suggests that adopting a feminist methodology was fitting.

Using art materials, his work gave women a chance to think about their futures and to depict them, to create a literal embodied vision of what they were hoping for: a picture of the aims they were striving towards. Given that financial independence was highlighted as a concern for many participants, his work has not stopped there and he is working, with an occupational therapist, on interventions that aim to help women who have experienced domestic violence to gain financial independence through enhancing their employment prospects. This is an aim that fits with the current UK government's agenda of moving people off benefits and into work, but done in a way that is sensitive to the particular needs of those who have encountered domestic violence.

Arts-based research has also been used to produce evocative case studies. One example of this is Huss and Alhaiga-Taz's (2013) work on Bedouin children, which looked at cultural differences between those children who lived in townships set up in Israel (in Hura, near Be'er Sheba), and those who had refused to be relocated (in Abu Rinat). The different physical realities of the locations were depicted. Furthermore, a different conceptualisation of what 'home' means was also evident in the two groups: this was evident in 'special organisation and symbolic meanings attributed to specific objects' (p. 16). The latter group conceptualised the entire village, rather than a specific house, as their home, with more similarity and proximity between houses, indicating a different set of values (p. 13). A flaw of the study was that only a limited record of the children's narratives about the pictures was recorded. Similar work has been produced by an art therapist, J.A. Fletcher, who has collaborated with psychologists interested in looking at children's views of mental illness using visual methods, producing revealing images which are in many ways more telling than the spoken words.

Social action takes many forms, not all of it with an obvious practical end. In a grim-sounding Kenyan women's prison, Gloria Simoneaux instigated expressive art therapies for HIV-positive inmates. Describing her work she proclaims, 'Occasionally we discuss the action that landed them in prison, although we don't ask about this . . . [our] goal is to provide *time for the women to experience their humanity and their beauty*, without having to explain the reasons for their incarceration' (Simoneaux 2011, p. 165; my italics).

## Conclusion

Although the general tone of this book has been not to promote one theory over another, but to render each as cogent, social art therapy is inherently political. As noted above, it takes many forms. Some of these approaches focus on power relations and social critique within a therapeutic frame; or breaking out of that frame, social art therapy may make proclamations, often via public exhibition.

Another strand of activity is using participatory frameworks, which hand over the direction of the enterprise increasingly to the participants themselves; such approaches may be particularly compatible with community development strategies and ethnography. There is also a social science research agenda, often politicised, which increasingly uses the arts to enable communities to represent themselves, or as an elicitation tool, or to communicate research findings. The value of such methods is being increasingly recognised and the International Visual Sociology Association (IVSA), for example, though nevertheless film and photography inclined, is interested in the use of all the arts. There are also emerging performance-based social science networks which seek to integrate experiential art techniques.

Arts and health research, interrogating the use of, and using, visual methods, is increasingly gaining recognition and funding is forthcoming from mainstream bodies such as funding councils and the National Centre for Research Methods. We live in exciting times.

# Chapter 11

# A critical glossary of terms

**Amplification**  This is a technique derived from Carl G. Jung in which the mood tone or symbolic content of a picture is entered into in an imaginative way. For example, the therapist (looking at a picture of a boat at sea) might ask how it feels in the boat, or where the boat is going, or even whether the boat has a voice! Originally, the term referred to the symbolic quality of dreams: 'Compared to free association, amplification is a more narrowly defined, more controlled and more focused type of association where one attempts to search for analogies that would expand upon the symbol in question' (Laine 2007, p. 129).

For example, Irene Champernowne, an early pioneer of art therapy in Britain, talked about 'dreaming the dream onwards on paper' and advocated 'entering into the language' of her client's art works (Hogan 2001, p. 240). She wrote, 'It is possible to accept the material in the state of the subject at the moment, and discuss it from the experimental point of view, rather than from the intellectual interpretation of the symbols used' (1949, cited in Hogan 2001, p. 271). By this she meant entering into the mood tone of the piece and asking speculative questions. For example, a house lashed by a storm might provoke a question about whether the house could stand up to such a beating. This is a useful elicitation technique.

**Analogy**  An analogy is 'a comparison between one thing and another, typically for the purpose of explanation or clarification' (oxforddictionaries.com). There can be 'a partial similarity in particular circumstances on which a comparison may be based' (*Macquarie Dictionary* 1981, p. 103), for example, the 'analogy between the workings of nature and those of human societies' (oxforddictionaries.com). It may be 'an 'illustration of an idea by means of a more familiar idea that is similar or parallel to it in some significant features, and thus said to be *analogous* to it. Analogies are often presented in the form of an extended simile' (Baldick 2001, p. 12).

**Biological determinism**  This theory suggests that shared behavioural patterns and the social and economic differences between groups (primarily races, classes and sexes) arise from inherited, inborn distinctions. Certain sets of social relations have existed and evolutionary theory was (and is) used to justify them. In the nineteenth century, the application of evolutionary theories was often simply a matter of analogy. Equated through supposed likenesses were women, criminals, children, beggars, the Irish and the insane – all of whom were lacking in social power and were likened to 'primitives' or to 'savages'. Biological determinism has changed over time, but is still evident in psychiatric discourses, especially in relation to gender 'norms'.

**Countertransference (see 'projection' first)**   Countertransference is the therapist's projection to the client, which is a potentially distorting aspect of treatment. The term is also used to mean 'the analyst's emotional attitude towards the patient, including his response to specific items of the patient's behaviour' (a reflection upon which may be therapeutically useful in illuminating the therapist's understanding of the client) (Rycroft 1968, p. 25).

**Discourse**   Referring to debate, or communication of thoughts in words, this term has a specific meaning within cultural theory. This is Foucault's idea of discursive practice, which is a highly organised and regulated set of practices and statements that serve to create and maintain definitions, for instance of 'madness' or 'femininity'. This has a history and a set of rules which distinguish it from other discourses establishing both links and differences. In other words:

> the term has been used to denote any coherent body of statements that produces a self-confirming account of reality by defining an object of attention and generating concepts with which to analyse it (e.g. medical discourse, legal discourse, aesthetic discourse). The specific discourse in which a statement is made will govern the kinds of connections that can be made between ideas, and will involve certain assumptions about the kind of person(s) addressed.
>
> (Baldick 2001, pp. 68–9)

The literary theorist Catherine Belsey defines 'discourse' eloquently thus:

> A *discourse* is a domain of language-use, a particular way of talking (and writing and thinking). A discourse involves certain shared assumptions which appear in the formulations that characterise it. The discourse of common sense is quite distinct, for instance, from the discourse of modern physics, and some of the formulations of the one may be expected to conflict with the formulations of the other. Ideology is *inscribed* in discourse in the sense that it is literally written or spoken *in it*; it is not a separate element which exists independently in some free-floating realm of 'ideas' and is subsequently embodied in words, but a way of thinking, speaking, experiencing.
>
> (Belsey 1980, p. 5)

We can see in this definition that here 'discourse' is embodied in ways of experiencing, and that as a particular 'domain of language-use' (thinking, talking and experiencing) it resembles a paradigm, and moves beyond the small 'd' discourse 'language-in-use' concept that the theorist Gee describes (1999, p. 7).

**Displacement**   This is a psychoanalytic idea used to describe the 'process by which energy (cathexis) is transferred from one mental image to another . . . for instance in dreams one image can symbolise another' (Rycroft 1968, p. 35).

**Elicitation**   This refers to a range of techniques used to draw out further meaning from art works.

**Embodied images**   Arguably, any image which carries with it a strong mood tone is an embodied image; art can become imbued with another person's feelings in a tangible manner, or at least in what appears to be a tangible manner. As Tolstoy put it, 'Art is a human activity consisting in this, that one man consciously, by means of external signs, hands on to others feelings he has lived through, and that others *are infected by these feelings and also experience them*' (Tolstoy 1987, cited in Harris 1996, p. 2; my italics).

Joy Schaverien suggests that, 'no other mode of expression can be substituted for it', and that 'in the process of its creation, feeling becomes "live" in the present' (2011, p. 80). In Chapter 8 I discussed how we *feel* other people's emotions; sometimes we can even feel engulfed by them; alternatively, the intended meaning of the painter *does not* necessarily hold a privileged position, so art therapists must always be circumspect about whether they really are experiencing what was intended, and seek clarification from the person who created the art work. This is because we bring our own experience and 'habitus' (our embodied way of being) to the experience of viewing an art. Art objects in general are inherently open to multiple meanings and interpretations. Context too is important in how we see art works (Hogan 1997).

**Empathy**   'This is the ability to identify [with] and thereby understand another person's feelings or difficulties' (Wood 2011, p. 81). Art therapists would wish to demonstrate an *empathetic* response to the art works produced in sessions.

**Feminism**   This is a much maligned and misused term. Feminism is the principle of advocating the social, political and other rights of women as equal to those of men. Most of us (practising art therapists) are feminists, whether we embrace the term or not, because we advocate equality of opportunity. Feminism is necessarily interested in the question of fairness (Hogan 2011a). In academic writing, feminism refers to a mode of analysis that seeks to examine the function of sex in societal relations. This mode of analysis sees the construction of sex (or writers may use the term 'gender') as historically and geographically situated and subject to change. In terms of feminist art therapy, this is primarily an enhanced awareness of misogynist discourses (particularly negative psychiatric discourses about women's inherent inborn 'instability') and women's issues. Sometimes, when using directive art therapy, it is possible to introduce exercises that can help participants reflect on their sex and sexual orientation. For example, I offer a workshop in which I ask men and women to bring in two images from any sources (newspapers, art books, magazines etc.) of a man if they are a man, and of a woman if they are a woman, or if they regard themselves as gay, lesbian, transgender or questioning they may reflect that in their choice of images. I ask them to bring in one image they like and another that makes them feel uncomfortable. These images form the basis of the session, and it is an opportunity to look at how people are represented, and to explore how participants feel about these images which surround us in our daily lives.

Some art therapists work with women-only groups to readily allow women to explore unique aspects of their experience, such as pregnancy and childbirth (Hogan 2003, 2008a, 2008b, 2012a), or collective trauma such as breast cancer or rape (Malchiodi 1997), or the experience of ageing (Hogan and Warren 2012). However, maintaining a feminist awareness is, arguably, an important aspect of good practice in general and should form an integral part of training.

(Hogan 2011b, p. 87)

**Field theory**   This is a theory taken from physics and applied to the study of human beings 'that explains physical phenomena in terms of a field and the manner in which it interacts with matter or with other fields' (oxforddictionaries.com). Hence, in branches of psychology influenced by field theory, a person and his or her context are indivisible.

**Group resonance**   Group members can sometimes show empathy towards each other by adopting a similar pictorial style or particular symbols or motifs. This may be done quite unconsciously, and has been called 'group resonance' by Gerry McNeilly and others (1983, 2005); this is an idea (a metaphor taken from physics) that describes the way members' images can seemingly influence each other and 'resonate' or reverberate together. Richardson explains, 'that resonance makes the group more than the sum of its parts, rather like the moment when the individual voices in a choir lend to a spine-tingling complex chord' (2011, p. 202).

**Habitus**   Habitus is an 'embodied history, internalised as a second nature and so forgotten as history – is the active presence of the whole past' (Bourdieu 1990, p. 56).

**Hegemony**   Hegemony has been used to mean political prominence. In cultural theory, from the work of Gramsci, it is often used to mean what is taken for granted as 'common sense' or it refers to unquestioned assumptions. It is also used to refer to the dominant ideology. Taking the example of the concept of taste, Douglas writes:

taste is always going to be harnessed to the *struggle for hegemony* in a particular community . . . although good taste claims to rest on universal principles, it is always challengeable; the challenge comes from those who wish to subvert the established order.

(Douglas 1994, p. 29)

This introduces the idea of a plurality of hegemonies linked to different 'community' interests, which is a more sophisticated usage than one suggesting a single overarching oppressive hegemony.

**Icon**   Within the discipline of semiotics, an icon possesses an actual resemblance between the signifier and the signified. For example, a portrait signifies the person depicted less by arbitrary convention than by resemblance (Culler 1983); however, the resemblance can be through analogy.

**Iconography**   Iconography is 'the branch of knowledge concerned with pictorial or sculptural representations' or 'symbolical representation' (*Macquarie Dictionary* 1981, p. 865). It is concerned with 'the visual images and symbols used in a work of art or the study or interpretation of these' (oxforddictionaries.com).

**Identification**   In psychoanalytic terms, identification is a process in which an individual '(a) extends his identity *into* someone else, (b) borrows his identity *from* someone else, or (c) fuses or confuses his identity *with* someone else' (Rycroft 1995, p. 76). Thus, in group work, through a process of *projective identification*, a person can imagine himself or herself to be inside or part of an object which is external to him or her. This can give the individual 'the illusion of control over the object' (Rycroft 1995, p. 76). Laplanche and Pontalis note it as a psychological defence mechanism 'in which the subject inserts himself – in whole or in part – into the object in order to harm, possess or control it' (1973, p. 356). Though characterised negatively as 'primitive', Segal notes that projective identification is important to symbol-formation: projecting parts of the self into an object and identifying parts of the object with parts of the self, the ego forms symbols (Segal 1978, p. 36).

**Ideology**   Hadjinicolaou writes of ideology that:

The very function of ideology . . . is to hide the contradictions in life by fabricating an illusory system of ideas which shapes people's views and gives them a perspective on their experience of life . . . this system . . . extends to myths, taste, style, fashion, and the 'whole way of life' of a particular society.

(1978, p. 10)

In this example, ideology represents a false consciousness, a lack of awareness of ideas conditioning one's experience and actions. The term has also been used to describe a system of ideas appropriate to a specific social group such as 'bourgeois ideology' (Williams 1983, p. 157).

**Introjection**  Introjection is a psychoanalytic concept that forms part of the idea of transference (hence its inclusion):

> It describes the process by which the functions of an external object are taken over by its mental representation, by which the relationship with an object 'out there' is replaced with an imagined object 'inside'. The resulting mental structure is variously called an *introject*, an *introjected object*, or an *internal object.*
>
> (Rycroft 1995, p. 87)

**Metaphor**  Metaphor is 'The figure of speech in which a name or descriptive term is transferred to some object to which it is not properly applicable' (Oxford Dictionaries 1973, p. 1315). For example, when we talk of gene maps and gene mapping, we use a cartographic metaphor; or it is 'a thing regarded as representative or symbolic of something else' (oxforddictionaries. com). A point of comparison may be made with an otherwise unrelated object. Henzell claims that, for a metaphor to have real power, it must be concerned with more than simple truth or analogy: 'the comparison affected by it must scandalise current perceptions and so doing jolt them into a new frame of reference' (Henzell 1984, p. 23). He defines a metaphor as 'the illumination of one realm of related facts, associations, history, and orderings in terms of another. This is accomplished by the interaction of at least two conceptions of different things in one symbol which refers to them both' (p. 22). A simple example would be the idiomatic expression, 'to lay one's cards on the table' to denote frankness. Metaphors are used abundantly and eloquently in art therapy, as well as in literature. The use of metaphor to produce new combinations of ideas is important in art therapy, where multiple metaphors can interlink to produce manifold meanings.

**Motif**  A motif is 'a recurring subject or theme . . . a distinctive figure in a design' (*Macquarie Dictionary* 1981, p. 1118), 'a dominant or recurring idea in an artistic work' (oxforddictionaries.com).

**Parataxic distortion**  This concept derives from the work of Harry Stack Sullivan, and refers to our tendency to distort the perceptions we have of others. These distortions are the result of relating to another person, 'not on the basis of the real attributes of the other, but wholly or chiefly on the basis of the person we see in our fantasy' (Molnos 1998). Parataxic distortions result from the individual's propensity to shape his or her responses in relation to previous experiences; this may also serve as a defence against anxiety. It is a broader concept than 'transference'. See also 'habitus'.

**Projection**  This means literally 'throwing in front of oneself', hence 'its use in psychiatry and psychoanalysis to mean 'viewing a mental image as objective reality'. In psychoanalytic theory there are two further meanings. The first is 'a general misinterpretation of mental activity as events occurring to one, as in dreams and hallucinations', so that a hallucination is thought to be reality. The other 'involves a process in which wishes or impulses or other aspects of the self are imagined to be located elsewhere in an object external to oneself' (Rycroft 1968, p. 125). Projection is often linked with reversal, in that the emotion or wish felt is denied, but asserted to belong to someone else. Disavowed aspects of the self might be imagined in another person: 'Projection of aspects of oneself is preceded by denial, i.e. one denies that one feels such and such an emotion, has such and such a wish, but asserts that someone else does' (Rycroft 1995, p. 139).

**Psychodynamic**   This refers to schemas of mental structures in which movement is a part, for example, the dynamic tensions inherent in the relationship between the id, ego and super-ego in psychoanalysis, or the compensatory dimensions of the function types of psyche in the analytic (Jungian) model, to give another example. Ideas about the workings of a mind are referred to as dynamics; models interested in postulated inter-psychic processes are referred to as psychodynamic. Group work which uses certain theoretical formulations may be called psychodynamic group work and therapists will talk about group dynamics. This is in contrast to types of psychology 'which merely enumerate and define attributes of the mind' (Rycroft 1995, p. 42). Some writers use the word psychodynamic as a synonym for psychoanalytic.

**Reification**   Reification is a tendency to think of abstract concepts as concrete entities. This tendency is applied to complex and multi-faceted human capabilities. The 'shorthand' for these intelligences is then reified. Alternatively, sophisticated ideas about human interaction can be 'reified' in the design of buildings. For example, a ranked lecture theatre with a lectern is a physical design that illustrates assumptions about the transmission of knowledge.

**Representation**   In cultural theory, images and texts are not viewed simply as 'mirrors' which simply reflect reality. Rather, representations are seen as conventions and codes which articulate practices and forms that condition our experience.

**Resonance** *see* **group resonance**

**Scapegoat transference (***see also* **transference)**   Joy Schaverien describes the concept of transference, that is, the idea of the magical transferability of attributes and states, as the main pivot of psychoanalytical theory. Schaverien argues that the biblical scapegoat may be seen as representing a 'ritualised transference' – the goat having become a talisman, in that it is magically invested with the power of the sins (1987, pp. 74–5). When the goat is killed the sins are absolved. A similar process takes place in art therapy when there is a transference of attributes and states to an object which, subsequently empowered, becomes a talisman. Once an object is experienced as a talisman, any act of resolution in relation to it becomes significant and might be seen as an act of 'disposal' (p. 75).

Schaverien points out that 'scapegoating' can occur in groups, where a person is punished or ostracised for something which is not their own fault; for example:

for exhibiting or expressing behaviours which those doing the rejecting might fear, or need to display themselves. The group fantasy may be that once this individual is removed, everyone else will relate harmoniously. The bad is all invested in one person.

(p. 80)

However, if recognition of transference can take place prior to 'disposal' then Schaverien argues that disposal can be positive rather than negative. Making an art work can enable 'acknowledgement' of the process of projection to take place, since the art work has undeniably been made by the client – although such acknowledgement may be a fleeting phenomenon (p. 86).

Schaverien describes the destruction of the art object as a potentially 'meaningful act [which] offers a genuine opportunity to enact the scapegoating process in full. Keeping the art object is also a meaningful act which offers the solution of a different type of disposal'. The client, she argues, 'has dominion over the picture or art object, in a way that would never be possible with a person' (p. 87).

**Semiotics**   This is the study of signs and symbols and their use or interpretation (oxforddictionaries.com). This is also a field of study.

**Sign**   A sign is something that can be interpreted as having a meaning. The relationship between the signifier and the signified is arbitrary and conventional; for example, a red cross on a white background denotes a first-aid kit (medical supplies) in the UK.

**Simile**   A simile is a figure of speech in which there is an explicit comparison of two unlike things, for example 'she was like a rose'.

**Surrealist**   The word surrealistic has acquired an idiomatic popular meaning, replacing the rather 1970s' 'zany'; it can refer to iconoclastic images – images that jolt us out of our usual lazy sensibilities. Examples of iconic surrealistic images are perhaps Méret Oppenheim's fur-covered cup, saucer and spoon, Salvador Dali's melting clocks or René Magritte's *This is Not a Pipe*.

In a more academic context, and with a capital 'S', it is a cultural movement dating from the 1920s in which artists sought to apply the psychoanalytical idea of 'free association' to art, harnessing thought 'freed from logic and reason' (Breton 1924, cited in Hogan 2001, p. 94). Initially, a technique called 'automatic writing' was developed, and then these ideas were applied to images. Surrealism was a contributing influence to the development of modern art therapy (Hogan 2001).

**Symbol**   A symbol is 'something that stands for, represents, or denotes something else (not by exact resemblance, but by vague suggestion, or by some accidental or conventional relation); *esp.* a material object representing or taken to represent something immaterial or abstract' (Oxford Dictionaries 1973, p. 2220); for example, a wedding ring is a symbol of marriage or a big office can denote rank.

In psychoanalytic theory, symbolism is seen as arising out of an *inter-psychic* conflict between the repressing tendencies of the unconscious mind and the repressed . . . 'only what is repressed is symbolised; only what is repressed needs to be symbolised' (Rycroft 1968, p. 162). Furthermore, the object or activity symbolised is theorised as 'always one of basic, instinctual, or biological interest' (p. 163). Therefore, the word 'symbolic' is used in a particular way by psychoanalytically orientated writers.

It is not necessary to get bogged down in the fundamentally reductive psychoanalytical theory of symbolism here. However, symbolic representation is immensely important in all forms of art therapy (not just psychoanalytically orientated work), as feeling states and ideas which would be difficult or impossible to articulate verbally can be depicted in symbols and metaphors (these can express, through suggestion, an idea or mood which would otherwise remain inexpressible or incomprehensible). Symbols are often 'mysteriously indeterminate' with many possible meanings, or multiple meanings. Baldick speaks here of literary symbols, but his point applies equally to images when he suggests that it is:

> usually too simple to say that a literary symbol 'stands for' some idea as if it were just a convenient substitute for a fixed meaning; it is usually a substantial image in its own right around which further significances may gather according to differing interpretations.
>
> (Baldick 2001, p. 252)

Thus, symbols offer a rich and complex mode of communication.

**Systems theory**   This is the interdisciplinary study of systems in general. In group psychotherapy the entire group is viewed as an entity; within it the specific roles and interrelated concerns of individual members that are adopted during group processes are scrutinised to illuminate patterns of being.

**Transference**   Transference is the 'process by which a patient displaces onto his analyst [or art therapist] feelings, ideas, etc., which derive from previous figures in his life' (Rycroft 1968, p. 168) via a process called displacement. In this process the client relates to the therapist as if the therapist 'were some former object in his life' (p. 168). In psychoanalysis these are called 'object-representations [the *mental representation* of an object] acquired by earlier introjections' (p. 168). Or put more simply, clients 'tend to re-experience emotional reactions which were originally directed towards members of their own families [or significant others] . . . in relationship to their doctor' (Tredgold and Woolf 1975, p. 22). These feelings are projected on to the therapist, and to the image. Broadly, the term can be used to describe the client's emotional attitude towards her or his therapist (Rycroft 1968, p. 168). In art therapy the client's demeanour towards her or his art work is of crucial importance, as well as the client's feelings about her or his therapist. However, in my view, seeing all aspects of the therapeutic relationship in terms of shifting transference is potentially reductive.

**Unconscious**    Being unconscious is not being aware of the existence or occurrence of something, or being 'temporarily insensible' (Oxford Dictionaries 1973, p. 2406). In psychoanalytical theory, unconscious processes refer to psychic material, which is only rarely accessible to awareness and which is repressed or pre-conscious (the latter may arise into the conscious mind more easily). It is believed that such psychic material can have a profound influence upon behaviour: 'When used loosely, the unconscious is a metaphorical, almost anthropomorphic concept, an entity influencing the SELF unbeknownst to itself' (Rycroft 1968, p. 173). In the 1920s, Freud renamed the conscious mind as the 'ego' and the unconscious mind as the 'id' (a potentially useful distinction), the id being associated with 'instinctual' energy and the gratification of basic needs, the 'ego' being the more cultivated, civilised and socialised aspects of the psyche. Rycroft discusses why the use of the term 'unconscious' is potentially problematic:

First it can be and is used to obliterate a number of other distinctions, e.g. voluntary and involuntary, unwitting and deliberate, unself-conscious and self-aware. Secondly, it can be used to create states of sceptical confusion; *if a person (patient) accepts the general proposition that he may have unconscious motives, he may then find himself unable to disagree with some particular statement made about himself*, since the fact that it does not correspond to anything of which he is aware does not preclude the possibility that it correctly states something of which he is unaware. As a result he may formally agree to propositions (interpretations) without in fact assenting or subscribing to them.

(1968, p. 173; my italics)

As discussed in the main text, it is potentially problematic for art therapists to offer interpretations for precisely these reasons: that the therapist's view may be hard to resist, especially if unconscious motivations are invoked. Rycroft (1968) also discusses the potential problem that a client may 'entertain an indefinite number of hypotheses about their unconscious motives without having any idea how to decide which of them are true'. It makes much more sense, I'd maintain, for any interpretation of an art work to be undertaken by the art therapy participant, as thoughts and feelings reach his or her awareness. The other, very serious, reason for avoiding focusing on 'unconscious' motivations for clients' behaviour is, as Rycroft suggests above, that it is simply too crude, and can distract from the more helpful task of enabling clients to explore their psychological motivations and complexities. Anyway, it is not my intention to try to re-convert the psychoanalytically inclined here, but rather to point out the conceptual pitfalls implicated in the use of this term. Making assumptions about what might be unconscious in art or discourse is potentially problematic as has been discussed in the main text.

In Chapter 10 I discuss the contribution of Pierre Bourdieu, who has highlighted another way to think about what we 'unconsciously' bring with us, giving it the name *habitus*. This is an 'embodied history, internalised as a second nature and so forgotten as history – is the active presence of the whole past' (Bourdieu 1990, p. 56). It conjures up our habitual ways of being that are not necessarily in our conscious minds, or even in our consciousness. With an increasing emphasis on embodiment in art therapy, Bourdieu's ideas may be useful to us and offer a non-psychoanalytic way of conceptualising 'unconscious' processes.

# Bibliography

Adamson, E. 1970. *Art as Healing*. London: Coventure.

Agazarian, Y. and Peters, R. 1981. *The Visible and the Invisible Group*. London: Karnac Books.

Allen, P.B. 2014. 'Intention and Witness: Tools for Mindfulness in Art and Writing', in L. Rappaport (ed.) *Mindfulness and the Arts Therapies*. London and New York: Jessica Kingsley, pp. 51–64.

Anyanwu, C.N. 1988. 'The Technique of Participatory Research'. *Community Development Journal*, 23: 11–15. Online at http://cdj.oxfordjournals.org/cgi/reprint/ (accessed 23 January 2011).

Appignanesi, L. 2008. *Mad, Bad and Sad: A History of Women and the Mind Doctors from 1800 to the Present*. London: Virago Press.

Arts Council England. 2011. *Arts Audiences: Insight Report*. Online at www.artscouncil.org.uk/media/uploads/Arts_audiences_insight.pdf (accessed 29 April 2015).

Aveline, M. and Dryden, W. 1988. *Group Therapy in Britain*. Milton Keynes: Open University Press.

Baldick, C. 2001. *Concise Oxford Dictionary of Literary Terms*. Oxford: Oxford University Press.

Banks, S. and Armstrong, A. (eds). 2012. *Community-based Participatory Research: A Guide to Ethical Principles and Practice*. Centre for Social Justice and Community Action, Durham University, and National Co-ordinating Centre for Public Engagement. Online at www.publicengagement.ac.uk/how/sites/default/files/publication/cbpr_ethics_guide_web_november_2012.pdf (accessed 9 May 2015).

Beck, A.T. 1963. 'Thinking and Depression. Part 1: Idiosyncratic Content and Cognitive Disorders'. *Archives of General Psychiatry*, 9: 324–33.

Beck, A.T., Freeman, A., Davis, D.D. and Associates. 2004. *Cognitive Therapy of Personality Disorders* (2nd edition). London: The Guilford Press.

Belsey, C. 1980. *Critical Practice*. London: Routledge.

Bennett, F. and Roberts, M. 2004. *Participatory Approaches to Research on Poverty: Findings Report*. Online at www.jrf.org.uk/sites/files/jrf/334.pdf (accessed 14 May 2015).

Betts, D.J. 2003. *Creative Arts Therapies Approaches in Adoption and Foster Care: Contemporary Strategies for Working with Individuals and Families*. Springfield, IL: Charles C. Thomas.

Bhasin, M.K., Dusek, J.A., Change, B-H., Joseph, M.G., Denniger, J.W., Fricchione, G.L., Benson, H. and Libermann, T.A. 2013. 'Relaxation Response Induces Temporal Transcriptome Changes in Energy Metabolism, Insulin Secretion and Inflammatory

Pathways'. *Plos One* (open access), 1 May. Online at www.plosone.org/article/info%3Adoi%2F10.1371%2Fjournal.pone.0062817 (accessed 21 April 2015).

Birch, M. and Miller, T. 2002. 'Encouraging Participation: Ethics and Responsibilities', in M. Mauthner, M. Birch, J. Jessop and T. Miller (eds) *Ethics in Qualitative Research*. London: Sage, pp. 91–106.

Bird, J. 2010. 'Gender, Knowledge and Art: Feminist Standpoint Theory Synthesised with Arts-Based Research in the Study of Domestic Violence'. Adaptation of paper presented at Vital Signs 2 Conference, Manchester University, 7–9 September, pp. 1–9.

Birtchnell, J. 1998. 'The Gestalt Art Therapy Approach to Family and Other Interpersonal Problems' in D. Sandle (ed.) *Development and Diversity*. London: Free Association Press, pp. 142–53.

Birtchnell, J. 2003. 'The Visual and the Verbal in Art Therapy'. *International Arts Therapies Journal*, 2. Online at www2.derby.ac.uk/vart/vol-2-200203-international-arts-therapies-journal/42-refereed-articles-/58-the-visual-and-the-verbal-in-art-therapy-by-dr-john-birtchnell (accessed 30 January 2014).

Bleier, R. 1984. *Science and Gender: A Critique of Biology and its Theories on Women*. New York: Pergamon Press.

Bloch, S. and Crouch, E. 1985. *Therapeutic Factors in Group Psychotherapy*. Oxford: Oxford Medical.

Bourdieu, P. 1990. *The Logic of Practice*. Cambridge: Polity Press.

Breitbart, M.M. 2003. 'Participatory Research Methods', in N. Clifford and G. Valentine (eds) *Key Methods in Geography*. London: Sage, pp. 161–78.

Briers, S. 2009. *Brilliant Cognitive Behavioural Therapy*. London: Prentice Hall.

Brown, L.S. 2010. *Feminist Therapy*. Washington, DC: APA.

Bugental, J. 1964. 'The Third Force in Psychology'. *Journal of Humanistic Psychology*, 4: 19–26.

Burt, H. (ed.). 2012a. *Art Therapy and Postmodernism: Creative Healing Through a Prism*. London: Jessica Kingsley.

Burt, H. 2012b. 'Women, Art Therapy and Feminist Theories of Development', in S. Hogan (ed.) *Revisiting Feminist Approaches to Art Therapy*. London and New York: Berghahn Books, chapter 5.

Butler, J. 1990. *Gender Trouble: Feminism and the Subversion of Identity*. New York and London: Routledge Classics.

Campbell, J. and Gaga, D.A. 1997. 'Black on Black Art Therapy: Dreaming in Colour', in S. Hogan (ed.) *Feminist Approaches to Art Therapy*. London: Routledge, pp. 216–28.

Campbell, J. and Gaga, D.A. 2012. 'Black on Black: Dreaming in Colour', in S. Hogan (ed.) *Revisiting Feminist Approaches to Art Therapy*. London and New York: Berghahn Books.

Champernowne, H.I. 1949. *British Red Cross Conference Report*. London: British Red Cross.

Champernowne, H.I. 1963. 'Psychotherapy and the Arts at Withymead Centre'. *American Bulletin of Art Therapy*, Spring Issue.

Champernowne, H.I. 1973. *Creative Expression and Ultimate Values* (pamphlet). London: The Guild of Pastoral Society.

Champernowne, H.I. 1974. *Searching for Meaning: The One and Only Me*. Nutfield: Denholm House University Press.

Champernowne, H.I. and Lewis, E. 1966. 'Psychodynamics of Therapy in a Residential Group'. *The Journal of Analytical Psychology*, 11(2): 163–80.

Chang, F. 2014. 'Mindfulness and Person-Centred Art Therapy', in L. Rappaport (ed). *Mindfulness and the Arts Therapies*. London and New York: Jessica Kingsley, pp. 219–35.

Chesler, P. 1972. *Woman and Madness*. Garden City, NY: Doubleday.

Chipp, H.B. 1968. *Theories of Modern Art: A Source Book by Artists and Critics*. Berkeley, CA and London: University of California Press.

Corey, G. 2009. *Theory and Practice of Counseling and Psychotherapy*. Belmont, CA: Brooks/Cole.

Corrie, J. 1927. *ABC of Jung's Psychology*. London: Kegan Paul, Trench, Trubner & Co.

Crimp, D. and Rolston, A. 1990. *AIDS Demo Graphics*. Seattle, WA: Bay Press.

Culler, J. 1983. *On Deconstruction: Theory and Criticism after Structuralism*. London: Routledge & Kegan Paul.

Cunningham Dax, E. 1948. 'Art Therapy for Mental Patients'. *The Nursing Times*, 14 August: 592–4.

Darwin, C. 1871. *The Descent of Man and Selection in Relation to Sex*. New York: Modern Library (unabridged).

de Beauvoir, S. 2011. *The Second Sex* (1949). (New translation by C. Borde and S. Malovany-Chevallier). London: Vintage.

Dictionary.com. 2015. 'Metaphor'. Online at http://dictionary.reference.com/browse/metaphor (accessed 21 May 2015).

Douglas, M. 1970. *Natural Symbols* (2nd edition 1996). London: Routledge.

Douglas, M. 1994. 'The Construction of the Physician', in S. Budd and U. Sharma (eds) *The Healing Bond*. London: Routledge.

Douglas, M. 1996. *Thought Styles*. London: Sage.

Douglas, M. 2001. 'Foreword', in S. Hogan, *Healing Arts: The History of Art Therapy*. London: Jessica Kingsley.

Duvvury, V.K. 1991. *Play, Symbolism, and Ritual: A Study of Tamil Brahmin Women's Rites of Passage*. New York: Peter Lang.

Eagle Russett, C. 1989. *Sexual Science: The Victorian Construction of Womanhood*. Cambridge, MA: Harvard University Press.

Eastwood, C. 2012. 'Art Therapy with Women with Borderline Personality Disorder'. *International Journal of Art Therapy: Formerly Inscape*, 7(3): 98–114.

Edwards, C. 2007. 'Art as Witness', in S.L. Brooke (ed.) *The Use of the Creative Therapies with Sexual Abuse Survivors*. Springfield, IL: Charles C. Thomas, pp. 44–59.

Edwards, D. 2004. *Art Therapy*. London: Sage.

Fausto-Sterling, A. 1985. *Myths of Gender. Biological Theories about Women and Men*. New York: Basic Books.

Forrester, J. 1980. *Language and the Origins of Psychoanalysis*. London/New York: Macmillan/Columbia University Press.

Franklin, M.A. 2014. 'Mindful Considerations for Training Art Therapists: Inner Friendship–Outer Professionalism', in L. Rappaport (ed.) *Mindfulness and the Arts Therapies*. London and New York: Jessica Kingsley, pp. 264–76.

Freud, S. 1939. *Moses and Monotheism* (trans. Kathleen Jones). New York: Knopf.

Freud, S. 1949. *An Outline of Psychoanalysis* (trans. James Strachey). New York: Norton.

Freud, S. 1963. *Introductory Lectures on Psycho-Analysis (1916–1917). The Standard Edition, Vol. XV* (trans. James Strachey). London: Hogarth Press.

Freud, S. 1973. *New Introductory Lectures on Psychoanalysis*. London: Pelican. (Originally published in *The Standard Edition of the Complete Works of Sigmund Freud, Vol. XXII*, Hogarth Press, 1964.)

Freud, S. 1977. *The Interpretation of Dreams*. Harmondsworth: Penguin.

Frosh, S. 2002. *Key Concepts in Psychoanalysis*. London: The British Library.

Furth, G.M. 2002. *The Secret World of Drawings: A Jungian Approach to Healing Through Art* (2nd edition; originally published 1988). Toronto: Innercity Books.

Gee, J.P. 1999. *An Introduction to Discourse Analysis: Theory and Method*. London: Routledge.

Gilman, S.L. 1988. *Disease and Representation: Images of Illness from Madness to AIDS*. New York: Cornell University Press.

Gould, S.J. 1981. *The Mismeasure of Man* (revised and expanded). New York: W.W. Norton.

Greenburg, J.R. and Mitchell, S.A. 1983. *Object Relations in Psychoanalytic Theory*. Cambridge, MA and London: Harvard University Press.

Hadjinicolaou, N. 1978. *Art History and Class Struggle*. London: Pluto.

Hall, K. and Iqbal, F. 2010. *The Problem with Cognitive Behavioural Therapy*. London: Karnac Books.

Haraway, D. 1992. *Primate Visions: Gender, Race, and Nature in the World of Modern Science*. London: Verso Press.

Harding, S. 2004. 'Rethinking Standpoint Epistemology: What Is "Strong Objectivity"?', in S. Harding (ed.) *The Feminist Standpoint Theory Reader: Intellectual & Political Controversies*. London: Routledge, pp. 127–40.

Hare-Mustin, R.T. and Marecek, J. (eds). 1990. *Making a Difference: Psychology and the Construction of Gender*. New Haven, CT: Yale University Press.

Harris, R. 1996. *Signs, Language and Communication*. London: Routedge.

Henderson, J.L. 1980. 'Foreword', in I. Champernowne, *A Memoir of Toni Wolff*. San Francisco, CA: C.G. Institute of San Francisco.

Henzell, J. 1984. 'Art, Pychotherapy and Symbol Systems', in T. Dalley (ed.) *Art As Therapy: An Introduction to the Use of Art as a Therapeutic Technique*. London: Tavistock Publications.

Hess, E. 2007. *Gestalt Therapy*. Video. Online at www.youtube.com/watch?v=ZbOAdMdMLdI (accessed 21 August 2013).

Hill, A. 1945. *Art Versus Illness: A Story of Art Therapy*. London: George Allen & Unwin.

Hill, A. 1951. *Painting Out Illness*. London: Williams and Norgate.

Hocoy, D. 2007. 'Art Therapy as a Tool for Social Change', in F.F. Kaplan (ed.) *Art Therapy and Social Action*, London and New York: Jessica Kingsley, pp. 21–40.

Hogan, S. (ed.). 1997. *Feminist Approaches to Art Therapy*. London: Routledge.

Hogan, S. 2001. *Healing Arts: The History of Art Therapy*. London: Jessica Kingsley.

Hogan, S. 2003. *Gender Issues in Art Therapy*. London: Jessica Kingsley.

Hogan, S. 2004a. 'An Introduction to Art Therapy: Further Reflections on Teaching Art Therapy at an Introductory Level: Part One'. *Journal of the Australian National Art Therapy Association*, 15(3): 15–23.

Hogan, S. 2004b. 'Reflections on Experiential Learning'. *Journal of the Australian National Art Therapy Association*, 15(2): 16–20.

Hogan, S. 2006a. 'The Tyranny of the Maternal Body: Maternity and Madness'. *Women's History Magazine*, 54: 21–30.

Hogan, S. 2006b. *Conception Diary: Thinking About Pregnancy and Motherhood*. Sheffield: Eilish Press.

Hogan, S. 2008a. Angry Mothers in M. Liebmann (ed.) *Art Therapy and Anger*. London: Jessica Kingsley.

Hogan, S. 2008b. 'The Beestings: Rethinking Breast-feeding Practices, Maternity Rituals, & Maternal Attachment in Britain & Ireland'. *Journal of International Women's Studies*, 10(2): 141–60.

Hogan, S. 2009. 'The Art Therapy Continuum: An Overview of British Art Therapy Practice'. *International Journal of Art Therapy: Formerly Inscape*, 12(1): 29–37.

Hogan, S. 2011a. 'Post-Modernist but Not Post-Feminist: A Feminist Post-Modernist Approach to Working with New Mothers', in H. Burt (ed.) *Current Trends and New Research in Art Therapy: A Postmodernist Perspective*. Waterloo, ON: Wilfred Laurier Press.

Hogan, S. 2011b. 'Feminist Art Therapy', in C. Wood (ed.) *Navigating Art Therapy. A Therapist's Companion*. London: Routledge, pp. 87–8.

Hogan, S. (ed.). 2012a. *Revisiting Feminist Approaches to Art Therapy*. London and New York: Berghahn Books.

Hogan, S. 2012b. 'Post-modernist but Not Post-feminist! A Feminist Post-modernist Approach to Working with New Mothers', in H. Burt (ed.) *Art Therapy and Postmodernism: Creative Healing Through a Prism*. London: Jessica Kingsley, pp. 70–82.

Hogan, S. 2012c. 'Ways in which Photographic and Other Images are Used in Research: An Introductory Overview'. *International Journal of Art Therapy: Formerly Inscape*, 17(2): 54–62.

Hogan, S. 2013a. 'Your Body is a Battleground: Women and Art Therapy'. *The Arts in Psychotherapy*, Special Issue on Gender and the Creative Arts Therapies, 40(4): 415–19.

Hogan, S. 2013b. 'Peripheries and Borders: Pushing the Boundaries of Visual Research'. *International Journal of Art Therapy: Formerly Inscape*, June: 1–8.

Hogan, S. 2014. 'Lost in Translation? Inter-cultural Exchange in Art Therapy', in C.E. Myers and S.L. Brooke (eds) *Creative Arts Across Cultures*. Springfield, IL: Charles C. Thomas.

Hogan, S. 2015. 'Mothers Make Art: Using Participatory Art to Explore the Transition to Motherhood'. *Journal of Applied Arts & Health*, 6(1): 23–32.

Hogan, S. and Cornish, S. 2014. 'Unpacking Gender in Art Therapy: The Elephant at the Art Therapy Easel'. *International Journal of Art Therapy: Formerly Inscape*, 19: 122–34.

Hogan, S. and Coulter, A. 2014. *The Introductory Guide to Art Therapy*. London and New York: Routledge.

Hogan, S. and Pink, S. 2010. 'Routes to Interiorities: Art Therapy, Anthropology and Knowing in Anthropology'. *Visual Anthropology*, 23(2): 158–74.

Hogan, S. and Pink, S. 2011. 'Visualising Interior Worlds: Interdisciplinary Routes to Knowing', in S. Pink (ed.) *Advances in Visual Methodology*. London: Sage, pp. 230–48.

Hogan, S. and Warren, L. 2012. 'Dealing with Complexity in Research Findings: How Do Older Women Negotiate and Challenge Images of Ageing?' *Journal of Women & Aging*, 24(4): 329–50.

Hogan, S. and Warren, L. 2013. 'Women's Inequality: A Global Problem Explored in Participatory Arts'. *International Perspectives on Research-Guided Practice in Community-Based Arts in Health (UNESCO Observatory Multi-Disciplinary Journal in the Arts)*, Special Issue, 3(3): 1–27.

Hogan, S., Baker, C., Cornish, S., McCloskey, P. and Watts, L. 2015. 'Birth Shock: Exploring Pregnancy, Birth and the Transition to Motherhood Using Participatory Arts', in N. Burton (ed.) *Natal Signs: Representations of Pregnancy, Childbirth and Parenthood*. Toronto: Demeter Press (in press).

Holloway, M. 2009. British Australian: Art Therapy, White Racial Identity and Racism in Australia. *Australian and New Zealand Journal of Art Therapy*, 4(1): 62–7.

Home Office. 2012. 'Body Confidence Campaign'. Online at www.homeoffice.gov.uk/equalities/equalities/equality-government/body-confidence (accessed 4 August 2013).

Hopkins, J. 1996. 'The Dangers and Deprivations of Too-Good Mothering'. *Journal of Psychotherapy*, 22(3): 407–22.

Houston, G. 2003. *Brief Gestalt Therapy*. London: Sage.

Howell, E. and Baynes, M. (eds). 1981. *Women and Mental Health*. New York: Basic Books.

Hubbard, R. 1990. *The Politics of Women's Biology*. New Brunswick, NJ: Rutgers University Press.

Huet, V. 1997. 'Ageing: Another Tyranny? Art Therapy with Older Women', in S. Hogan (ed.) *Feminist Approaches to Art Therapy*. London: Routledge, pp. 125–40.

Huet, V. 2012. 'Ageing: Another Tyranny? Art Therapy with Older Women', in S. Hogan (ed.) *Revisiting Feminist Approaches to Art Therapy*. London and New York: Berghahn Books, pp. 159–73.

Huss, E. and Alhaiga-Taz, S. 2013. 'Bedouin Children's Experience of Growing Up in Illegal Villages, Versus in Townships in Israel: Implications of Social Context for Understanding Stress, and Resilience in Children's Drawings'. *International Journal of Art Therapy: Formerly Inscape*, 18(1): 10–19.

Isis, P.A. 2014. 'Mindfulness-based Stress Reduction and the Expressive Arts Therapies in a Hospital-based Community Outreach Programme', in L. Rappaport (ed.) *Mindfulness and the Arts Therapies*. London and New York: Jessica Kingsley, pp. 155–67.

Iveson, C. 2002. 'Solution-Focused Brief Therapy'. *Advances in Psychiatric Treatment*, 8: 149–56.

Jones, S.L. 2012. 'Visual Voice: Abusive Relationships, Women's Art and Visceral Healing', in S. Hogan (ed.) *Revisiting Feminist Approaches to Art Therapy*. London and New York: Berghahn Books, pp. 173–210.

Joyce, S. 2008. 'Picturing Lesbian, Informing Art Therapy: A Postmodern Feminist Autobiographical Investigation'. Thesis. Southern Cross University, New South Wales (e-publication).

Jung, C.G. 1928. *Two Essays on Analytical Psychology* (trans. H.G. and C.F. Baynes). London: Baillière, Tindall and Cox.

Jung, C.G. 1936. *The Integration of the Personality* (trans. Stanley Dell). New York: Farrar and Rinehart.

Jung, C.G. 1953. 'The Structure of the Unconscious', in R.F.C. Hull (trans.) *The Collected Works of C.G. Jung, Vol. 7*. Princeton: Princeton University Press. (Original work published in 1916.)

Jung, C.G. 1960. *The Structure and Dynamics of the Psyche (Collected Works of Jung, Volume 8)*. London: Routledge & Kegan Paul.

Jung, C.G. 1963. *The Secret of the Golden Flower*. London: Routledge & Kegan Paul.

Jung, C.G. (ed.). 1964. *Man and His Symbols*. London: Aldus.

Jung, C.G. 1967. *The Spirit in Man, Art, and Literature*. London: Ark.

Jung, C.G. 1971. *C.G. Jung Letters, Volume 1*. London: Routledge & Kegan Paul.

Jung, C.G. 1976. *Collected Works*. New York: Pantheon Books.

Jung, C.G. 1983a. *Dictionary of Analytical Psychology*. London: Ark.

Jung, C.G. 1983b. *Memories, Dreams, Reflections*. London: Flamingo.

Jung, C.G. 1984. *Modern Man in Search of a Soul* (trans. C.F. Baynes). London: Ark.

Junge, M.B. 1999. 'Mourning Memory and Life Itself: The AIDS Quilt and the Vietnam Veterans' Memorial Wall'. *The Arts in Psychotherapy*, 26(3): 195–203.

Junge, M.B., Alvarez, J.F., Kellogg, A. and Volker, C. 1993. 'The Art Therapist as Social Activist: Reflections and Visions'. *Art Therapy: Journal of the American Art Therapy Association*, 10: 148–55.

Kaplan, F. (ed.) 2007. *Art Therapy and Social Action*. London and New York: Jessica Kingsley.

Kavaler-Adler, S. 2011. *Object Relations Clinical Theory*. Film. Online at www.youtube.com/watch?v=CWRhB2IQvbc (accessed 12 October 2013).

Kernberg, O. 1994. 'Validation in the Clinical Process'. *International Journal of Psychoanalysis*, 75: 1195–6.

Kirschenbaum, H. and Land Henderson, V. (eds). 1990. *The Carl Rogers Reader*. London: Constable.

Korb, M.P., Gorrell, J. and Van De Riet, V. 1989. *Gestalt Therapy: Practice and Theory* (2nd edition). New York and Oxford: Pergamon Press.

Kris, E. 1953. *Psychoanalytic Explorations in Art*. London: George Allen & Unwin.

Laine, R. 2007. 'Image Consultation', in J. Schaverien and C. Case. *Supervision of Art Psychotherapy: A Theoretical and Practical Handbook*. London: Routledge, pp. 119–37.

Lala, A. 2011. 'Seeing the Whole Picture: A Culturally Sensitive Art Therapy Approach to Address Depression Amongst Ethnically Diverse Women', in H. Burt (ed.) *Art Therapy and Postmodernism: Creative Healing Through a Prism*. London and Philadelphia: Jessica Kingsley, pp. 32–49.

Landes, J. 2012. 'Hanging By a Thread: Articulating Women's Experience via Textiles', in S. Hogan (ed.) *Revisiting Feminist Approaches to Art Therapy*. London: Berghahn Books, pp. 224–37.

Landy, R.J. 1994. *Drama Therapy: Concepts, Theories and Practices*. Springfield, IL: Charles C. Thomas.

Laplanche, J. and Pontalis, J.B. 1973. *The Language of Psychoanalysis*. London: Hogarth Press.

Layard, R. 2006. *The Depression Report: A New Deal for Depression and Anxiety Disorders*. London: London School of Economics.

Levine, E.G. and Levine, S. (eds). 2011. *Art as Social Action*. London: Jessica Kingsley.

Lewin, K. 1935. *A Dynamic Theory of Personality*. New York: McGraw-Hill.

Lewin, K. 1951. 'Field Theory in Social Science', in D. Cartwright (ed.) *Field Theory in Social Science: Selected Theoretical Papers*. London: Harper & Row.

Lewontin, R.C., Rose, S. and Kamin, L.J. 1984. *Not In Our Genes: Biology, Ideology, and Human Nature*. London: Penguin.

Liebmann, M. (ed.). 1996. *Arts Approaches to Conflict*. London: Jessica Kingsley.

Lodge, O. 1911. *The Position of Women: Actual and Ideal*. London: James Nesbit.

Lofgren, D.E. 1981. 'Art Therapy and Cultural Difference'. *American Journal of Art Therapy*, 21(1): 25–32.

Long, C. 1920. *Collected Papers on the Psychology of Phantasy*. London: Baillière, Tindall and Cox.

Lusebrink, V.B. 1990. *Imagery and Visual Expression in Art Therapy*. New York: Plenum.

Mackewn, J. 1997. *Developing Gestalt Counselling*. London: Sage.

Maclagan, D. 2001. *Psychological Aesthetics*. London: Jessica Kingsley.

*Macquarie Dictionary*. 1981. Chatswood: Macquarie University.

Malchiodi, C.A. 1997. 'Invasive Art: Art as Empowerment for Women with Breast Cancer', in S. Hogan (ed.) *Feminist Approaches to Art Therapy*. London: Routledge, pp. 49–65.

Malchiodi, C.A. (ed.). 2012. *Handbook of Art Therapy* (2nd edition). New York: The Guilford Press.

Malchiodi, C.A. and Rozum, A.L. 2012. 'Cognitive-Behavioral and Mind–Body Approaches', in C.A. Malchiodi (ed.) *Handbook of Art Therapy* (2nd edition). New York: The Guilford Press, pp. 89–103.

Manuel, M. 2013. 'Shame and Powerlessness: Feminist Art Therapy with Black Female Prostitutes'. Paper presented at the annual meeting of The Association for Women in Psychology, San Diego, CA, 15 December. Online at http://citation.allacademic.com/meta/p230896_index.html (accessed 4 July 2014).

Martin, E. 1987. *The Woman in the Body: A Cultural Analysis of Reproduction*. Boston, MA: Beacon Press.

Martin, R. 1997. 'Looking and Reflecting: Returning the Gaze, Re-enacting Memories and Imagining the Future Through Phototherapy', in S. Hogan (ed.) *Feminist Approaches to Art Therapy*. London: Routledge, pp. 150–77.

Martin, R. 2012. 'Looking and Reflecting: Returning the Gaze, Re-enacting Memories and Imagining the Future Through Phototherapy', in S. Hogan (ed.) *Revisiting Feminist Approaches to Art Therapy*. London and New York: Routledge, pp. 112–40.

Maudsley, H. 1873. *Body and Mind*. London: Macmillan.

McGee, P. 2012. 'A Feminist Approach to Child Sexual Abuse and Shame', in S. Hogan (ed.) *Revisiting Feminist Approaches to Art Therapy*. London: Berghahn Books, pp. 281–93.

McNeilly, G. 1983. 'Directive and Non-Directive Approaches in Art Therapy'. *The Arts in Psychotherapy*, 10(4): 211–19.

McNeilly, G. 2005. *Group Analytic Art Therapy*. London: Jessica Kingsley.

McNiff, S. 1984. 'Cross-cultural Psychotherapy and Art'. *Art Therapy: Journal of the American Art Therapy Association*, 1(3): 125–31. (Work republished in 2009 – doi: 10. 1080/07421656.2009.10129379.).

McNiff, S. 1998. *Art-based Research*. London: Jessica Kingsley.

McNiff, S. 2004. *Art Heals: How Creativity Cures the Soul*. Boston, MA: Shambhala Press.

Mearns, D. and Thorne, B. 2000. *Person-centered Therapy Today*. London: Sage.

Menninger, K. 1958. *Theory of Psychoanalytic Technique*. New York: Basic Books.

Milner, M. 1957[2010]. *On Not Being Able to Paint*. London: Routledge.

Molnos, A. 1998. 'A Psychotherapist's Harvest: Parataxic Distortions'. Online at www.net. klte.hu/~keresofi/psyth/a-to-z-entries/parataxic_distortions.html (accessed 23 November 2011).

Monti, D.A., Peterson, C., Kunkel, E.J., Hauck, W.W., Pequignot, E., Rhodes, L. and Brainard, G.C. 2006. 'A Randomized, Controlled Trial of Mindfulness-based Art Therapy (MBAT) for Women with Cancer'. *Psycho-Oncology*, 15(5): 363–73.

*New World Encyclopaedia*. 2013. 'Defense Mechanism'. Online at www.newworldencyclo pedia.org/entry/Defense_mechanism#Repression.2FSuppression (accessed 30 August 2013).

Oakley, A. 1981. *From Here to Maternity: Becoming a Mother*. London: Penguin.

O'Neill, M. 2008. 'Transnational Refugees: The Transformative Role of Art?', *Forum: Qualitative Social Research*, 9(2) (Art. 59): 1–21.

O'Neill, M. 2010. *Asylum, Migration and Community*. Bristol: Polity Press.

O'Neill, M. 2012. 'Ethno-Mimesis and Participatory Arts', in S. Pink (ed.) *Advances in Visual Methodology*. London: Sage, pp. 153–73.

Oppenheim, J. 1991. *Shattered Nerves: Doctors, Patients, and Depression in Victorian England*. Oxford: Oxford University Press.

Oudshoorn, N. 1994. *Beyond the Body: An Archaeology of Sex Hormones*. London: Routledge.

Oxford Dictionaries. 1973. *Shorter Oxford English Dictionary*. Oxford: Oxford University Press.

oxforddictionaries.com. 2015. 'Oxford Dictionaries Definitions'. Online at www. oxforddictionaries.com/definition/english/ (accessed 12 May 2015).

Pailthorpe, G.W. 1938–9. 'The Scientific Aspects of Surrealism'. *London Bulletin*, 7: 10–16.

Perls, F.S. 1942. *Ego, Hunger and Aggression. A Revision of Freud's Theory and Method*. New York: Gestalt Journal Press. (Reprinted 1992.)

Perls, F.S. 1947. *Ego Hunger and Aggression: A Revision of Freud's Theory and Method*. Gouldsboro, ME: The Gestalt Journal Press.

Perls, F.S. 1969. Reproduction of 'Here and Now: Gestalt Therapy' Lecture 1969. Online at www.youtube.com/watch?v=9_voss41dyA (accessed 1 June 2015).

Peterson, C. 2014. 'Mindfulness-based Art Therapy: Applications for Healing with Cancer', in L. Rappaport (ed.) *Mindfulness and the Arts Therapies*. London and New York: Jessica Kingsley, pp. 64–81.

Petocz, A. 1999. *Freud, Psychoanalysis and Symbolism*. Cambridge: Cambridge University Press.

Pink, S., Hogan, S. and Bird, J. 2011. 'Boundaries and Intersections: Using the Arts in Research'. *International Journal of Art Therapy: Formerly Inscape*, 16(1): 14–19.

Prison Reform Trust. 2014. *Why Focus on Reducing Women's Imprisonment?* London: Prison Reform Trust.

Prochaska, J.O. 2013. 'Transtheoretical Model of Behavior Change'. Online at www. prochange.com/transtheoretical-model-of-behavior-change (accessed 12 December 2013).

Rappaport, L. (ed.) 2014a. *Mindfulness and the Arts Therapies*. London and New York: Jessica Kingsley.

Rappaport, L. 2014b. 'Focusing-oriented Arts Therapy: Cultivating Mindfulness and Compassion, and Accessing Inner Wisdom', in L. Rappaport (ed.) *Mindfulness and the Arts Therapies*. London and New York: Jessica Kingsley, pp. 193–208.

Ratigan, B. and Aveline, M. 1988. 'Interpersonal Group Therapy', in M. Aveline and W. Dryden (eds) *Group Therapy in Britain*. Milton Keynes: Open University Press, pp. 43–65.

Redfern, C. and Aune, K. 2010. *Reclaiming the F Word*. London: Zed Books.

Rehavia-Hanauer, D. 2012. 'Habitus and Social Control: Feminist Art Therapy and the Critical Analysis of Visual Representations', in S. Hogan (ed.) *Revisiting Feminist Approaches to Art Therapy*. London: Berghahn Books, pp. 91–9.

Rhyne, J. 1996. *The Gestalt Art Experience*. Chicago, IL: Magnolia Street Publishers.

Richardson, L. 2011. 'Resonance', in C. Wood (ed.) *Navigating Art Therapy: A Therapist's Companion*. London and New York: Routledge.

Rogers, C.R. 1946. 'Significant Aspects of Client-centered Therapy'. *American Psychologist*, 1: 415–22.

Rogers, C.R. 1957. 'A Note on the "Nature of Man"'. *Journal of Counseling Psychology*, 4(3): 199–203.

Rogers, C.R. 1961. *On Becoming a Person: A Therapist's View of Psychotherapy*. London: Constable.

Rogers, N. 2000. *The Creative Connection: Expressive Arts as Healing*. Ross-on-Wye: PCCS Books. (Original work published 1993.)

Rogers, N., Tudor, K., Embleton Tudor, L. and Keemar, K. 2012. 'Person-Centered Expressive Arts Therapy: A Theoretical Encounter'. *Person-Centered and Experiential Psychotherapies*, 11(1): 31–47.

Rosal, M. 2001. 'Cognitive-Behavioural Art Therapy', in J. Rubin (ed.) *Approaches to Art Therapy: Theory and Technique* (2nd edition). London and New York: Brunner Routledge, pp. 210–25.

Ross, C. 1997. 'Women and Conflict', in S. Hogan (ed.) *Feminist Approaches to Art Therapy*. London: Routledge, pp. 140–50.

Ross, C. 2012. 'Women and Conflict', in S. Hogan (ed.) *Revisiting Feminist Approaches to Art Therapy*. London and New York: Berghahn Books, pp. 150–9.

Roth, E. 2001. 'Behavioural Art Therapy', in J. Rubin (ed.) *Approaches to Art Therapy: Theory and Technique* (2nd edition). London and New York: Brunner Routledge, pp. 195–209.

Royce, E. 2009. *Poverty & Power. The Problem of Structural Inequality*. Lanham, MD: Rowman & Littlefield.

Rubin, J. (ed.). 2001. *Approaches to Art Therapy: Theory and Technique* (2nd edition). London and New York: Brunner Routledge.

Russell, D. 1995. *Women, Madness and Medicine*. Cambridge: Polity.

Rycroft, C. 1968. *A Critical Dictionary of Psychoanalysis*. London: Thomas Nelson & Sons.

Rycroft, C. 1995. *A Critical Dictionary of Psychoanalysis* (2nd edition). London: Penguin Books.

Samuels, A., Shorter, B. and Plaut, F. 1986. *A Critical Dictonary of Jungian Analysis*. London: Routledge & Kegan Paul.

Sandler, J., Dare, C. and Holder, A. 1973. *The Patient and the Analyst*. London: Maresfield.

Sayers, J. 1982. *Biological Politics: Feminist and Anti-Feminist Perspectives*. London: Tavistock Publications.

Schaverien, J. 1987. 'The Scapegoat and the Talisman: Transference in Art Therapy', in T. Dalley, C. Case, J. Schaverien, F. Weir, D. Halliday, P. Nowell Hall and D. Waller (eds) *Images of Art Therapy: New Developments in Theory and Practice*. London: Tavistock Publications.

Schaverien, J. 1990. 'Triangular Relationship (2): Desire Alchemy and the Picture'. *Inscape* (now *International Journal of Art Therapy*), Winter: 14–19.

Schaverien, J. 1992. *The Revealing Image: Analytical Art Psychotherapy in Theory and Practice*. London: Routledge.

Schaverien, J. 1998. 'Inheritance: Jewish Identity, Art Psychotherapy Workshops and the Legacy of the Holocaust', in D. Dokter (ed.) *Art Therapists, Refugees and Migrants: Reaching Across Borders*. London: Jessica Kingsley, pp. 155–75.

Schaverien, J. 2000. 'The Triangular Relationship and the Aesthetic Countertransference in Analytical Art Psychotherapy', in A. Gilroy and G. McNeilly (eds) *The Changing Shape of Art Therapy: New Developments in Theory and Practice*. London: Jessica Kingsley.

Schaverien, J. 2005. *Desire and the Female Therapist: Engendered Gazes in Psychotherapy and Art Therapy*. London: Routledge.

Schaverien, J. 2011. 'Embodied Image', in C. Wood (ed.) *Navigating Art Therapy: A Therapist's Companion*. London and New York: Routledge.

Scheper-Hughes, N. 1991. 'The Rebel Body: The Subversive Meanings of Illness'. *Traditional Acupuncture Society*, 10: 3–10.

Segal, H. 1978. *Introduction to the Work of Melanie Klein* (2nd edition). London: Hogarth Press.

Seymour-Jones, C. 2008. *A Dangerous Liaison*. London: Arrow Books.

Shamdasani, S. 1995. 'Memories, Dreams and Omissions'. *A Journal of Archetype and Culture*, 57, Spring Issue: 115–37.

Shapiro, S.L., Carlson, L.E., Astin J.A. and Freedman, B. 2006. 'Mechanisms of Mindfulness'. *Journal of Clinical Psychology*, 62(3): 373–86.

Shazer, S. and Dolan, Y. 2007. *More than Miracles: The State of the Art of Solution-Focused Brief Therapy*. London: Routledge.

Sheldon, B. 2011. *Cognitive-Behavioural Therapy: Research and Practice in Health and Social Care* (2nd edition). London: Routledge.

Sherlock, A. 2012. 'Jo Spence'. *Frieze Magazine*, 149, September. Online at www.frieze.com/issue/review/jo-spence/ (accessed 21 May 2015).

Shiebinger, L. 1993. *Nature's Body: Gender in the Making of Modern Science*. New Brunswick, NJ: Rutgers University Press.

Shlien J.M. 1984. 'A Counter-Theory of Transference'. Online at www3.telus.net/eddyelmer/Tools/transf.htm (accessed 18 April 2015).

Showalter, E. 1985. *The Female Malady: Women, Madness and English Culture, 1830–1980*. London: Virago.

Showalter, E. 1992. *Sexual Anarchy: Gender and Culture at the Fin de Siècle*. London: Virago.

Sills, C., Lapworth, P. and Desmond, B. 2012. *An Introduction to Gestalt*. London: Sage.

Silverstone, L. 1997. *Art Therapy: The Person-Centred Way*. London. Jessica Kingsley.

Silverstone, L. 2009. *Art Therapy Exercises: Interpersonal and Practical Ideas to Stimulate the Imagination*. London: Jessica Kingsley.

Simmons, J. and Griffiths, R. 2009. *CBT for Beginners*. London: Sage.

Simoneaux, G. 2011. 'Creating Space for Change', in E.G. Levine and S. Levine (eds) *Art as Social Action*. London: Jessica Kingsley, pp. 159–73.

Skaife, S. 1990. 'Self Determination in Group Analytic Art Therapy'. *Group Analysis*, 23(3): 237–44.

Slater, N. 2003. 'Re-visions on Group Art Therapy with Women Who Have Experienced Domestic and Sexual Violence', in S. Hogan (ed.) *Gender Issues in Art Therapy*. London and New York: Jessica Kingsley, pp. 173–84.

Somers, J. and Querée, M. 2007. *Cognitive Behavioural Therapy: Core Information Document*. Vancouver: British Columbia Ministry of Health.

Sontag, S. 2003. *Regarding the Pain of Others*. London: Hamish Hamilton.

Sperber, H. 1912. 'Uber den Einfluss sexueller Momente auf Entstehung und Entwicklung der Sprach'. *Imago*, 1: 405–89.

*Stanford Encyclopaedia of Philosophy*. 2015. 'Buddha'. Online at http://plato.stanford.edu/entries/buddha/ (accessed 9 January 2015).

Stevens, A. 1986. *The Withymead Centre: A Jungian Community for the Healing Arts*. London: Conventure.

Stocking, G. 1987. *Victorian Anthropology*. New York: The Free Press.

Stopa, L. (ed.). 2009. *Imagery and the Threatened Self: Perspectives on Mental Imagery and the Self in Cognitive Therapy*. London: Routledge.

Talwar, S., Iyer, J. and Doby-Copeland, C. 2004. 'The Invisible Veil: Changing Paradigms in the Art Therapy Profession'. *Art Therapy Journal of the American Art Therapy Association*, 21(1): 44–8; doi: 10.1080/07421656.2004.10129325.

Tavris, C. 1992. *The Mismeasure of Woman: Why Women are Not the Better Sex, The Inferior Sex, or the Opposite Sex*. New York: Simon & Schuster.

10MinuteCBT. 2015. Online at www.10minutecbt.co.uk/?More_about_CBT:Basic_Principles_of_CBT (accessed 24 March 2015).

Tilakaratna, S. 1990. 'A Short Note on Participatory Research'. Online at www.caledonia.org.uk/research.htm (accessed 6 March 2015).

Tredgold, R. and Woolf, H. 1975. *UCH Handbook of Psychiatry*. London: Duckworth.

Ullman, D. and Wheeler, G. (eds). 2009. *Co-Creating the Field: Intention and Practice in the Age of Complexity*. London: Gestalt Press.

University of Sheffield. 2010. 'Look at Me! Images of Women & Ageing'. Online at www.representing-ageing.com/workshops.php (accessed 15 May 2015).

Ussher, J. 1991. *Women's Madness: Misogyny or Mental Illness?* Brighton: Harvester Wheatsheaf.

Ussher, J. 2011. *The Madness of Women: Myth and Experience*. London and New York: Routledge.

Wadsworth, Y. 1998. What is Participatory Research? *Action Research International*, November. Online at www.scu.edu.au/schools/gcm/ar/ari/p-ywadsworth98.html (accessed 4 March 2015).

Waldman, J. 1999. 'Breaking the Mould'. *Inscape* (now *International Journal of Art Therapy*), 4(1): 10–19.

Wallace, E.R. 1983. *Freud and Anthropology: A History and Reappraisal*. New York: International Universities Press.

Waller, D. 1991. *Becoming a Profession*. London: Routledge.

Waller, D. 2015. *Group Interactive Art Therapy: Its Use in Training and Treatment*. London: Routledge.

Waller, D. and Mahoney, J. (eds). 1998. *Treatment of Addiction: Current Issues for Art Therapists*. London: Routledge.

Waller, D. and Sibbett, C. (eds). 2005. *Art Therapy and Cancer Care*. Milton Keynes: Open University Press.

Weiner, E.T. and Rappaport, L. 2014. 'Mindfulness and Focusing-Orientated Arts Therapy with Children and Adolescents', in L. Rappaport (ed.) *Mindfulness and the Arts Therapies*. London and New York: Jessica Kingsley, pp. 248–64.

Weir, F. 1987. 'The Role of Symbolic Expression in its Relation to Art Therapy: A Kleinian Approach', in T. Dalley, C. Case, J. Schaverien, F. Weir, D. Halliday, P. Nowell Hall and D. Waller (eds) *Images of Art Therapy: New Developments in Theory and Practice*. London: Tavistock.

Wilkins, P. 2003. *Person Centred Therapy in Focus*. London: Sage.

Williams, R. 1983. *Keywords: A Vocabulary of Culture and Society*. London: Fontana.

Willis, F. 2009. *Beck's Cognitive Therapy*. London: Routledge.

Wittgenstein, L. 1958. *Philosophical Investigations* (3rd edition) (trans. G.E.M. Anscombe). Upper Saddle River, NJ: Prentice Hall.

Wood, C. 2011. 'Empathy', in C. Wood (ed.) *Navigating Art Therapy: A Therapist's Companion*. London and New York: Routledge.

World Health Organisation (WHO). 2010. 'Gender, Women and Health. Section 2: Gender-based Discrimination Limits the Attainment of International Health and Development Goals such as the MDGs'. Online at www.who.int/gender/events/2010/iwd/backgrounder2/en/index.html (accessed 21 May 2015).

World Health Organisation (WHO). 2012. 'Gender and Women's Mental Health'. Online at www.who.int/mental_health/prevention/genderwomen/en/ (accessed 21 May 2015).

Wright, T. and Wright, K. 2013. 'Art for Women's Sake: Understanding Feminist Art Therapy as Didactic Practice Re-orientation'. *International Practice Development Journal*, 3(5): 1–8.

Yalom, I.D. 1975. *The Theory and Practice of Group Psychotherapy* (2nd edition). New York: Basic Books.

Yalom, I.D. 1980[1931]. *Existential Psychotherapy*. Basic Books. (Reprinted with revised introduction 1980.)

Yalom, I.D. 1995. *The Theory and Practice of Group Psychotherapy* (4th edition). New York: Basic Books.

Young, M. 1982. *The Elmhursts of Dartington Hall: The Creation of a Utopian Community*. London: Routledge & Kegan Paul.

Zinker, J. 1977. *Creative Process in Gestalt Therapy*. New York: Brunner/Mazel.

# Index

ageing 8, 114–116, 120, 125, 135–136, 145; *see also* women's issues
analytical (Jungian) art therapy 5, 38–51; amplification technique 49–50; compensation 38, 40–42; development of 39–40; function types 48–49; reductive interpretation 43–44, 50; spirituality and art therapy 48, 50–51; studio philosophy and approach 45–49; symbolism 38, 40–45, 50–51
anthropology 112, 128.

biological determinism 109–110, 118, 142
body image 19, 113, 117, 123, 132

CBT and art therapy 2–3, 10–23; art techniques 22–23; CBT and mindfulness techniques 25; critical discussion of 11; formulations 14–16; NATS 13, 18–21; solution-focused brief therapy 23–25
ceramics 49
children 12, 14–15, 24, 76, 88, 109–110; abuse 21; body image 113; children's views of mental illness 140
Christianity 108

death 51, 95, 98, 128
depression 12, 14, 16, 82, 88, 112, 119, 131; oppressive label 123
domestic violence: violence against women 8, 76, 110, 118, 123, 131, 139–141
DSM 12

empowerment 123, 125, 133
equality 7, 110, 111, 113–114, 116–117, 120–121, 124–125, 144
existentialism 94, 96, 105
expressionism 33

feminist art therapy 7–8, 180–152; consciousness raising 111, 123; ethnicity 122; intersectionality 121–122; misogyny 116; scholarship 116–120, 125; second sex 108; separatism 120; sexuality 110, 122, 125; structural inequality 111–112, 114–116, 123, 125

gestalt 6, 52–79; art therapy techniques 59–65; field theory 53; self-regulation 54–56; talking (to the picture) 60; techniques 56–59
grief 74
group-interactive art therapy model *see* integrative art therapy
Guerilla Girls 130

hope 24, 48, 59, 120; hopelessness 18, 81; installation of hope in group process 101–102

integrative art therapy: the group-interactive art therapy model 7, 93–107; curative features 102–103; critical discussion of 105–107; existentialism 94–99; habitus 99; psychodynamic aspects 104–105; roles 105; social microcosm (group as) 100; symbolism 103–104 love 17, 19, 47, 63, 67–69, 80, 91, 95; death of loved one 28; of self 11

migration 136–139
mindfulness art therapy 6–7, 80–92; art psychotherapeutic 85–86; CBT orientated 82–83; compassion 81–84, 91; FOAT 83–85, 88; foundation of 80–82; integration into art therapy 86–90; physiological effects (stress reducing) 90

participatory approaches 133–135; PAR (Paulo Fréire) 134–135, 139, 141
person-centred (Rogerian) therapy 5, 66–79; art based therapy 73–78; basic principles 66–69; key therapeutic features (congruence, unconditional positive regard and empathy) 70–73, 79; transference 69–70
prosopopeia 1
poverty 110–112, 133
psychoanalysis and art therapy 3–5; 26–38; basic principles (id, ego,

superego etc.) 26–27; critical discussion of 32–34; object relations 26–27, 34; reductive interpretation 32–34, 36–37; symbolism 29–34; unconscious processes 27–29

racism 100; internalised 122
re-enactment phototherapy 115, 121, 134–136

social art therapy 8; 126–141; critical discussion of 141; habitus 127; HIV 131, 141; phenomenological 129; reflexivity 140; social justice 126, 133; standpoint theory 139; symbolism 140
Surrealism 33, 149

World Health Organisation (WHO) 110–112
women's issues: ageing 114–115, 135; childbirth 112; equality 111; motherhood and art therapy 112–113; pregnancy 133; Suffrage 111; violence 118, 123, 131, 141

# eBooks
## from Taylor & Francis

Helping you to choose the right eBooks for your Library

Add to your library's digital collection today with Taylor & Francis eBooks. We have over 50,000 eBooks in the Humanities, Social Sciences, Behavioural Sciences, Built Environment and Law, from leading imprints, including Routledge, Focal Press and Psychology Press.

**Choose from a range of subject packages or create your own!**

Benefits for you
- Free MARC records
- COUNTER-compliant usage statistics
- Flexible purchase and pricing options
- All titles DRM-free.

Benefits for your user
- Off-site, anytime access via Athens or referring URL
- Print or copy pages or chapters
- Full content search
- Bookmark, highlight and annotate text
- Access to thousands of pages of quality research at the click of a button.

REQUEST YOUR **FREE** INSTITUTIONAL TRIAL TODAY

**Free Trials Available**
We offer free trials to qualifying academic, corporate and government customers.

## eCollections

Choose from over 30 subject eCollections, including:

| | |
|---|---|
| Archaeology | Language Learning |
| Architecture | Law |
| Asian Studies | Literature |
| Business & Management | Media & Communication |
| Classical Studies | Middle East Studies |
| Construction | Music |
| Creative & Media Arts | Philosophy |
| Criminology & Criminal Justice | Planning |
| Economics | Politics |
| Education | Psychology & Mental Health |
| Energy | Religion |
| Engineering | Security |
| English Language & Linguistics | Social Work |
| Environment & Sustainability | Sociology |
| Geography | Sport |
| Health Studies | Theatre & Performance |
| History | Tourism, Hospitality & Events |

For more information, pricing enquiries or to order a free trial, please contact your local sales team: www.tandfebooks.com/page/sales

**www.tandfebooks.com**